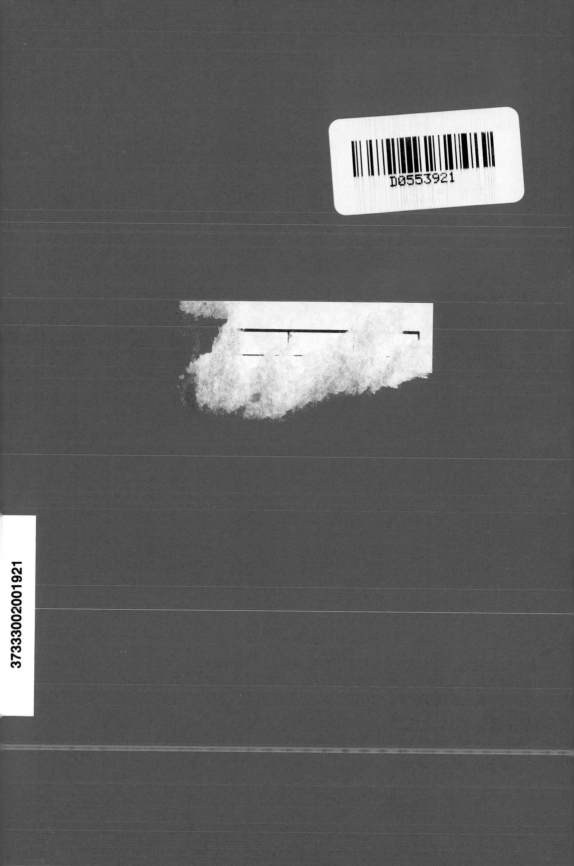

Autumn Cloud

From Vietnamese War Widow to American Activist

Jackie Bong-Wright

CAPITAL
BOOKS, INC.

Sterling, Virginia

Capital Books, Inc.
P.O. Box 605
Herndon, Virginia 20172-0605

ISBN 1-892123-52-5

Library of Congress Cataloging-in-Publication Data

Bong-Wright, Jackie, 1940–
    Autumn cloud: from Vietnamese war widow to American activist / Jackie
    Bong-Wright.
       p. cm.
    ISBN 1-892123-52-5
    1. Bong-Wright, Jackie, 1940–2. Vietnamese Americans—Biography. 3. Ref-
    ugees–United States—Biography. 4. Vietnamese Conflict, 1961–1975—Per-
    sonal narratives, Vietnamese. I. Title.

E184.V53 W758 2001
973'.049592'0092—dc21

                                                                    2001025572

Printed in the United States of America on acid-free paper that meets the American National Standards Institute Z39-48 Standard.

First Edition

10 9 8 7 6 5 4 3 2 1

Illustrations by Vu Hoi

CONTENTS

Dedication

To my grandparents and parents, who left me the legacy that is this account of four generations of our family.

To Bong and Lacy, my two loves, past and present, who constantly give me the *khi,* strength and energy, to survive.

To my children, my grandchildren, present and to come, and those of my friends who will live long enough to learn from history's mistakes. May they neither succumb to hatred nor foment war, whether in their own heart or against others. May they defend their own rights and the universal rights of others in a peaceful way.

ACKNOWLEDGMENTS

Lacy Wright not only polished my English, but he also pushed me to write, rewrite, and see clearly into my stories and into myself. This book could not have been finished if it were not for the infinite patience and persistence of a great husband.

All my brothers and sisters who, through innumerable exchanges in letters, and overseas phone calls, have fed me the insightful stories and anecdotes that inspired my writing.

Special gratitude to dear friends for their invaluable thoughts and encouragement, and to many other people whose names I cannot possibly cite. To Leon Galanos, who assisted me with the technological intricacies of the computer.

FAMILY TREE

Duong & Chieu   (grandparents)   Gia & Thom

Hanh (mother 1904–1996) ————————●———————— Thong (father 1899–1959)

1 Hai Duc, number Two (eldest) sister, 1922–1997, sign of the Dog, 10 children, 13 grandchildren, 2 great-grandchildren

2 Hoai, alias Anh Ba, number Three brother, 1924, sign of the Rat, 9 children, 7 grandchildren; lives in Houston, Texas

3 Hue, also called Madame Tao, 1927, number Four sister, sign of the Cat, 4 children, 7 grandchildren; lives in Paris, France

4 Nam Ly, number Five sister, 1929, sign of the Snake, 4 children, 3 grandchildren; lives in Ho Chi Minh City, Vietnam

5 Trung, number Six brother, 1930, sign of the Horse; died in Communist prison camp in 1979 at Vinh, near Hanoi, North Vietnam

6 Thu Ha Bell, number Seven sister, 1932, sign of the Monkey, 1 daughter, 2 granddaughters; lives in Orange County, California

7 Thu Cuc, number Eight sister, 1934, sign of the Dog, 6 children, 9 grandchildren; lives in Houston, Texas

8 Thu Thuy Mennessier, number Nine sister, 1937, sign of the Buffalo, 2 children, 2 grandchildren; lives in Nice, France

9 Thu Van, alias Jackie Bong-Wright, number Ten sister, 1940, sign of the Dragon, 3 children, 1 granddaughter; lives in Falls Church, Virginia

10 Khanh, number Eleven brother, 1942, sign of the Horse, 1 daughter; killed in battle by the Vietcong in 1967 in South Vietnam

CHRONOLOGY

Year	Family/Author	General
248 BC		Trieu Au defeats Chinese
111 BC–39 AD		1,000 years of intermittent Chinese rule over Vietnam
39 AD		The sisters Trung defeat Chinese
1300		Vietnamese defeat Mongols
1500		Vietnamese overrun Champa
1515		Portuguese come to Vietnam (VN)
1600		Vietnam conquers Mekong Delta
1615		French Jesuits arrive; Alexandre de Rhodes transposes Vietnamese into roman alphabet
1637		Dutch establish trading center
1672		British come to Hanoi
1680		British launch a trading center
1830s		Opium War in China
1840s		China accords Most-Favored-Nation status to Europeans
1850s		Russia takes over Manchuria & Korea
1858		France conquers northern VN
1859		France conquers southern VN
1879		First French governor in VN
1880s		British conquer Nepal & Burma Japan controls Taiwan & Korea
1883–1945		Vietnam is a French Protectorate
1893		France annexes Laos & Cambodia; calls Vietnam, Laos, Cambodia "Indochina"; rules there until 1945
1870s	Grandparents born	
1899	Father, Le Van Thong, born	
1904	Mother, Nguyen Thi Hanh, born	

1907		Indochinese University founded in Hanoi, North VN
1918		All instruction in Indochina is in French
1919		Cao Dai sect founded
1920		Ho Chi Minh (Ho) goes to Europe, joins French Communist Party
1921	Parents married	
1922	Hai Duc, eldest sister, born	
1924	Father moves to Saigon	
	Anh Ba, number Three brother, born	
1925	Family moves to Peamcheang, Cambodia	
1927	Chi Tu, number Four sister, born	
1929	Nam Ly, number Five sister, born	
1930		Ho sets up VN Communist Party
1931	Anh Sau, Trung, number Six brother, born	
1932	Mother opens store in Kompong Cham	
	Chi Ha, number Seven sister, born	Emperor Bao Dai in power
1934	Thu Cuc, number Eight sister, born	
	Mother sells store, buys farm	
1935	Father receives medal, becomes Mandarin	

1937	Thu Thuy, number Nine sister, born	
1939		Hoa Hao Sect formed
		Dai Viet Party established
1940	Hai Duc married to Phuoc	France surrenders to Germany
		Japanese occupy Southeast Asia and Indochina:
	Thu Van born	24 million Indochinese & 40,000 French in Indochina;
		6,000 Japanese troops in North VN
		Tokyo recognizes French sovereignty over Indochina
1941		Ho sets up Viet Minh Party
		20,000 Japanese troops in Indochina
1942	Khanh, youngest brother, born	
1945	Father becomes head of Terres Rouges plantation	**March:** Indochina under Japanese protection with 60,000 Japanese troops
	Kobayashi marries Nam Ly	Truman sends OSS to help Ho
		August: Atomic bomb on Hiroshima;
		World War II over;
	Father & Nam Ly raised funds for Ho Chi Minh's "Gold Week"	VN declares Independence
		September: Ho is President
		Kobayashi & Nam Ly go to Saigon
		Allied Forces monitor deportation of Japanese
	Nam Ly has baby at "Great House" on father's island	French troops return to VN; Famine in VN; Viet Minh return to maquis & to father's island
	Kobayashi deported to Japan	
1946	Family deported to Saigon, VN	Chi Tu joins the Dai Viet
		Nam Ly joins Viet Minh
	Father becomes part-time accountant	Cochin-China is free state within French Union; French Governor in VN; Indochina War starts

	Mother becomes diamond broker	
	Hai Duc's family moves to Saigon	
	Anh Ba works for Esso	
	Jacqueline Thu Van enrolled at Marie Curie	
1947	Chi Tu marries & goes to Paris	
1948	Bibiche born in Paris	
1949	Chi Tu & Bibiche come back to Saigon	Defeat of Chiang Kai-Shek Mao Tse Dong of China sends aid to Ho
1950		Pres. Truman sends troops to Korea & gives $15 M in aid to France to fight in VN
1951	Nam Ly marries Binh, a Viet Minh cadre Thu Cuc joins Viet Cong in maquis Father has stroke	
1952	Thu Cuc marries Hao, a militant Viet Cong	Pres. Eisenhower gives $3 B in aid to France
1953	Nam Ly pregnant	France defeated at Dien Bien Phu. Bloody Land Reform by Ho in North
1955		Hoan Van Chi, a Communist cadre, becomes a dissident
1954	Thu Van visits Thu Cuc in maquis; Thu Cuc's family moves to Saigon; Nam Ly delivers son in Saigon & becomes a	Geneva Accords divide VN: North is Communist under Ho; South is Republic under Ngo Dinh Diem

	Communist operative; husband, Binh, goes to North	
	100,000 Communist cadres go north but 10,000 stay in South; 900,000 northern Catholics come south as refugees	
	Binh studies navigation in China	
	Thu Cuc & family move to Saigon	
1955	Thu Van & Bibiche in boarding school at Les Oiseaux, Dalat	
	Trung drafted into army of the Republic (South VN)	Diem gets aid from U.S.
1956	Nam Ly flees to Cambodia	Last French soldier leaves VN
		Land Reform "Rectification of Errors" in North; General elections not held in South
1957	Nam Ly joins husband in North VN	
1958		Ho sends troops to Laos
1959	Father dies	Ho sets up COSVN & sends 4,000 troops South on Ho Chi Minh trail
	Thu Cuc's husband, Hao, jailed	
1960	Thu Van studies in Paris	National Liberation Front (NLF) established in maquis
		Coup attempt against Diem

1961	Thu Van studies in London	
1962	Thu Van & Bong meet at wedding in Paris Khanh, 19, joins the Army of the Republic	
1963	Thu Van returns to VN	Pres. Kennedy sends $1/2 B and 16,000 Americans to South Coup d'etat against Diem; he & brother Nhu killed
1964	Bong & Thu Van married Twins, Victor & Annie, born	24,000 American advisors
1965	Khanh wounded	Pres. Johnson sends 125,000 troops to South VN B-52s attack North
1966	Khanh killed in action Youngest son Alex born	300,000 Allied Troops in VN Thieu & Ky in power
1967	Trung retires as Major from Army and teaches Vietnamese at Fort Bliss, Texas	500,000 American troops in VN
1968	Attempt against Bong's life	1968 Tet Offensive
1969		NLF sets up Provisional Revolutionary Government (PRG) Bong sets up Progressive Nationalist Movement (PNM) American troops pulled out
1971	Bong is assassinated Jackie Bong works at VAA	Kissinger in VN PNM wins twenty-one seats in Lower House

1972	Workshop at University of Chicago	Kissinger & Le Duc Tho win Nobel Peace Prize
	Founding member of "Family Happiness Assn."	
	Founding member of "Business and Professional Women's Club"	
	Lunch with Nancy Reagan in Saigon	
	Trung moves to the Washington area; Victor stays in Virginia	
1973	Jackie Bong interviewed by New York Times;	Paris Peace Accords
		250,000 Northern troops infiltrate South VN
	Attends UN conference on "Status of Women" in Indonesia	
	Bronze bust erected in honor of Bong	Congress cuts funding for war
1974	Jackie Bong quoted by Newsweek in "Year of the Women" article	Pres. Nixon resigns
	Article in Vietnam Magazine on Jackie Bong	
	VN House repeals Family Planning Law	
	Trung returns to Saigon	

1975	Jackie & children flee to the U.S.	Panic in South VN
		Evacuation of foreigners
	Works in vocational school in Washington	North Communists overrun South VN
	Nam Ly & family resettle in Saigon	
	Trung jailed in Northern camp	
1976	Lacy & Jackie married	Publication of *Decent Interval* by Frank Snepp
	Wright family moves to Milan, Italy	300,000 detained in "re-education camps," in South
	Jackie in depression	
1978	Wright family in Virginia;	VN troops in Cambodia
	Jackie works for Department of Social Services, Fairfax County	
	Thu Cuc visits husband & Trung in prison camp	
1979	Jackie founds Indochinese Refugees Social Services (IRSS) to resettle refugees	*The White House Years* by Henry Kissinger
		American embargo in VN
	Trung dies while incarcerated in North	
1980	Mother migrates to U.S.	*Vietnam Gulag* by Doan Van Toai
1981	Board member, Asian Pacific American Women's Club (APAWC), Washington	

	Meets Nancy Reagan at White House	
	National Award by US–Asia Institute	
	Victor goes to Duke and Annie to George Washington University	
1982	Mother moves to Senior Citizens' Home;	
	Thu Thuy visits Washington	
	Jackie studies at Georgetown University	
1983	Alex starts at Yale	
1984		*VN Logistics: Who's to Blame?* by Gen. John Murray
		A Vietcong Memoir by Truong Nhu Tang
1986	Hoai Lang migrates to U.S.	"Renovation" policy in VN
1987		Gen. Vessey mission to Vietnam on POW/MIA issues
1989	Madame Tao migrates to France	Berlin Wall comes down
		3,000 Soviet advisors left in Vietnam
		Lost Victory by William Colby
1991	Thu Cuc migrates to U.S.	
1992		U.S. "road map" in VN
1993		*The End of a Dream* by French Amb. Jacques de Folin
1994	Visit to de Folin in Spain	U.S. embargo lifted
1995	Hai Duc migrates to Canada	U.S.–VN resume diplomatic relations

	Hoai Long travels to VN to cremate Trung's remains	*In Retrospect* by Robert McNamara
1996	**May:** Mother dies at 92 in Houston	
	June: Little Lacy born to Annie	
1997	Lacy retires from the Department of State	
	Resettling in Falls Church, Virginia	
1999	Jackie founds National Foundation for Vietnamese American Voters (VFVAV), becomes President and CEO	
2000	Jackie registers Vietnamese Community members to vote at state and federal levels; works for Census Bureau to recruit and train enumerators	

PREFACE

I first met Henry Kissinger at a reception in Saigon, in July 1971. Kissinger was President Nixon's National Security Advisor and the prime architect of his Vietnam policy. I was married to Nguyen Van Bong, the head of the Progressive Nationalist Party, the primary opposition party in South Vietnam.

Twenty-four years later—and twenty years after I was forced to flee Vietnam—I met Kissinger again in Brazil. I was married to Lacy Wright, Charge d'Affaires at the American Embassy in Brasilia, and we were hosting a luncheon for Kissinger. As I greeted him, I mentioned that I was from Vietnam. He looked at me and uttered a simple sentence, "I am sorry the U.S. let Vietnam down." Those words motivated me to write about Vietnam. Before, I only wanted to suppress painful memories of the war.

Two months later I saw Robert McNamara, Secretary of Defense under Presidents Kennedy and Johnson, on CNN. He was in Hanoi, apologizing to Vietnam and the world for America's failure in Vietnam. That night I could not sleep. I went to my computer and wrote until 3:00 a.m., and have not stopped since.

I wanted to tell the story of Vietnam as I saw it. From hundreds of discussions, I knew Americans were eager to know more about Vietnam. The war was deeply ingrained in a generation of Americans, but even those for whom it was a pivotal event, knew mostly of Ho Chi Minh, the Viet Cong, corrupt generals, and Saigon bar girls. They knew little about the history of Vietnam or about its ordinary people. Vietnam had not been described from the point of view of those who lived there, whether poor farmers or middle-class people, struggling to make a success of their lives amidst chaos and upheaval. I wanted to help redress that.

Autumn Cloud, the English translation of my Vietnamese name, is about my family from the French colonial period, through what we now call the Vietnam War, to the present. Born in 1940, at the beginning of

World War II, I stand in the center of the Indochinese drama, which started in the last century and has yet to be fully played out. By telling my family's story, I am portraying countless Vietnamese families who survived foreign occupation and successive wars against the Chinese, the French, the Japanese, and the Vietnamese Communists. They struggled to save their self-esteem, their identities, and their lives. I am telling the story, too, of those who did not survive, who sacrificed their lives for their country. My book pays tribute to my mother and father, their ninety descendants, and the spirit and strength of the Vietnamese people.

FOREWORD

Tin is the glue that both holds Vietnamese together and keeps them apart. *Tin* is loyalty to one's family, friends, and country. It is a good Confucian virtue, rooted in the Vietnamese soul. The saying "trung quan, ai quoc," means "loyalty to the king equals loyalty to the country." The king had the "mandate of heaven," and was perceived as a god on earth. In the Vietnam of the last hundred years or so—the period since my grandparents were born—*tin* has meant loyalty to a variety of leaders, whether on the throne, or at the head of a village or of a family. *Tin* could involve blind, stubborn devotion to an idolized figure.

The Communists in the North brought a discipline to Vietnam that was strong enough to turn *tin* to their advantage, and make them powerful in war. They deified Ho Chi Minh, the Bringer of Light, to the point where every household in the North and many in the deep South worshipped the portrait of him on their altars as a savior next to Buddha. People were ready to sacrifice themselves for this deity, and die in the name of patriotism. Ho Chi Minh appealed to their nationalism when he called on the Vietnamese to fight the French, never mentioning that, in fact, he also wanted to expand Communism.

In the South, we tended to be more restrictive where *tin* was concerned. We were subject to an ancient, clannish code of behavior that produced families which were sanctuaries in a hostile world but also inward-looking and self-protective. We did not produce a god-like leader. Instead, we tried to nourish the seed of democracy, but we did not have the discipline or political tradition to make it work. That is one of the main reasons South Vietnam lost the war.

The story of four generations of my family is a story of loyalties—divided loyalties, shifting loyalties, loyalties sustained, loyalties betrayed. The wars we Vietnamese lived through presented us with choices that were so complicated that some of us chose one side, some another. We learned how hard it was to satisfy the demands of *tin* amidst the confusion of war.

ONE

My Family's Rise and Fall under the French and the Japanese

In the war-torn year of 1940, as Germany, Italy, and Japan stepped up their efforts to conquer Europe and South Asia, I announced my arrival on the far eastern side of planet Earth noisily, with loud cries. My parents and my eight brothers and sisters stared intently at my tiny eyes, slanted into imperceptibility, and communicated their warmth and love at my birth. It was November. We were in a remote and still untouched area of Cambodia, well cocooned in a setting of rich farmland, with red earth, fertile vegetation, and rubber plantations all around. I was unaware that far away, on the rim of the Atlantic Ocean, Norway, the Netherlands, and France had surrendered that fateful summer to Hitler, following Poland's fall the year before. In September, German planes had bombed England in a series of raids called the "Blitz." Closer to home, Japanese troops had descended southward from their country and entered Indochina. What a tumultuous and bloody year.

A *Vu Van* (nanny of the cloud) took care of me until I was five. My ninth sister, Thu Thuy, and my younger brother, Khanh, each had a nanny, as well. *Vu*, which means "breast" in Vietnamese, was a woman who nursed babies. After seven children, my mother wanted to preserve her health and hired nurses to breastfeed the last three. Two of the nannies came from Saigon, Vietnam; mine was from Go Cong, my mother's hometown. They all had their own babies and were healthy enough to nurse them. But because of their circumstances—either because they had lost their babies or because they needed the money to care for their children—they nursed those of other people.

It was my grandmother from Go Cong who sent Vu Van, then in her

1

late twenties, to my mother. She nursed me for six straight months before starting to alternate nursing me with feeding me the bottle. She was with me constantly, day and night, and served as my nurse and guardian angel.

My name was Le Thi Thu Van. My first name, Thu Van, was pronounced, "too young," if one uses the accent of the South, or "too van" in the North. It means "Autumn Cloud." I had the impression that I could fly freely in outer space, in a higher position than my older two brothers and six sisters. The connotation of my name gave me an edge. Although I was the youngest girl, I saw myself elevated in the air, above my siblings, looking down on them all from a distance. A place had been carved out for me that seemed detached from the daily worries of the world.

Born in the season of autumn, I could be cheerful or moody. Just as the fall changes the green of summer into a rainbow of colors, from the brightest golden red to the darkest bluish-gray, I could be happy one minute and moody the next. My temperament swung back and forth like a metronome. I could taste sweet, bitter, sour, or spicy, or be all of them together. I could not be bored or boring.

According to the Eastern horoscope, I was born in the Year of the Dragon (*Nam Thin*) and blessed with the basic element of the metal gold (*Mang Kim*). Earth and water would enrich me. I was predestined to lead a solitary internal life (*Canh*), even when surrounded by crowds of people. That was my fate, already determined, my parents told me. They had consulted an astrologer after my birth.

My bad stars showed that I would be envied, that I would have two names, two identities, two husbands, two separate lives. I would have to struggle. I would be challenged, and obstacles would stand between me and what I wanted. My good stars, on the other hand, showed that I would receive a higher education and achieve a higher position in society than my siblings, and would travel all over the world. I would be fortunate in many things.

I would never be too rich or too poor. I would aspire to go to the top, but would not attain the apex. There was a pedal, like a brake, that would keep me from going overboard, from reaching any extreme, whether acquiring too much wealth or succumbing to bad health. The pedal would serve to balance my life.

A chart with twelve squares, each representing a cycle of the year and filled with indecipherable, handwritten astrological terminology, was handed to me to keep when I became a teenager. "Look at it from time to time and check your future," my parents instructed me. My mother added, "You are like a majestic dragon. You will fly high and far and will have an exceptional life. But, my poor child, for that you will have to pay a dear price." I did not pay much attention to all these predictions and superstitions. I kept the chart hidden in a compartment of my brain and forgot all about it until the day disaster struck. The first part of my life would turn out to be a Shakespearian tragedy, with a joyful beginning and a traumatic ending. When I finally consulted the chart, it was right.

At the time I was born, my parents were enjoying a period of prosperity. My mother had also been born in the year of the Dragon, in the same autumn month of November, more than three decades earlier. She was thirty-six at that point; my father, Le Van Thong, forty-three. He was with a French company of rubber plantations, *Les Terres Rouges* (Red Lands), where he worked for more than twenty years. He rose to the highest position a Vietnamese could hold in the company in colonial Indochina. As deputy director of a plantation, he kept track of the finances and hired and supervised the personnel, about four thousand people. We lived in Cambodia, in the province of Kompong Cham, district of Peam Cheang.

We had one of two villas inside the plantation compound. The French director, Monsieur Goblet, lived alone in the larger one. His wife had stayed in France to oversee their children's education. We shared tennis courts, a swimming pool, and a horse track. M. Goblet trusted my father as his right hand, and valued his efficiency and diligence. He considered us to be part of his family.

When my father had worked at Les Terres Rouges for ten years, M. Goblet rewarded him for his excellence by recommending to the French governor general of Indochina, headquartered in Saigon, the capital of South Vietnam, that he be made a mandarin. So my father was given the honorary rank of *Huyen*, the equivalent of a District Chief. He was also awarded the gold metal of *Kim Tien* for his excellent performance.

There was more. For his good relations with his Cambodian personnel, his many friendships, his hard work, and his contributions to the development of Cambodia, my father became a Knight of the Royal Order of Cambodia, *Chevalier de l'Ordre Royal du Cambodge*, as well. His support for various social causes also made him a Life Member of the Red Cross.

I can still picture Ong Huyen Thong—the honorable Mr. District Chief Thong, as he was called until he died—wearing a black tunic with a big medal pinned next to a large golden ribbon running from his shoulder to his waist. People would bow when talking to him. He often attended official functions, receptions, and dinner parties, frequently with ballroom dancing. He and my mother socialized with the cream of Cambodian, Vietnamese, and French society in their community.

When M. Goblet was sent back to France, a M. Simon came to replace him. He had the same appreciation for my father's performance.

Well situated for a Vietnamese in colonial Indochina, my father had an elevated position and made a good salary. To add to his income, he and an associate, an engineer, set up a construction company in the late 1920s. They built roads, about a thousand houses, a school, and a health unit that later became a hospital in an unexploited jungle area.

My father brought his parents to Cambodia, as well, and they lived with us. My grandfather was happy at what his son had achieved—rank, honor, wealth. He was proud to be the father of a mandarin. By association, he, too, rose in status, though I am told he remained a simple, humble man. I did not know him; he died, a respected elder, a year after I was born. His wife had died earlier.

But money and honors spoiled my father. Like most successful men of that period, he took up gambling and opium. He started going out with friends after dinner to play cards and smoke at opium dens or in private houses—the kinds of places where girls, too, abounded. The rich, successful men of that period, called *cong tu* (princes), were enticed by procurers, and encouraged by their friends, to take well-known *wantons* as mistresses, and to see whose was the most beautiful.

My father's coming home late at night did not make my mother happy. At that time, it was taken for granted that men had mistresses, and she suspected that he had one, too. In fact, there was at least one woman in his life, a famous beauty queen in Saigon named Co Ba Tra (Miss Tra number three), renowned for her glamour and her opium smoking. My father's friends introduced him to the elegant courtesan in her opium den and bordello in Saigon. She became so attached to my father that she came to visit him and stayed many times as a houseguest on the plantations. He showered her with money and jewelry.

But, although my mother was jealous, her most important worry was not women. The opium concerned her more.

A wife in those days could do little. She certainly could not divorce or leave her husband. That would have brought shame to her parents, her family, and her home village. All she could do was to cry her heart out and accept the situation—or commit suicide.

With five children to care for, my mother at first begged my father to desist. But smoking opium with his friends was my father's favorite pastime in that remote area. So she agreed to let him bring his opium pipe and equipment to our house. To keep him at home, she turned the library room into a smoking area for him and his friends. It was fashionable after a function to invite one's guests to smoke opium—an upper-class phenomenon—in addition to offering cigarettes or cigars.

My grandfather, my father's father, was very close to my mother and held her in high esteem. He understood how much she had to go through when my father was poor, and how hard she had to work to keep my father's love and raise a family. It was he who made my father promise, after a several-year, on-and-off relationship with Miss Ba Tra, to give her up for good. And my father did. He knew that he could not give up my mother for anyone else. The affair was just a temporary escapade.

My mother was a strong, exceptional woman, not only in how she handled her husband, but in everything else, as well, like the way she helped support our family. She had her own farm, fifty acres of fertile land a few miles from our house, that my father bought for her and that she later enlarged when business blossomed.

She hired laborers to plant soya, corn, beans, peas, sugar cane, and fruit trees. She sold the crops in the local markets and as far away as Saigon, four hundred fifty miles distant. Every day, she drove to the farm in her Italian Fiat convertible, which we called a *decapotable*, to manage and supervise. My father had taught her how to drive, and she was the only woman I knew in those days who drove herself around in her own vehicle.

All of this hard work resulted in good earnings, and my parents invested them wisely. They bought twenty-four houses in Go Vap, a suburb of Saigon, and rented them out. The money went to board and educate my brothers and sisters in private French Catholic schools in Saigon.

Three months after I was born, my father sold his houses and bought a small island at Can Gio in the province of Cap St. Jacques, southeast of Saigon. Land had always been thought of as a source of prosperity. He later used most of his savings to build a village of two hundred thatched-roof dwellings that he rented to tenant farmers who then worked the land. The income was to finance his retirement in his old age.

The honorable Madame Huyen Thong, as my mother was called, was among the first Vietnamese ladies to wear trousers and to run a farm and a business. She was graceful, too, with refined tastes. She smoked French cigarettes, and her prowess on the dance floor earned her the name, "Miss Tango." She could waltz until the man who invited her to dance became dizzy. She not only drove a car, but she taught all of us to drive, too. It was a daring thing at that time for a woman to show herself as Westernized or emancipated, and my mother was one of the few who did.

She also paid close attention to our education. Although we went to foreign schools and acquired a Western mentality, she taught us to value Vietnamese traditions. She insisted that we base our actions on *phuc duc*. *Phuc* means "happiness," and *duc*, "virtue and merit." We were to be devoted to the Celestial god, our ancestors, our family, and our elders. We were to show a good heart by treating people well. She made us respect and obey older people, even when they were wrong. We were not supposed to question them or display any sign of arrogance, although we could disagree with them. We had to observe social and family customs at times of birth, marriage, and death. We were expected to be close to others in the family, even distant relatives, and to lend support to people in need.

We were taught to be grateful to people who gave us a glass of water. Misdeeds and wrongdoings would be punished. *Nhan* (cause) and *qua* (effect) would determine our fate, based on how we observed *phuc duc*. There was an old saying that man was a *tieu thien dia* (a small Heaven and Earth—that is, a small universe). Therefore, we could not escape the forces of the *yin* (*am*, female or earth) and the *yang* (*duong*, male or sky), the two irreconcilable and antagonistic principles that eventually would bring harmony or imbalance to our lives. We could not ignore, either, the five basic elements of mutual generation and destruction—fire, water, metal, earth, and wood—that affected our environment and mankind's destiny. But that belief in destiny and fate did not lead to fatalism, my father told me. You could change your fate by your will and your *phuc duc* comportment.

We also learned that good fortune flowed from righteous behavior, and that a person blessed with good fortune could in turn bless members of his family. This held true not only during a person's lifetime, but also in one's future life and for generations to come. A *phuc duc* life was the best inheritance one could leave to one's descendants.

Tin (trustworthiness, faithfulness, or loyalty) was also ingrained in our culture. A person lost face and honor if he forgot this basic precept. Everyone was obligated to protect his relatives, friends, and those involved with him in a party or association or some other face-to-face relationship. It was *tin* that made it possible for the people who made up extended families or political parties to stick to each other for life, even fanatically. Loyalty to family, party, and country was sacrosanct, a divine duty. Vietnamese leaders routinely appealed to *tin* to keep their followers in line.

That kind of ethical behavior—self-control that paved the way for self-government—was in this view the most democratic way a society could function; it was better than relying on the legal system that regulates people's lives in the West. Confucius taught that individuals had to rectify their hearts and thoughts first to cultivate their persons. Then they could manage their families. Only then were they fit to govern their states and bring peace to mankind. That always sounded to me like the simplest principle and best guide to moral conduct one could imagine, but it was also the hardest to live by.

As is normal for a Vietnamese wife, my mother wielded the power of the purse. She held and dispensed all the family money. My father came home every month and handed her his salary in an envelope, and she handed him back his pocket money. In this and other ways, her role was well defined. She was looked upon as a *noi tuong*—an "indoor general." She had total power, for example, to make daily decisions concerning the household, the children, and the family business without consulting my father as long as she had his general consent. She was at once chief executive officer, chief justice, minister of the Interior, and minister of Finance. Of course, my father made other important decisions, but they were outside the house.

My mother was born Nguyen Thi Hanh, in 1904 in Go Cong, a fertile little town, rich in rice, a hundred miles southeast of Saigon. The oldest of four children, she only finished two years of high school. At that time, girls were not allowed much education. As a young woman, she applied at the City Hall for a permit to be a schoolteacher, and started at a public school teaching third grade, including French as a second language. That was where she met my father. He was working there as an interpreter of French and an accountant. She said my father knew where she lived and, every day after work, would follow her home like a shadow, not daring to speak.

After a couple of months, she said, my father tried to reach her through notes that he asked her students to pass to her. It would have created a scandal for a girl to be caught speaking to a boy on the street. Although my mother said that her heart melted when she first saw him, and my father said he fell in love at first sight, it was a long, silent, Charlie Chaplinesque courtship.

My father said that she was the loveliest of all the girls back then, and that people exclaimed at her natural beauty. At fifteen, still innocent and naïve, she was in full bloom. Many people called her "Miss Go Cong." She was five feet tall, and weighed around ninety-five pounds, exactly my own height and weight when I was her age. My father had a number of competitors for a glance from her lovely eyes, and they made him jealous and more determined than ever to catch her attention.

Every day, my mother walked to and from her school, fifteen blocks from her house. Ladylike, svelte in her long, simple pastel *ao dai*, the tunic that is Vietnam's national dress for women, she floated along with her umbrella, her long hair done up as a *chignon*, a beautiful bun held together in spirals with a coil. A serious girl, she spoke to no one. She told me that she often felt male shadows behind her, but when men tried to talk to her, she ignored them.

Her parents wanted her to marry a teacher, a son of one of their friends. Her mother, Mrs. Chieu, was a devout Buddhist who spent hours every day praying and meditating to do away with the desires of the senses, which she thought generated endless unhappiness. That was her philosophy. My mother's father, Nguyen Duy Duong, a career teacher, was more inclined to Confucianism. That meant that he professed a strict code of ethics and engaged in ancestor worship through various rites and ceremonies.

Mr. Duong's Confucianism also led him to prize learning and to cultivate wisdom, focusing on literature and art. He wanted to be a superior man, calm and at ease, elevated above animal instincts, known for virtue, trustworthiness, and loyalty. He taught his children to have a strong sense of *jen* or *hieu* (filial piety), a total respect for and devotion to one's parents. He thought it was his social obligation to consider his best friends sworn brothers, and my older brothers and sisters called his friends, "grandfather," as they did him.

My grandfather was well-off, having inherited rice fields and a row of three houses from his father, former principal of a Go Cong school. His houses occupied a block on Forestier Street, which intersected with the main avenue. My grandparents rented out two of their houses and lived in the largest, which sat in the middle of the block. Like most large houses in the provinces, theirs had a covered veranda in the front, decorated with huge *trau ba* (philodendron leaves) that climbed all the way to the eaves on one side. Tall, carved wooden doors formed a middle entrance. Inside them was a spacious area with two mahogany columns on either side supporting a high, red-tiled roof that covered the whole living area. Tall mahogany panels inscribed with Chinese characters adorned the columns. There was no ceiling.

Two living rooms went off the front area, and each contained hand-carved mahogany living room sets, encrusted with mother of pearl and complete with marble coffee tables and end tables. There was an imposing *bo ngua* (mahogany plank) on the right side, placed against the wall. Women liked to sit on it and chew betel nut with my grandmother when they visited. At night, it also served as a king-size bed for guests. Behind the two living room sets and the wooden plank, three tall chests engraved with mother of pearl served as altars facing the entrance, one in the center and two against the two walls. On top of the right altar was a drawing of Confucius; on the center altar, a big statue of Buddha; and, on the left altar, large portraits of my mother's ancestors.

Beyond the center altar was a corridor, with blue and white antique vases on stands down its length. Behind the right and left altars were bedrooms. In the back were the kitchen, a dining area with a round table and chairs, storage space for rice for the year, and the bathrooms. Farther back, behind the dining area, there was another big rosewood plank where women and children sat during the day, and used as a bed at night. At siesta time, my grandmother hung a hammock on top of the plank and rested there. She and her children spent most of their time in the spacious back area that served as the family room, leaving my grandfather in peace in the front area.

Mr. Duong was chairman of the Confucius Society of Go Cong. He spent his days writing poems on the Confucian virtues of piety, fidelity, honesty, and harmony. He also wrote poems about patriotism and inde-pendence veiled under metaphors, symbols, and emblems of freed womanhood and an independent motherland. He was not a subversive, however, and played no role in attacks on the Chinese, who had dominated Vietnam for centuries, nor on the French, who had been colonizing his country for five decades. He liked to invite his friends in for tea in the larger living area on the left. They used to spend their afternoons reciting Chinese and Vietnamese poems and writing. He was well versed in Chinese characters and Vietnamese ideographs. Although the Chinese stopped mandatory study of Confucianism in 1905, the Vietnamese intelligentsia blindly maintained it until 1917. They refused to send their children to bilingual Franco-Annamite schools for fear of corrupting them with Western education.

Mr. Duong had other talents, too. He had learned from his Vietnamese teachers how to write herbal prescriptions and cure certain illnesses, although he had no office and practiced only on people who had heard about him and asked for help. Still, he was considered an herbal doctor. He also learned how to repair his own grandfather clocks, and did so for others, upon request.

A versatile generalist, the typical elitist of his time, my grandfather was at once teacher, doctor, poet, landlord, and clocksmith. With a secure income from his houses and his rice fields, he lived a comfortable, peaceful life, happy to render services when they were needed.

Today, there is a street in Saigon named after my grandfather, the result of his association with Ho Bieu Chanh, a well-known writer in Vietnam who attended a literary conference in Go Cong organized by my grandfather's Confucius Society. Impressed with my grandfather's talent in poetry, his integrity, his devotion to Confucianism, and, perhaps, his elite lineage, Mr. Chanh persuaded the city government to name a street in Saigon's District 10, near Chinatown, "Nguyen Duy Duong street," after my grandfather. That was in the late 1950s. The street, near the Nhat Tao market, still bears his name, even though the names of most streets in the capital were changed when the Communists took over the city in 1975.

My father's constant efforts to attract my mother's attention and win her favor finally paid off. She sent him a note telling him of her love, and of her parents' intention to marry her to another young man they had chosen for her. Immediately, he came with his parents to ask for her hand. Her parents refused, saying that she was already engaged. His parents were of a different class; they were not intellectuals, then considered to be at the top of Vietnamese society.

Furthermore, my father and his father, Mr. Le Van Gia, both worked for the French and had what were considered decadent Western values, another strike against them in the eyes of the Vietnamese elite. Nor did they come from the same province or from wealthy or well-known families. Nor had they inherited land or rice fields or houses. To top it all, my father was five years older than the girl he wanted to marry, without the house or the money he would need to provide a comfortable life for my mother and her future children.

The real problem was social class. Mr. Le Van Gia was from the neighboring province of Ben Tre. Married to a quiet woman named Mrs. Thom, who tended only to the rearing of her two boys and her household chores, Mr. Gia was drafted at a certain point into the French army in his home province. He was injured on the battlefield during a fight with the Viet Minh, the southern Communists who were the Viet Cong's predecessors. While recovering in the army hospital, Mr. Gia befriended his unit's French chef, who taught him how to cook French cuisine. He became the chef's assistant and cooked so well that the French governor of neighboring Go Cong province asked him to come and work at his residence.

That was how my father ended up—after he had graduated from a Franco-Annamite high school and learned accounting in Ben Tre—with a job in the Go Cong City Hall. He also served as a translator, from French into Vietnamese and vice versa, for the court, which conducted all of its business in French.

My father begged my mother's parents to reconsider and let him marry their daughter. He promised that he would be prosperous one day, and he would be able to provide for my mother. For my grandfather, these were empty words. Fortunately, my mother had the support of my grandmother. Every day, she would ask her husband to treat their daughter with generosity, tolerance, and love, and to pardon her, as Confucius had taught him.

But my grandfather retorted that it was unfilial for a child to disobey her parents' wish that she enter a suitable, prearranged marriage. She was not practicing the Confucianist virtue of *hieu*, "total obedience," as she should. Furthermore, he had given his word of honor to the friend whose son had been promised my mother's hand, and he did not want to break the Confucian code of trustworthiness and integrity and lose face. He could not violate his *tin*. He threatened to disown his daughter if she married anyone else, and said he would not give her away at the wedding.

In those long-ago times, it was the giving-away ceremony—witnessed by the two families, their relatives and friends, and the rest of the town— that constituted a legitimate marriage. Afterward, all considered the bride and groom to be husband and wife. The couple did not need to legalize their vows at City Hall if they preferred not to; the traditional rites were more important. A marriage without this particular bit of fanfare would be a loss of face for both families.

In the end, my grandfather relented. Seeing his daughter constantly in tears, with no appetite or enthusiasm for life, he reluctantly let my mother do as she wished. My mother and father were finally united, more than two years after they had first stared at each other, talking the same heart language, without uttering a word. She was seventeen. My eldest sister would be born a year later, and my parents would have nine more children, at intervals of every two to three years thereafter.

Despite his victory, my father felt rejected by his father-in-law because of his class. He decided to take his sweetheart away from small, bucolic Go Cong and seek his fortune in a new place.

He went first to Saigon, alone, in 1924, and stayed with his older brother, Bac Hai, who had a wife and a son, Hai Buu. He found a position in a firm as an accountant, but he did not earn enough to send for his wife, who was expecting another child. He could not support a family in the capital, where food and rent were too expensive.

My mother, living at my father's parents' home in Go Cong, missed my father, and when her second child was born in 1924, she chose to name him Hoai Lang, "Longing for One's Husband." My father could only visit my mother from time to time, on weekends.

After a long year in Saigon, my father met a friend who told him that the Terres Rouges plantation company in Cambodia needed people to work there. It was 1925. At that time, Vietnam was partitioned into three states, all under the French, a situation that dated from 1884. The northern region, Tonking, was a French protectorate, and its capital was Hanoi. The central part, Annam, was also a protectorate, with its capital at Hue, where the Vietnamese emperor, Khai Dinh, lived and reigned symbolically. The two protectorates were ruled by a French administrator, who, in theory at least, governed according to a local Annamite system with a severe judicial code. Finally, there was Cochin-China in the south, covering Saigon and the Mekong Delta and governed directly from Paris.

The Vietnamese at that time were called Annamese or Annamites, or, pejoratively, "Mit." The Chinese, who had occupied the country earlier, had changed its name from Nam Viet, "Land of the Southern Viet People," to An Nam, "the Pacified South."

These three regions of Vietnam, along with the two neighboring protectorates of Laos and Cambodia, formed the French Union of Indochina, which in the 1920s was administered from Saigon by a French governor-general. The Vietnamese part of this entity was heavily influenced by the Chinese, while Indian culture was the main influence in Cambodia and Laos. The Annamese mountain chain that ran down the middle of Indochina (along which the Ho Chi Minh trail would run) extended from north to south and served as the area's strategic backbone. In their material resources and economies, the three nations, united under French supervision, complemented each other. A thousand years of Chinese domination had given way to a new era of French colonialism.

The French always proclaimed that they had come to the three backward nations on a *mission civilisatrice*, to help them move into the industrialized twentieth century. But that did not keep them from exploiting the mines, rubber plantations, and rice fields and selling in Europe for their own benefit what was produced. It was also said that the French, while creating a union of the five dependent states and exerting administrative and military control over them, kept them apart politically. Thus, they fostered hatred and division among the Vietnamese, Cambodians, and Laotians, and even between the Vietnamese of north and south. Their practice was to divide and rule. To the Vietnamese resistance movements, however, the French were regarded as "suckers of blood."

My father applied for a job with the Terres Rouges plantations and got it. He worked a few months in Phnom Penh, Cambodia's capital, and then was transferred to a jungle area, Peam Cheang, Chup, where there was nothing but thousands of young rubber trees and a few houses. Undaunted, he agreed to stay and help build a settlement. Working as a translator and accountant, he was put in charge of hiring and supervising the administrative staff and the workers, called "coolies." He was given a small cabin to live in. He was willing to suffer hardship in the beginning for the chance to prosper later and fulfill the dream of a suitable life for my mother and their family.

A few months later, my father asked to return to Go Cong to bring back his wife, children, and parents to live with him. His mother died not long after she arrived at the plantation, perhaps of malaria. But more children were born, and his small cabin became a bigger cabin, and then a house, as more of my brothers and sisters came into the world.

Ironically, forty-five years later, in 1972, I would pioneer the first population and family planning effort in Vietnam. It is still hard for me to believe that my mother had delivered ten children by the time she was thirty-eight, and had ninety descendants when she died in 1996 at the age of ninety-two.

When my three older brothers and sisters reached school age, my father rented a house for the whole family in Kompong Cham, the nearest city, over three hours away by car, where schooling was available. He remained on the plantation to work and visited his family as often as he could. By that time there were five children. To lighten the financial burden of providing for two households, my mother opened a store, called Maison Nghia Loi, in 1932.

My mother was the exclusive representative for various Western drugs and for Vietnamese medicinal herbs that her father and his friends sent her from Go Cong. She also sold items like school and household supplies. Her father-in-law, Mr. Gia, and an employee helped her.

Having made a good deal of money—my father made extra pay as a construction contractor in the area of the plantation—my parents decided, after two years, to sell the store so the family could be back together again. My father was lonely staying in another part of that remote hinterland, and neither he nor my mother wanted to go on living in two different places. So my mother went back to the plantation, bought a farm, and ran it. Later, my parents sent three, and then five, of my older siblings to French Catholic boarding schools in Saigon, where the education was of better quality.

The Vietnamese say, "The more children, the more prosperity." That held true for my father and mother in Cambodia. Industrious and resilient, my parents worked hard all their lives to support their family and keep it together.

In Vietnam, people's names describe different parts of nature: flowers, fruits, birds, seasons, winds. To a Vietnamese, these names evoke a range of sounds, colors, and fragrances. Traditionally, you can also call people by the cardinal virtues: wisdom, piety, loyalty. You rarely find names that do not have interesting meanings. In the countryside, even illiterate people with simple vocabularies give their children vivid names that describe how they looked at birth, names that are sometimes unflattering: *Ti* (tiny), *Map* (fatty), *Lung* (dwarf), *Coc* (frog), *Le* (cross-eyed), or *Be* (small).

In the home, children are ranked by number to show where they fit into the hierarchy among their siblings, starting with number two. A legend forbids the eldest child from being called number one. It is said that the evil spirit would be jealous if the first child were ranked at the top, in a higher position than the demon himself. He might give the child a bad destiny. Therefore, parents simply call their first child, "number two."

Your number also serves as your pet name. These names show the affection you have for one another, and the respect accorded to your position. Therefore, we all addressed my eldest sister as "Sister Number Two."

It was in this tradition that my parents named their ten children. They decorated our house with colorful names and symbolic flowers. Hue, the name of my number four sister, means "lily." Cuc, my number eight sister, is "marguerite." And Ly, my number five sister, is "plum," as though the two flowers were surrounding a fruit tree. My parents carefully landscaped their garden and gave it a three-dimensional, panoramic view, adding to it my number nine sister, Thuy, meaning "waterfall," my number seven sister, Ha, which means "mountain," and Van, myself, which means "cloud." They fertilized their garden with Duc, or "virtue," my number two sister; Hoai Lang, "longing for one's husband," my brother number three; Toan Trung, "total fidelity," my brother number six; and Truong Khanh, "unending love," my youngest brother.

We children formed an exquisite painting from which an array of aromas, colors, and sounds emerged. We embodied the essential elements of the Universe, from the Earth to the Sky.

If we needed animals to complete our cosmos, we had those, as well. Each of us represented a different creature, according to the year we were born—dog, cat, rat, buffalo, horse, snake, monkey, boar, tiger, dragon, and so on.

My mother was thirty-six when I was born. A family picture taken some months before my birth shows her, splendid in her Vietnamese *ao dai*, sitting next to my father, a handsome man in an elegant suit. Behind them stand my brothers and sisters, all nicely dressed. Prosperity allowed my parents to order our clothes, shoes, and other apparel from Paris.

My eldest sister, Hai Duc, was eighteen years older than I, and she stands in the back row of that now-ancient photo. I often sought her wise advice, or cried on her shoulder when I ran into problems. She was less strict than my mother and easier to talk to. I considered her both my number two sister and my number two mother. Being the ninth child, or number ten in rank, I was also called Co Ut, "Miss Littlest."

Another sign of our prosperity was the company house we lived in, which sat on a large piece of land. An expanse of grass separated our villa from a big kitchen, a pantry, and storerooms in back. Farther behind was a row of rooms for the servants. This was the setting of my early childhood and the backdrop for my pleasant memories of my first years.

One day, when I was about three, Vu Van took me for a walk, and then cleaned my feet and hands in the back yard. I dared her to race me through the kitchen to the living room to see who was faster. We started off at the gardener's signal and burst into the kitchen just as the cook was moving a big pot of boiling soup from the burners to the table.

I do not know how, but I ran into her. Off balance, she poured the boiling soup on top of me. I fell on the floor, my arms and legs kicking hard in all directions like a furious wrestler. Years later, when I was visiting Vu Van in her sickbed in Go Cong, my beloved nanny recounted the whole incident to me, weeping. She said I had screamed with all my might. People came to my rescue, and the assistant cook ran to tell my parents. My father wrapped a towel around me and rushed me to the hospital.

Leaving me lying in the hospital with second degree burns, my father came home and fired all the bullets from his hunting rifle into the air to vent his anger. The cook had to run away, deep into the forest. She hid for three days and nights, Vu Van continued. She came back to ask my father to pardon her for having committed such an offense. He realized by then that it was I who was the culprit, not she.

When I was a year older, but not a year wiser, I was involved in another situation that the Vietnamese call *lien khi*, a "monkey-style joke." I remember being near a horse, and my eldest brother, Anh Ba, was helping my younger brother, Khanh, into the saddle. He told Khanh to hold on tightly to the reins, and he walked slowly alongside. Standing near and holding a branch, I tried to imitate what I had seen people do while riding horses and hit the horse hard on its rear leg. Rearing up, the horse galloped forward, throwing poor Khanh like a ball. Whoa! I received *une bonne fessée*, a "big slap on my rear," from my brother. Khanh and I were crying as loud as we could at the same time.

Another memorable event was my first funeral. Anh Ba had always had a special love for dogs. Most of the time he could be seen with a huge, white dog with black spots, Medor, that was much taller than I was. The immense dog somehow died suddenly. People said he might have drunk water mixed with insecticide. Anh Ba organized a funeral ceremony to bury him.

I recall walking slowly and sobbing, lined up in a procession with a dozen other kids, the children of our servants, and all my brothers and sisters. Anh Ba, two gardeners, and a housekeeper put the dog, wrapped in a white sheet, into a small coffin. As our beloved hound lay there, next to the open grave that was to receive him, I said my last farewell. "I loved you very much, but I won't have to be scared of you any more. You won't be pushing me around or throwing me down on the ground with your long legs any longer. Sleep tight, and have sweet dreams. *Au revoir*." I patted him and shook his enormous right paw.

Medor was lowered into a small hole. We all bowed our heads and looked down at him, lying motionless. The gardeners filled the hole with dirt until it was flat, then they made a mound above it. Anh Ba put three incense sticks in front of the little tomb to ensure that Medor's soul would be blessed, and we prayed that he would be reincarnated into a higher and better being.

We all believed that everything—humans, animals, even trees and rocks—had a soul and would be reincarnated. Vu Van had told me many times, "If you don't behave, you will turn into a pauper or a ferocious animal in your afterlife instead of a princess."

"How can I turn into an animal?"

"Everything has to do with a person's karma, or *nhan qua* [cause and effect]. That is why some people came back as house servants, like myself.

Others are reborn into royalty, and still others become wild animals or loving pets."

All these supernatural concepts were beyond my mental reach, so I accepted what Vu Van said. On the way back from the funeral, I asked her, "Do you think Medor is going to be reborn a wealthy prince or a hard-working buffalo?"

"That is up to God to determine. He has to receive a report on Medor's whole life before He makes a decision."

"How can He do that?"

"Well, He will find out from many people whether Medor was compassionate with others. He will take into account whether Medor fought with other animals, whether he bit people, and whether he killed any lizards, rats, or cats. If he had a lot of sinful desires, he will be punished. But if Medor put up with suffering and was a good dog, he will be rewarded. He will enjoy freedom and bask in light."

"I never saw Medor killing anything, but sometimes he barked a lot and chased after people. That was one bad thing he did. I saw him one time run after a boy and bite him."

"Yes, that was very bad."

"Sometimes he pushed and shoved me, too. That was another bad thing to do. But I don't think he did it on purpose."

"The rascal was also greedy with his food," Vu Van added. "He never shared anything with the other dogs."

"Yes," I had to agree. That wasn't very good either.

That was our final report to God on Medor's behalf. I hoped He would make allowances for Medor's mistakes, and that Medor's *karma*, the rule governing punishment for wrongdoing in a preceding life, would be a favorable one.

On that note, I imagined I would see Medor again one day.

In Asia, we used to take an hour of siesta after lunch. The nap was a feature of life, especially for us children, a regulation we could not disobey. Adults came home for lunch at noon, also took a nap, then returned to work at two and stayed until six.

Every day Vu Van put me in my bed for my nap, but I could never sleep. It bothered me that I could not go to the library room where my father took his siesta. He went there every day with the same *boi*, one of our three male housekeepers. They stayed in there until my father went back to work. When I asked if I could go in with him, too, he and my mother both told me that he read books and newspapers in there, and then took a nap. I was not supposed to disturb him. But why, I wondered, could the *boi* go in and not me? Were they trying to hide something from me?

I wanted to know what was going on. One day, after Vu Van thought I had gone to sleep, she went off to the kitchen to have lunch with the other domestic staff. As soon as she had left, I tiptoed in my bare feet to the library. The door was closed but not locked. I looked around to make sure that no one saw me.

I pushed the door quietly and slipped inside. The room was dark, and the windows were closed. I lowered myself onto my hands and knees, like Medor, and soon found myself under the thick plank of mahogany that served as my father's tall bed. The bed was supported by two forked wooden stands underneath. I had to hide quickly so he would not discover me.

I looked around and found a place, just big enough for me, behind a huge blue and white cachepot containing a tall plant. I counted something like eight to fifteen small ceramic tiles separating the plant from me. It did not look too far. Still on the floor, I turned my hands to the left, then my knees, and finally my feet. I crept slowly toward the cachepot.

Suddenly, my father, who had been sleeping, called, "*Boi*, one more." I flattened myself on the floor, trembling. The *boi* answered, "*Da bam Quan Lon,*" "Yes, your Honor."

My heart was pounding, but the two men did not seem to be paying any attention to me. I was safe, but I had to get to my hiding place. On my elbows and toes, I crawled slowly, then faster. Finally, I reached my destination and positioned myself behind the vase. Oof! I felt safe now. I squatted on the floor carefully, so no one could see my little body.

But I had the impression that someone was watching me, and looked up to the right wall, my heart hammering.

Sitting on a stand, a big metal Buddha was staring at me. He was affable and looked merciful. I bowed to him to show my respect. I had seen my mother and Vu Van do it often. Then I crossed my legs in the same position as the Buddha. That way, I thought, I might look like one of his disciples, and He would protect me. Vu Van had told me He was a generous God and did not harm good children. So I prayed that He would approve of my hiding behind the plant and not punish me for being disobedient. I hoped he would understand that I had not done anything wrong, but was just curious.

I then stood up carefully and stuck my head out from behind the left side of the vase. I wanted to see what was happening on that wooden bed. There was no mattress on top, just a *chieu* (thick mat) with colorful designs. *Aii*, it would hurt me to lie on that tough piece of lumber, I imagined. There seemed to be a faint oil lamp on top of a big wooden tray in the middle, with the *boi* lying on one side and my father on the other, facing each other. Their necks were propped up on small, square headrests, not the comfortable pillows I was used to. Their feet stretched out in my direction.

The *boi* was holding a wooden pipe as long as my whole arm. It looked like a dark, engraved flute. On one side, there was something protruding, about the size of my little fist. That look-alike fist was like a tiny, covered coffee cup, with a little hole in the center. The other side of the flute had an open hole, too.

With a minuscule knife, the *boi* scooped what looked like a dark, thick coffee bean out of a round, engraved, silver box, the size of my mother's powder box. He put the coffee bean on the cover of the tiny coffee cup. He lifted the flute to put the coffee cup on top of the fire of the oil lamp. He then moved the gluelike coffee bean around a few times with his knife, still holding the flute near the fire. The coffee bean melted and swelled up. It made a faint hiss, as one hears at a barbecue. He immediately pushed the melted coffee bean inside the hole of the cup and handed it to my father. My father puffed a few times on the flute. A strong, long-lasting aroma perfumed the whole room.

The compelling scent of the smoke glided toward me. I inhaled, closed my eyes, and felt good. It was a strange smell, not like coffee at all. The strong, attractive odor became milder, wrapping around me and making me sleepy. I saw both my father and the *boi* falling asleep, so I did the same. Lying on the floor, I turned myself sideways like they were and took my nap. Vu Van could not reproach me for not having taken my siesta, I thought. I would tell her that the Buddha could testify to it.

Then I heard Vu Van calling my name from the corridor. I sprang to my feet and jumped around the plant. My father and the *boi* had already left the room, and the oil lamp and flute had disappeared. Excited, I called out to Vu Van and ran to her. Nestled in her arms, I put my hands to her ear and said, "Oh, Vu Van, I want to tell you a big secret!"

"Where have you been, naughty Co Ut, Miss Littlest? I've been looking for you everywhere. You gave me a scare. Don't do it again. I don't know what I'd do if something happened to you."

"But, Vu Van, I didn't do anything wrong. I just went to father's library and took my nap there. The Buddha knows that I went to sleep. I was a good girl."

"What? Where did you go? Heaven and Earth, you mean you disobeyed your parents and went to the library?"

"I found out the secret. It was the coffee. Instead of boiling the coffee, the *boi* grilled it on the oil lamp. And Father puffed on it from a long pipe."

"What? You saw him puffing a long pipe? Oh, my Buddha!"

"Yes, with my own eyes. But why is it such a secret?" I could not understand why the houseboy had resorted to such a time-consuming and complicated procedure, and why my father wanted to smoke his coffee instead of drinking it. "Also, it didn't smell like coffee at all."

"Don't tell anybody. I hate to think what your parents would do to you and to me if they knew what you did."

"All right. I don't want to get into trouble, either. But, you know what? When I grow up, I'm going to learn how to grill coffee for my father."

"Don't say that! I could lose my job! This is serious!"

Instead of being pleased, Vu Van was upset with me. Disappointed and half-crying, I told her I could not understand why I was in trouble simply for watching my father smoke coffee instead of drinking it.

I also recall that one day I escaped from my normal routine to play alone with the servants' children near the rubber trees. I was forbidden to touch the rubber milk. We were told it was poisonous and it could kill children if we happened to get it in our mouths or blind us if it got into our eyes. Although surrounded by rubber trees, I rarely went near one; Vu Van often pulled me away from them. But those big trees, lined up methodically row after row, one row evenly spaced from the next, made a strong impression on me. When I drove by them with my parents, the trees seemed to open their huge arms to invite us to penetrate deeper into their midst. It was like flying into clouds: you seemed to collide with them without their ever touching you.

I often saw workers, the coolies, with their sharp knives, carve a dark, descending spiral into the trunk, an inch deep and an inch wide. Suddenly, a white liquid would appear, and each tree would seem to be wearing a white ribbon swirling around its waist, its long arms holding an immense, green, patched umbrella over its head with the sun's rays filtering through. The milk was precious, my father told me. It would be made into rubber and then shipped to France, known as our "motherland," to make things like tires and shoes. How marvelous to know that these little drops of milk would produce such magic.

The children I was with, using their index finger, touched the white milk that slid down slowly from the trees and dropped into a tin bowl. They spread the milk onto the palm of their left hand, where it formed a thin layer. When the layer dried up, it tightened the palm, as if they were wearing a glove. They pressed it and made a circle with the other palm, rolling it as if making meatballs. After a while, the substance became rounder, thicker, and harder.

I did the same, and was amazed to find that drops of liquid could transform themselves into a round piece of gum. Repeating the process many times made the rubber ball bigger and bigger, but it was a long and patient operation. It required many missed siestas for me to make something the size of a Ping-Pong ball. We had a lot of fun throwing these balls at each other, and I never got caught skipping my nap.

So it went. I lived in a world of naïveté and innocence, isolated from and untouched by the war that was engulfing the world around me.

In Vietnam, the Viet Minh leader, Ho Chi Minh, changed his name a dozen times, like a chameleon changes colors, as he traveled to different parts of the world asking for help to get rid of the French colonizers. My father told us one evening at dinner that his French boss had warned him of Ho. M. Simon said that Ho had gone to France in the early 1920s and joined the French Communist Party. After that, he went to further his Communist studies at the Stalin Institute for the Toilers of the East in the Soviet Union. In China, he assisted the Chinese revolution. In 1930 Ho had set up the Vietnamese Communist Party, a resistance group, to wage war against the French. A decade later, Ho saw a golden opportunity to collaborate with the Japanese, who had come in 1940 to free Vietnam of French rule. In 1941, Ho established the Viet Minh, short for *Vietnam Doc Lap Dong Minh*, the League for the Independence of Vietnam. He borrowed from the league name a pseudonym, Ho Chi Minh (Bringer of Light). Instead, long, dark years of deadly violence were to unfold under his reign.

When my father complained to M. Simon that the French were raiding the island in Vietnam that he had bought and where he had invested his savings, his boss would say, *"Après la pluie, le beau temps,"* "After the rain comes the good weather." He advised my father to write to the Service for War Damage at the *Haut Commissariat de France Pour l'Indochine* (High Commission of France for Indochina) to seek reimbursement for damage caused by the French army. My father did, but he never got reimbursed. Each time French bombs rained down from the sky, destroying houses and crops, my father and his tenants tenaciously rebuilt, and the sun shone again on new crops and new dwellings.

The peasants kept growing their rice, sugar cane, and fruit trees, and they kept harvesting their fish and shrimp. They transported what they produced to the ports of Saigon and nearby Cholon by sampan. That was how they earned the rent to pay my father, and it was how they secretly supported the Viet Minh.

My father was apolitical; all he wanted was to lead a peaceful life. He was content to show his patriotism by doing his job conscientiously, providing work for others, and helping people as he could, without discrimination. When Vietnamese who had fled the French or the Viet Minh in Vietnam came to him to ask his assistance, he would board them on his plantation and give them work to do. It was not an easy role to play. The Viet Minh regarded him as both a landlord exploiting the proletariat and a traitor collaborating with the French.

In the summer of 1940, as France surrendered to Germany, the Japanese rolled into Southeast Asia, bringing their fleet, bombs, and troops, and establishing military bases. In Vietnam, Japan signed a treaty in July 1941 with the French that provided for the common defense of Indochina. Its terms allowed the Japanese to station troops at railroads, ports, airfields, and all other important strategic positions. They also committed the French to sell food to Japan for its troops at minimal prices. At the same time, Japan was encouraging the Vietnamese resistance groups in their struggle against the French.

In March 1945, Vietnam was proclaimed independent under Japanese "protection" after nearly five years of Japanese occupation. The Japanese then took control of the whole of Indochina—that is, of Laos and Cambodia, as well. As a result, the Japanese jailed the French colonial officials and took over their positions. The yellow masters replaced the white masters. They did exactly what the French had done, and worse.

Like feudal lords, the Japanese made the dominated countries send their most valuable resources as tribute to the Japanese Emperor. Most of our agricultural and mineral wealth—coal, timber, rice, and corn— were shipped to the new fatherland at one-tenth of the market price.

Famine ensued in Vietnam. The Japanese were called the "Yellow Fascists."

Nearly a hundred years of French influence and seventy years of official French colonialism were ending, and the Japanese policy of "Asia for the Asians" was in effect in Indochina. In Vietnam, a surge of patriotism raced through the streets. Our last emperor, Bao Dai, a ceremonial ruler educated in France and kept in power by the French since 1932, declared Vietnam's independence from France in March 1945.

Around this same time, in Cambodia, M. Simon was imprisoned, and the Japanese had to replace him. The Japanese officer in charge of the province of Kompong Cham and the Terres Rouges plantations came to see my father, bringing with him one of his subordinates, a civilian Japanese interpreter, Kobayashi Khensaboro, who knew Vietnamese. The commanding officer had put Kobayashi in charge of the plantation at Krek, 70 miles from ours. He also asked my father to stay on as head of the Peam Cheang plantation, replacing M. Simon. We were to move into Simon's residence. Resistance meant jail or death. My father had no choice but to accede, going about his daily work under the eyes of the Japanese guards with apprehension.

Kobayashi was in his late twenties, and he came several times to visit my father. Gradually, he took to my number five sister, Nam Ly. At sixteen, the sister whose name meant "plum" looked very much like a Japanese, short and round, attractive wearing her shorts and carrying a tennis racket.

One day, Kobayashi, his Japanese commander, and a Vietnamese go-between came to our house to ask my parents for Nam Ly's hand. The commander politely laid his long, sharp sword on the coffee table while his troops waited outside. I suppose my parents could see all of us decapitated, or our abdomens cut open in *hari kiri* fashion. They had no recourse but to agree to Kobayashi's proposal.

After the Japanese left, my parents went inside their bedroom. We children could hear my father shouting and cursing, and my mother wailing. After fifteen minutes, my father emerged, red-eyed, and called Nam Ly to his room. She eventually emerged, shrieking, and ran to her bedroom, where she locked herself in, crying loudly. Alarmed, I hung myself tightly around Vu Van's neck, asking what had happened. She did not know, or did not want to tell me.

That day was like a funeral: the whole house was in tears and in a state of alarm. Later, after other marriage offers had been made to our number four sister, Hue, our parents made her go into hiding. My eldest sister, Hai Duc, told me that Hue took refuge in the city of Kompong Cham at the house of Madame Soza, a Vietnamese lady married to a Frenchman. My other sisters were too small to be considered "marriageable."

After three weeks of preparation, Nam Ly underwent a two-day wedding to Kobayashi attended by five hundred guests. That remote area of Cambodia had not yet been reached by war or famine.

Although the marriage was forced on my parents, they asked that it be conducted according to Vietnamese tradition. They consulted an astrologer to determine the date and time of the wedding, which was held on the second and third of April 1945. A Vietnamese marriage mediator, an elderly, respected lady called a *ba mai*, explained to Kobayashi what to do.

It was the first time I was old enough to take part in a wedding ceremony, and I was very excited. My brothers and sisters and I were told to wear our best clothes and shoes, as if it were New Year's.

Early in the morning, I had to take a shower. I did not complain, because Vu Van had told me that it was an unlucky omen to cry or have bad feelings on a happy occasion like a wedding. So I was to behave the best I could and be completely obedient. Although we were losing Nam Ly to her husband, we all had to show our most cheerful faces to everyone on that day. There could be no sign of sorrow.

Vu Van chose my most beautiful dress. It was a three-tiered, bouffant white dress, hand-embroidered with pink and blue flowers all around the top, that my parents had ordered from Paris. She pulled my hair into a hibiscus-style arrangement that sat elegantly on the top of my head like a bouquet. She tied it with a rubber band, which she then covered with pink and white roses. My curly hair floated down my neck and around my ears.

I had tall, white socks embroidered with pink and blue flowers and new white shoes. Vu Van was wearing her best *ao dai*, her hair done into a higher bun than usual, and she was adorned with a golden necklace and earrings my mother had given her. She explained to me that I should behave like a well-brought-up girl, and should not run around disrupting the ceremony. I promised that, this time, I would obey her.

At eleven in the morning, all of us were dressed up and ready to welcome Mr. Kobayashi and company. His commander was first in the procession, elegant in his military uniform, complete with medals, sword, and hat. Then came an elderly man in a black Vietnamese tunic, holding a pair of huge red candles, with golden dragons carved on the sides. The candles were to light up the altar and to call on the gods and ancestors to witness the wedding. Next, a lady had in her hands an engraved silver betel box, filled with six pieces of betel leaves topped with six areca nuts, neatly displayed. They represented the two families and the newly engaged couple. Betel and areca were symbols of family union and loyalty.

A fourth man was carrying a silver platter with two bottles of whiskey covered with transparent red paper. Another man carried two bottles of French Bordeaux wine on another silver platter. Two men carried a huge red barbecued pig on a decorated tray. Two ladies each held a tray of candies and cookies, presents for the bride's family. Last came the groom, neatly dressed in a suit and tie, holding a square box encrusted with mother-of-pearl and covered with a red silk cloth. It contained gifts of jewelry for the bride.

The ten of them were ushered in and introduced as the groom's party by the *ba mai* (go-between). They all bowed to my parents' party, also ten people, and placed the boxes and trays on two coffee tables and a carved trestle. An elderly friend of my parents introduced the bride's party to the groom's party, and invited them to sit. The groom was still standing.

The two elderly men set the two candles on tall brass candlesticks on the altar, magnificently decorated with a shining brass statue of Lord Buddha sitting on a platform in the center, and portraits of my parents' ancestors on both sides. On the left side was a huge platter of fresh fruit, and, on the right, a tall antique vase with red and yellow gladiolas. From a side doorway, perched in Vu Van's arms, I peered in awe at the impressive spectacle.

Then the ceremony started. An elderly woman from the bride's side went to get Nam Ly, who slowly came out and bowed to everyone. She wore a red brocade *ao dai* that fit her tightly, and a loose, transparent, gold-colored *ao dai* on top of that. On her head was a golden turban, her hair tied inside it in the back. Her hands were clasped together at chest level, ready to pay respect to the guests.

The *ba mai* and my mother, in a bright gold silk *ao dai*, helped my sister don the earrings and necklace the groom had given her. The gold earrings had small diamonds in the middle, and the *kien* (the round, gold necklace) was engraved with dragons. The earrings were a symbol of the bride's virginity and blossoming beauty and took precedence over all other gifts. They showed honor to the bride's family.

Nam Ly was then led to her place near the groom, and both of them went to the altar to pay their respects to their ancestors. Each was given three lit incense sticks, which they held close to their foreheads. They prayed, asking their ancestors to bless them. They handed the incense sticks to the old men, who stuck them into a large censer filled with sand. The couple kowtowed four times to the altar to honor Buddha and their ancestors, pressing their heads to the floor each time.

Then the two went to my father, who was sitting solemnly on a rosewood settee, and my mother sitting next to him, and kowtowed twice to them. My father wore a long, dark blue tunic with Chinese characters on it. My parents welcomed Kobayashi as their son-in-law and invited the guests to stay for lunch.

That evening, the five hundred Cambodian, Chinese, and Vietnamese dignitaries coming from the capital and surrounding cities were invited to a seven-course dinner followed by ballroom dancing at our residence.

It was another grand occasion for me. Coquettish in a long, light pink dress with a huge ribbon tied around my waist, I was having a splendid time.

It was late when the dance music started. My parents came out to open the ball with the usual *passo doble*. Kobayashi and Nam Ly followed them, and then the other guests joined in, until the room was very crowded. Nam Ly wore a long, Western gown with lace, and a diamond diadem on her head. I stared at how elegantly the guests moved around the floor in their sumptuous attire. After the first dance, the orchestra stuck up the magic tango. My father and mother stayed on the floor while all the others returned to their seats. Everyone knew that they excelled at the tango, their favorite dance. A thousand luminous eyes— the guests, the crickets, the frogs, even the trees and flowers and moon and planets—focused on the dance partners, erect, center stage, directly under the spotlight. My parents' four legs moved as gracefully as swans' necks, and their heads were as rigid as Egyptian mummies'.

They strode back and forth with rhythm and passion, now in four-quarter time, now in two-quarter, slow-quick-slow-slow movements. They pranced and dipped, three legs down and one leg up. They turned their heads high, their cheeks glued to each other's, their eyes transfixed, in an abrupt, deadly serious about-face, their arms extended to the west. Then they swaggered arrogantly to the south, legs entwined, with long gliding steps. Now joined at the hip, then at the elbow, they kicked up their heels. They swayed with excitement to the north, and took provocative, syncopated steps backward and forward. The guests clapped loudly.

Suddenly, my father stopped short, his hand holding my mother's hand high in the air. Standing in one place and looking straight into his eyes, my mother turned fast in a semicircle—her right leg taking playful steps to the left, her left leg taking stirring steps to the right. The audience was breathless. Finally, my father hooked his foot with hers, and bent her backward with his body on top of her for the finale. My mother was curled in a crescent-moon shape under my father, scintillating in a thousand points of light in her red, sequined *ao dai*.

By then, I was perched on Vu Van's shoulders, my legs held tight by her two arms, my hands swinging above her head. Applause, shouts, and whistles hit the radiant sky like rockets. I waved my two arms high to join the crowd of admirers, while my parents bowed to the guests and glided off the dance floor.

Vu Van pulled me down and swept me away, telling me to go to bed. I was in no way ready for such an absurd idea. My eyes started to get moist, and I was about to cry. I broke away from her and ran to my father. I looked back and saw Vu Van panting far behind me. She had on wooden clogs with high heels and found it hard to run. I zigzagged my way around people, and found myself at my parents' table. I went to my father's side, avoiding my mother's stare.

I pulled my father's black coattail and begged him to let me stay, babbling and stomping my feet. He looked down, and pulled me up into his arms. He entwined the fingers of his left hand with the tiny fingers of my right hand, and started to dance with me, turning me around in slow circles. We moved toward the dance floor. I giggled and flirted with him, and my head spun like a merry-go-round. We were on fluorescent clouds, swirling around under the scintillating stars. Ecstasy enveloped me and spread its fire inside me. I sank my head onto his warm chest, under his black bow tie, and my face rested on his satin sash. My eyes blinked like a flickering torch. I was exhilarated. It was the happiest moment of my nearly five years.

The next day, after an early brunch, Kobayashi's party came to pay their last homage to the bride's party. This going-away ceremony was no less important than the one the day before. The gathering, all dressed up, lined up in the living room. One more time, the couple kowtowed to their ancestors and bowed to the assembly to bid farewell. A smaller altar was set at the front entrance with flowers and candles. A special platter of *ngu qua*—(five fruits including golden papaya, yellow pineapple, vermillion pomegranate, green coconut, and ripe mangoes)—was offered to the Celestial god and the Terrestrial god. This was meant to wish the couple prosperity and success on their way to their new home.

The groom left the house first, followed by his tearful bride in the midst of the rattling, bursting, and banging of the firecrackers. The louder the firecrackers, the better they were at routing the evil spirits. They were also a sign of good luck to the new couple. I could not understand why, after such festivities, my mother and Nam Ly wept as my new Japanese brother-in-law carried his trophy away. I wished there could be more weddings. I had had a wonderful time, and I would never forget my first dance with my father. He made me feel like a lady.

In the departing motorcade, the commander's car was first. The married couple's car, adorned with red flowers and ribbons, was the second in line, followed by a third car from the groom's party. My father's car was next, with my two eldest brothers. Finally, a long line of my father's friends' cars completed the convoy. They drove for nearly two hours to Kobayashi's quarters at the plantation at Krek. The crowd of a hundred, mostly men, ate an early dinner there before departing.

So Nam Ly became the wife of my father's counterpart on another Terres Rouges plantation. The marriage did not last long. Four months after the wedding, in mid-August of 1945, the Americans dropped the atomic bomb on Hiroshima. World War II was over.

My father heard the long-awaited news on the radio. Independence fever hit the countries of Europe, now freed from Germany, and those of Asia, liberated from the Japanese. A strong current of patriotism united all Vietnamese everywhere. In Vietnam, Emperor Bao Dai, under pressure from the Viet Minh, abdicated, renouncing his hereditary title. He conferred his "mandate of heaven"—the divine right to rule—on Ho Chi Minh.

By then Ho was considered his country's liberator. He proclaimed himself president in Hanoi on September 2, 1945, and formed the Provisional Government of the Democratic Republic of Vietnam. It was a coalition government composed mostly of the Communist Viet Minh, with a few representatives of the nationalist parties. Faced with opposition, Ho made a show of "disbanding" the Communist Party to demonstrate his devotion to the nationalist cause. The noncommunist leaders formed the *Lien Viet* (the Vietnamese Alliance Front) and cooperated willingly with Ho to thwart the French. In fact, though, Ho continued to operate in secret, promoting his Communist activities via a vast net-

work of secret cells among farmers, workers, small landlords, and educated people alike.

The word, "Communist," was not mentioned. Ho masked his Communism behind a patriotic front that he felt would have wider appeal to
Vietnamese and foreigners alike.

Ho hid his real name. "Ho" was a common family name, but he used
a pseudonym for the other two parts: *Chi* means "aspiration," and *Minh*,
"enlightment." He kept his origins and identity secret, denying he had
used other names, like Nguyen Ai Quoc (Nguyen the Patriot), for instance.
He never used Nguyen Van Cung, or Nguyen Tat Thanh, the two names
given him at his birth in Nghe An province, central Vietnam, in 1890.
Using astute subterfuges and displaying formidable endurance, he continually outwitted the Vietnamese National Police, the French security services, and Chinese, British, and American intelligence.

As head of state, Ho maintained the respect and confidence of the
whole nation because of his high moral posture. He lived an ascetic life,
renouncing the comfort of a family, dressing like a peasant in black
pajamas, and wearing sandals made from old tires. Ho had become an
icon during the years of resistance, a model of virtue and revolution. His
photograph, seen often on family altars, was worshipped like an idol by
peasants and his resistance followers.

Ho was helped by the fact that every Vietnamese citizen, no matter
how young or old and no matter what religion or party, felt it a duty to
help salvage a country ravaged by hunger and war, and newly freed
from foreign conquerors. Again, *tin* played a role. Ho used the slogan,
"Fatherland above All," to rally the whole population behind his government.

My father himself became associated with the Communists. He was
elected chairman of the patriotic Viet Minh Movement at the Terres
Rouges plantations. One of his main tasks was to raise funds during
"Gold Week," when Ho Chi Minh appealed for contributions to aid the
people in central and northern Vietnam hardest hit by the war and famine.
My sister, Nam Ly, and a cousin, Hai Buu, were made co-leaders of the
Viet Minh Auxiliary Youth Movement, comprising one hundred twenty

young people. Nam Ly organized shows to raise funds for the Viet Minh. Every Vietnamese saw it as his or her responsibility to preserve the nation and rid it of the last vestiges of outside domination.

Nam Ly also had problems of her own. Now expecting a baby, she went to Vietnam with the Youth Movement at the end of September and took refuge on my father's island. She stayed at Rung Sat, my father's plantation, in the large, plantation-type house he had built there for his retirement. We called it the "Great House." With her in the house were two cousins, Hai Buu and Ba Lua, whom my father had hired to manage his business. There, too, the Viet Minh contacted her, and asked for support. Like the many others who donated money, gold, jewelry and rice, she gave willingly. Filled with nationalistic fervor, she was eager to do anything she could to help regain Vietnam's freedom.

In due time, Nam Ly delivered Kobayashi's baby. The infant was premature and died of high fever a few months after its birth. Later, Nam Ly made a decision that would be a lifelong commitment: she joined Ho and the Viet Minh, and disappeared into the bush.

A master tactician, Ho played his friends and enemies against one another. After he had collaborated with the Japanese to get rid of the French, he sought to work with the Americans against the Japanese. Soon after the Japanese surrender, Major Archimedes Patti, an Office of Strategic Services (OSS) officer assigned to help with Allied prisoners, met with Ho in Hanoi. Ho promised to collaborate with the OSS and gave them information regarding the whereabouts of the Japanese. He also talked Patti into drafting Vietnam's Declaration of Independence, the first sentence of which was a copy of that of the United States: "All men are created equal, they are endowed by their creator with certain inalienable rights . . . " Ho even wrote President Harry Truman to ask for help, pleading for U.S. aid. American support came in mid-1945, with a team code-named Deer. The OSS agents supplied Ho with arms and trained about two hundred of his guerillas to assist in the rescue of American pilots downed by the Japanese.

Meanwhile, to grab sole power in Vietnam, Ho and his militant disciples tried to eliminate their Vietnamese political rivals.

Slowly, the Viet Minh crushed nearly all the nationalist movements. Theirs was a reign of terror, and the allegations of nationalist figures being killed by Ho threw my father into a state of confusion. He decided to retire and live quietly on his island south of Saigon. He made preparations to leave Cambodia.

It was now the fall of 1945, and over the radio came the news that the Allied Forces were disarming the Japanese troops. In North Vietnam, China played that role, bringing in two hundred thousand men to do the job. The British, with a smaller contingent, went to the South. President Franklin Roosevelt sent to Vietnam a small U.S. mission. Ho Chi Minh was trying to win the Allied Forces' support for his government, and a Vietnamese-American friendship society was formed in Vietnam. People thought they saw a peaceful future on the horizon.

All of the Japanese, including Kobayashi, had to go to Vietnam to surrender to the Allied Forces. Kobayashi was kept under guard for a period before being deported to Japan.

In September 1945, a contingent of French troops landed in Saigon, having been allowed to return by Britain and the United States. Again, fighting resumed between the French and the Viet Minh, reinforced by other Vietnamese resistance groups. The struggle spread across the whole country, and the Viet Minh were forced back to their base areas in the countryside.

It was during this period of resistance warfare that famine struck Vietnam. In the center and the north, and in some parts of the Delta in the south, a third to a half of the population died in some areas. It was reported that one million Vietnamese perished in the 1944–1945 famine; in fact, it might have been more.

My father still wanted to leave Cambodia and take all of us to the Great House on the island. But the island, too, was plagued with fighting and disorder. The French were bombing my father's part of the island, suspecting that Vietnamese resistance groups had infested it. The Viet Minh, in fact, had installed themselves clandestinely on the far side of the island, deep in the jungle. They, too, made life uncomfortable for the villagers, warning them not to collaborate with the French and asking them for assistance.

Back in Cambodia, my father bought a fishing boat to transport our household, including his collection of antique furniture and porcelain, back to Vietnam. The boat would go down the Mekong, out into the South China Sea, and to our grandfather's house in Go Cong. He let my brother number six, Trung, my sister number eight, Thu Cuc, and my sister number nine, Thu Thuy, go with the boat. They would stay with our grandparents. Then, to transport our clothes and smaller household items, he rented a big truck and put my brother number three, Anh Ba, in charge of taking it to Saigon. Anh Ba's destination was the house of Co Ba Tra, my father's old flame. So six of my brothers and sisters preceded me to Vietnam.

It was at this point that my father was deported from Cambodia. His French supervisor had been released from detention after the Japanese defeat. Once the French were back in power, they decreed that whoever had cooperated with the Japanese or the Viet Minh would be punished, and they considered my father a collaborator and a traitor. But because he had devoted twenty years, his whole working life, to Les Terres Rouges, they showed leniency. M. Simon dismissed him and ordered us deported to Vietnam at the end of 1945. I was still only five years old.

I did not understand why I had to be separated from my Vu Van. She held me tightly in her arms all night, sobbing. She kissed me and whispered that she hoped to see me again one day. She said that, because of the war, she had to go her own way, back to Go Cong to her family, after we left the rubber plantation.

It was late in the evening, after dinner, when we left. There was a direct bus that would take us overnight to Saigon, where we would arrive early the next morning. Our house, so magnificent a few months earlier for the wedding, now looked like a funeral home. My parents, stoically holding back their tears, said goodbye to the staff. Their eyes met, locked in a last adieu. Twenty years of good times and bad were being left in ashes. My sisters were sniffing noisily.

I shrieked and ran back into Vu Van's arms. "I don't want to leave you. I've always been with you. What am I going to do without you?"

"Please go back to your parents," she said. "You must go with them."

"Why? Don't you love me anymore? Come with me."

"Yes, I'll go later. Now, go back to your parents."

Tears fell from her puffy eyes. Without another word, she ran inside the house and hid behind the door. My father pulled me away, his hand holding mine tightly. All of our domestic staff, nearly ten of them, bowed their heads sadly, sobbing. They had packed their suitcases already and were to leave in the morning on another bus to their different villages.

Late in the evening, after dinner, my parents and the four of us who had remained behind got on the bus that would take us away forever. My mother carried my youngest brother, Khanh, and my father held me next to him. On the way to the border, I saw my parents sitting erect and dignified, silent tears flooding their faces. They did not turn their heads once. I slowly lay my head on my father's legs, and slept. We crossed the border at night, and arrived in Saigon in the early morning.

In March 1946, Ho signed an agreement with France that recognized the Republic of Cochin-China as a "free state" within the French Union. General Charles de Gaulle, the leader of France, granted Vietnam only restricted autonomy; instead of installing a French governor again, he sent a French high commissioner. In return, Vietnam was to allow fifteen thousand French troops to stay in the country for five years.

The French set about restoring order after the Japanese defeat. Life in the capital was still unstable, however, and it was hard for my father to find a new job or start a business. Fearing he might be on the French blacklist after his deportation from Cambodia, he felt he had to lead a quiet life, in the shadows.

My parents and we children stayed temporarily on Frères Louis Street with Miss Ba Tra, my father's old paramour, now married to a respectable man who worked at the Court of Saigon. My parents had become good friends with this couple, and decided to buy a house a mile away from them on the same street. Mortgages were unheard of, and my parents had to pay cash. But we were now living on our family's savings, and my parents were looking for ways to earn money. My parents' lives could be summed up in the words of Vietnamese poet Nguyen Du.

Tram nam trong coi nguoi ta
Chu tai chu menh kheo la ghet nhau

(Within the span of a hundred years, the limit of a human life,
Talent and destiny are apt to contradict each other)

The agreement between the French and Vietnamese with regard to Cochin-China was troubled from the start. Soon, French and Viet Minh troops were attacking each other again, not only in Cochin-China and the South, but throughout Vietnam. This was the start of the first Indochina War, which would last eight years and end with the French defeat at Dien Bien Phu in late 1953 and the Geneva Accords in early 1954.

During that period, rumors circulated that the Viet Minh had assassinated Huynh Phu So, leader of the Hoa Hao, an armed sect of reform Buddhists founded in 1939 in the South. In only eight years of preaching, Huynh Phu So had built up a tremendous following among common people who wanted to return to a purer form of Buddhism. At the same time, his followers were often armed, and they exerted strict control over their own areas. Huynh Phu So disappeared in 1947 and was never heard of again. Ta Thu Thau, leader of another resistance group; Ngo Dinh Khoi, brother of future president Ngo Dinh Diem; and many other political figures were also eliminated.

TWO

BROTHERS AND SISTERS ON OPPOSITE SIDES

The year 1946 was one of upheaval in Vietnam, with demonstrations, imprisonments, clandestine resistance groups, police searches, and assassinations. Fighting continued under the unsatisfactory treaty with the French, who refused to grant Vietnam total independence. In that feverish atmosphere, men and women, even high school students, tended to choose a political affiliation that they felt fit them. As secretly as possible, each resistance group tried to recruit members. Even people in the same family did not know exactly what the others were doing. They might suspect or guess that a parent, brother, or sister was going to meetings at night, but they did not know for sure, and they did not know why. Each person was sworn to silence.

Nam Ly ("plum") was my fifth sister and the one who was forced to marry the Japanese interpreter in 1945 during the Japanese occupation. After fleeing Cambodia for my father's island and losing her baby, she joined the Viet Minh as a sympathizer. That was in 1946; two years later, she became a sworn operative. During this period, she lived clandestinely on the island and dedicated herself to fighting the French colonialists. We lost track of her during most of the eight-year First Indochina War. She would reappear in Saigon near the end of the war, then go north when Vietnam was partitioned and not return for more than twenty years. In May 1975, when the victorious Northern Communists entered the South, Nam Ly and her family followed. They arrived in Saigon not long after my children and I had fled. She eventually would be the only one in our family to remain in Vietnam, and the only one to remain a convinced Communist.

As Nam Ly began her life as part of the Communist cadre in 1948, the Viet Minh were attacking French military strongholds throughout Vietnam, destroying bridges and blocking roads. They soon got help from China. With the defeat of Chiang Kai-Shek and the collapse of the Kuomingtang in 1949, Mao Tse-Dong took power in China, and Ho appealed to him for help. Within a few months, Mao sent to Vietnam General Lo Kwei-Po and a number of Chinese experts. Ho's generous Chinese brother also sent him arms, ammunition, and food.

During this period, Nam Ly was acting as a secretary, typing Viet Minh documents. She also taught children at the Youth Militants School in the bush. In 1951, she was transferred to another jungle area, at Duc Hoa, a small town in the Mekong Delta, where she married a passionate young Viet Minh comrade. Huynh Van Binh was a navy captain in the 308th Viet Minh Battalion. In 1953 Nam Ly became pregnant, left the bush, and went to Saigon to my parents' house to deliver her baby, named Long Nguyen. He was born in January 1954.

Was Nam Ly aware in 1953 that her comrades in the North were launching a land reform campaign that would later be condemned as zeal run amok and remembered for its cruelty and bloodshed? I recall documentaries and movies relating heinous scenes. Rich people, religious leaders, schoolteachers, former mandarins, and other "reactionary bour-geois" were gathered together in the evenings to discuss farm and trade taxes, and why they had evaded them. The cadres, the hard-core peasants who were the party faithful at the local level, set up "special people's courts" and held public trials. Armed with sticks and ropes, they arrested and tortured the alleged tax evaders until they signed confessions. It was rumored that these measures had been used in China and imported into Vietnam by the Chinese advisors.

Some victims had to kneel with a basket of stones balanced on their head. Some were hung by their feet from a rope thrown over a rafter, and jerked up and down. Some had their head immersed in a bucket of water until they confessed. Some had their thumbs wrapped in a cloth soaked in oil and lit on fire. Often the "traitors" had their feet chained together and their arms tied, and were dragged along dirty roads under the flaming sun.

Although most quickly confessed to whatever they were accused of, it was not enough: they were then beaten and sent to do hard labor in concentration camps or sentenced to death—either buried alive or put in front of a firing squad. At these executions, the reactions of the onlookers were orchestrated, with children beating drums and people shouting the usual slogans. They clapped their hands as these "public enemies" fell. The wives of the victims, now widows, were forced to marry party members. This way the party spread fear throughout the population and destroyed the middle class in the North. Hoang Van Chi, who had joined the French Socialist party in 1936 and the Viet Minh Resistance in 1945 and lived through the "land reform" campaign in the North, described it in his book, *From Colonialism to Communism—A Case History of North Vietnam*. He turned against the Communists in 1955 because of the brutal way some of his family members were treated. He dedicated a copy of his book to me in 1985.

Leaders of the party disclaimed any connection with the mass arrests and barbaric executions. It was the peasants who had to bear the guilt for the purging of their class enemies, and this, in turn, tied them even closer to the party. Their involvement was clear, and they had no choice but to stay loyal to the regime.

Finally, at the end of 1956, after three years of violent "land reform," the situation was so bad that the Communist leaders put a stop to it. They launched a "Rectification of Errors" campaign. Truong Chinh, secretary-general of the party, and Ho Viet Thang, vice-minister of land reform, resigned. At the tenth congress of the Party's Central Committee, General Vo Nguyen Giap, who had handed the French their monumental defeat at Dien Bien Phu in 1953, read a long list of "errors" committed. The party released twelve thousand people from jails and gave them back their confiscated properties.

Besides advising the Viet Minh on their land reform campaign, General Lo and his Chinese experts also counseled them on how to attack the French-occupied zones in the far north, along the border with Laos and

China. The Communists wanted to trap the French in the jungle areas, where the French were at a disadvantage. In April 1953, Viet Minh troops crossed the Annamese chain of mountains bordering Laos carrying ammunition and provisions on bicycles. In the mountains, they were protected from air attacks and fed by "walking grain carriers" from neighboring Thanh Hoa province. Every night, like ants, thousands of Vietnamese porters, male and female, each shouldering thirty pounds of rice, walked ten miles between sunset and sunlight to bring supplies to the troops around Dien Bien Phu.

Some Viet Minh troops then went to Luang Prabang, Laos's royal city, and proceeded on toward central and southern Laos, scattering and exhausting the French forces. The French had to defend Laos, particularly the capital city, so they had to halt the Viet Minh's advance at any price. To cut the enemy's supply route, the French made a fateful move: they parachuted six battalions into Dien Bien Phu, an outpost deep in the jungle, occupied it in November 1953, and then reinforced it with more troops.

Now the Viet Minh had the French in the jungle trap they had prepared so painstakingly. General Giap and his guerilla army laid siege, and, after a long and massive assault, the French garrison was overrun. This ended the French stay in Vietnam, a defeat formalized in May 1954 at the Geneva Conference. There, the Mendes-France government signed an agreement partitioning Vietnam at the seventeenth parallel and recognizing the Democratic Republic of Vietnam in the North. The South was left under the Emperor Bao Dai, still supported by the French.

After Dien Bien Phu and the Geneva Conference, the new Communist state in the North was supposed to bring home any troops it had left in the South. As part of this movement, Nam Ly's husband, Binh, piloted a boat carrying Viet Minh from the Mekong Delta province of Sadec to Hanoi. Binh told her that he would come back south to her and his child in two years, when the general elections called for in the Geneva Accords were to be held.

By this time, my family had moved to a bigger house on Paul Bert street in Tan Dinh, a section of Saigon. I was still in middle school at

Marie Curie. Nam Ly had come back to live with us. Although she did not have a steady job, she did a lot of volunteer work. She used to tell me she was going out to evening meetings to raise funds for the poor, and asked me to babysit for her son. I did not know that Nam Ly was in fact meeting with other Viet Minh cadres and working to recruit more adherents to the cause. Their aim was to make the French abide by the Geneva Accords and hold general elections in July 1956.

Whenever I asked questions about Nam Ly or her husband, my mother told me that young girls should not be too curious. I should concentrate on my studies and mind my own business.

Nam Ly's night outings became more and more frequent. On weekends, she helped to set up events for women's organizations and other groups. Besides meetings, these included fund-raising luncheons and dinners with shows and songs. Unaware of all the secret work, I attended some of them.

Meanwhile, Viet Minh agents were being sent to organize cells in the cities and towns of South Vietnam, and to infiltrate the government and the military. They mingled with all parts of the society, earned people's confidence, spread rumors, and fomented dissention. This was what Nam Ly and Anh Tam, the husband of my number eight sister Thu Cuc, and scores of their comrades had been doing all along in the capital city.

In early 1956, Nam Ly was called to the police station for questioning about her political activities. Released for lack of proof, but worried now that she would be caught and put in jail, she started to look for ways to leave Vietnam. Her chance came when she joined a tourist group to Cambodia to visit the famous temple of Angkor Wat, one of the Seven Wonders of the World. She did not return with the group to Saigon, but stayed on in Phnom Penh. She was able to speak some Cambodian, which she had learned as a girl on the rubber plantation.

The colorful Prince Sihanouk was then ruling Cambodia, as he would off and on for at least the next forty years. Nam Ly petitioned him to allow her to go to Hanoi to join her husband under the auspices of the International Control Commission, the Polish, Canadian, and Indian body supervising the Geneva Accords.

The accords provided for a period of free movement between North and South Vietnam for people who chose to use it. Many did. Some nine hundred thousand northern Catholics came south as refugees, and about one hundred thousand Viet Minh southerners moved to the North. Ominously, about ten thousand Viet Minh stayed in the South and continued their clandestine work.

After hearing the good news that Nam Ly could join her husband, Binh, in Hanoi, my mother asked an aunt of ours to take Ly's son, Long Nguyen, to Phnom Penh. The three were finally reunited in Hanoi in July 1957.

By then, Binh had spent time in China to further his studies in navigation. Back in Hanoi as a navy captain, he taught at the Naval Academy. When Nam Ly arrived, she went to work first for a factory manufacturing plastics, then for a metal factory in Hai Phong. She and Binh would have four children altogether.

Back in Saigon, my mother told me not to say anything to anyone about Nam Ly's whereabouts after she left for Cambodia. The police were ready to jail anyone with any connection to the Viet Minh, whether in the South or the North. So I kept my mouth shut. We hardly communicated with Nam Ly or talked about her. She had disappeared from our family. For us, she lived on another planet, carried away by the north wind.

Almost twenty years later, in the summer of 1975, the south wind would blow her back. The "liberation" of Saigon, now renamed Ho Chi Minh City, was a victorious homecoming for the Communists. Nam Ly, Binh, and their four children returned to live with my mother in Tan Dinh. She welcomed them with open arms, overjoyed to see them at long last. Poor herself, Nam Ly brought my mother gifts of a dozen ceramic rice bowls, two kilos of sugar, and two cans of condensed milk. She had been misinformed in the North that people in the South were much deprived; in fact, these items had always been commonplace in Saigon.

Nam Ly had sacrificed thirty years of her life to liberate our country from foreign domination. Now, at her homecoming, Vietnam was rid of the French colonialists, the Japanese conquerors, and the American "imperialists." All that remained were Soviet tanks and thousands of Russian advisors. She and her husband went to work for the Ministry of Transportation in Ho Chi Minh City, staying until they both retired in the late 1980s. She then established a folk theater troupe to propagate Communist ideology that performed all over Vietnam.

Nam Ly had paid a high price to see a unified Communist Vietnam, but the rest of our family had paid even more. My brother, Khanh, had been killed by the Viet Cong on the battlefield. My father had had his fortunes ruined and his life shortened by the war. My husband, Bong, had been assassinated by Communist terrorists. And now there was to be a new tragedy.

Even after the "liberation," the Communist victors continued to purge and eradicate the Vietnamese "lackeys" who had collaborated with the former regime and the Americans. It was said that they had enjoyed a corrupt life, paid for with the tears and blood of the Communist cadres. It was time for them to learn what they had done wrong and to repent. They had to acquire new, revolutionary ideas. So it became the policy of the new government after the unification of the two Vietnams in 1975 to retrain them in "reeducation" camps or, for higher-level sinners, to send them to prison.

This hit our own family in a terrible way. When my mother arrived in the United States in 1980 to live with us, she told me that she had heard a rumor that Nam Ly had denounced her younger brother, Trung, as a Central Intelligence Agency agent after she returned to Saigon. In fact, Trung was arrested, then sent to prison in the North. My mother said that Nam Ly devoted her *tin,* her "loyalty," to her party instead of to her family. Even though there was no proof, my mother was so heartbroken that she renounced Nam Ly and never talked about her or wrote to her again. At seventy-six, she had lived through enough turbulence, and could not bear the thought of such terrible divisions among her own children.

Nam Ly and her husband were among the first wave of Vietnamese Communists, the Viet Minh of the 1940s who fought the French. In the 1950s, another group of radicals emerged, well-educated, from the upper middle class, and disenchanted with the dictatorial regime of Ngo Dinh Diem and its American supporters. They, too, served as an extended arm of the Northern Communists in the South. Later, they became the Viet Cong. It was they who set up shop in the jungles in 1960 and established the National Liberation Front (NLF), a bogus grouping of "popular" organizations dedicated to bringing down the Diem government.

NLF members infiltrated the government at all levels, working their way into the ministries, the legislature, and the military. Once in position, they began to destabilize and sabotage. Among the best known were Albert Pham Ngoc Thao, Truong Nhu Tang, Nguyen Huu Tho, Trinh Dinh Thao, Duong Quynh Hoa, and Huynh Tan Phat. They all came from upper-class families, and they had a strong network of friends among the elite. They had left their comfortable lives in Saigon to join the Communist reformers and look for an ideal form of democracy. Then they came back as double agents.

Albert Thao was an admirer of Ho Chi Minh who was sent as an undercover agent to sow dissention in the South. Since the government was looking for him in the 1950s, his parents, strong Catholics, persuaded the Bishop of Hue, Ngo Dinh Thuc, to take their son under his wing and protect him. The Bishop was the elder brother of President Ngo Dinh Diem, and he accepted this charge as an extended gesture of *tin*, loyalty to his Catholic followers. Bishop Thuc introduced Albert to President Diem and his brother Ngo Dinh Nhu, describing him as the repentent son of devoted Catholics. Albert won their trust and was sent to Malaysia in 1957 to learn counterinsurgency techniques to help the government fight the Communist guerillas. Back home again, Albert was put in charge of the "strategic hamlet" program, a massive, nationwide effort to gather the farmers into self-contained compounds away from their villages, so they could be protected more easily from the Communist insurgents. The program was heavily assisted by American advisors.

Albert moved quickly to construct the hamlets and please his boss, Nhu, who was not only close to the president, but head of police intelligence. By then, Nhu was convinced both of Albert's loyalty and his capability. No one suspected that Albert was sowing confusion and instilling hostility among the peasants. But he was: he led them to believe they were being forced to leave their normal lives and herded into fortified outposts for reasons they could not understand.

The peasants resisted, and the government's program was a failure. But Albert was not. He gave new proof of his loyalty when he sped down to the Delta to urge Colonel Tran Thien Khiem, later President Thieu's prime minister, to lead his division to President Diem's rescue during the coup attempt of November 1960.

Albert's star rose higher, and in 1961 he was rewarded with the position of chief of Ben Tre province, a rich, rice-growing area in the Mekong Delta. Albert formed a quiet alliance with the guerillas there to keep the area stable, and Ben Tre became known as the model of a peaceful province. He won praise from Diem, Nhu, and the American advisors. In reality, Ben Tre was being used as a Viet Cong rest area and a place where they could plan their terrorist activities—using a wealth of intelligence passed on to them by the province chief himself, their enemy by day and secret ally by night. After Albert left, it became clear that Ben Tre was one of the most dangerous of the Delta's sixteen provinces. It was at the Lunar New Year, Tet, of 1968, when the Viet Cong launched their memorable nationwide attacks, that an American officer made the ill-fated remark, "We had to destroy Ben Tre in order to save it," a comment that was ridiculed forever afterward as showing the emptiness of the American war effort.

Albert kept being promoted, this time to Saigon to the general staff. He tried to keep his fellow generals' trust while fomenting trouble among them. He was able to attend the meetings of the various groups that staged the coup against Diem in 1963, and knew exactly what would take place. After Diem was murdered, Albert became the spokesman for the Revolutionary Council, and then chief of security for the armed forces. He was promoted to full colonel, and became the closest advisor of General Nguyen Khanh, chief of state in 1964.

But things finally turned sour among the bickering generals, and Albert was exiled to the Vietnamese embassy in Washington, D.C., where he served as military attaché. Also exiled was General Tran Thien Khiem, who went to Washington as ambassador.

Somehow, Albert managed to get back to Saigon and mount a coup against Nguyen Khanh with the support of a network of field commanders, Catholic leaders, and political groups. In February 1965, troops who backed Albert took over the radio station and post office and surrounded the military headquarters. In the end, Albert gave up the coup in exchange for Nguyen Khanh's resignation. Later, Albert disappeared, and it was rumored that he was caught and tortured to death in the summer of 1965 under the presidency of Nguyen Van Thieu. I remember reading with fascination the Saigon newspapers' descriptions of the double life of this master spy. It was like a detective novel. Albert had single-handedly succeeded in changing the fortunes of successive Saigon governments for a decade.

Another prominent Viet Cong figure was Truong Nhu Tang, a friend whom my husband, Bong, and I met occasionally at social functions. His older brother, Dr. Quynh, a doctor married to a French woman, and his younger brother, a well-known banker, were part of our circle. Tang and his five brothers were from a wealthy family, and all went to the French lycée, Chasseloup Laubat, then on to Paris to the university. They did well and were well placed in Saigon society. Right after the 1963 coup against President Diem, Tang became director general of the Société Sucriëre, Vietnam's national sugar company. Bong became head of the National Institute of Administration around the same time, so we saw a certain amount of Tang during this period.

Bong and I were not aware that Tang, as a student, had met Ho Chi Minh for tea in Paris in 1946, or that that meeting had converted Tang into a fervent partisan of the charismatic Ho. Against his father's will, Tang changed his major from pharmacy to political science and put all his effort into trying to liberate his country from French colonialism.

Once he was back in Vietnam, Tang, like Bong, rebelled against the iron rule of President Diem and his brother, Nhu. In 1958, he and others formed a secret society called the Mobilizing Committee. The group included my own gynecologist, Dr. Duong Quynh Hoa; a respected lawyer, Trinh Dinh Thao; and other politically minded people. Tang and others from the Committee founded the famous National Liberation Front (NLF) of South Vietnam, which was officially established in December 1960 in the jungle. Its president was Nguyen Huu Tho, the father of a very close classmate of mine, Jeanne Tho. Jeanne and I were at that moment studying together at Les Oiseaux high school in Dalat; our bedrooms were next to each other, divided only by a thin wall.

The NLF sought guidance and advice from Uncle Ho in the North. Its members called for an armed struggle to liberate the South from despotism. I never imagined that Tang, a shy, self-effacing man, could be working closely with Huynh Tan Phat, Vo Van Kiet, and other notorious members of the Communist Politburo whose names became prominent after the fall of Saigon to the Communists in 1975. Working in the political, military, and diplomatic arenas, they mobilized support within and outside Vietnam, aiming particularly to win the sympathy of the American people. They used a psychological warfare technique called *danh va dam, dam va danh,* meaning "fight and talk, talk and fight."

Within the South Vietnamese government, Tang worked under the supervision of Nguyen Anh Tuan, undersecretary for economic planning, who had been a friend of Bong in the School of Law and Political Science in Paris. His wife, Hoai Tran, taught political science with Bong at the School of Law in Saigon. Tuan, Hoai Tran, Bong, and I were together frequently at dinners and parties at our own houses and those of friends. None of us suspected for a moment that Tang was working feverishly at night and on weekends to get people he knew to form bogus front organizations like the Movement for Self-Determination, the Peace Committee, and the Catholic Youth and Buddhist Youth Associations, whose purpose was to denounce the government and criticize the American attacks in the North.

It was not until 1967, when Tang was betrayed by a Viet Cong agent and put in jail, that we learned that that soft-spoken, respected bourgeois seen often at Saigon parties and nightclubs was in fact part of the National Liberation Front brain trust. Tang was tortured in prison and put in solitary confinement. After eight months of incarceration, not long after the 1968 Tet Offensive, he and two women from the Front were exchanged for American prisoners. The transfer took place near the Gia Long high school, the area where Bong and I lived for eight years.

The three Vietnamese were ushered into an American Red Cross truck escorted by several American military vehicles. They stayed in an American safe house for a day, then were taken by a man from the Front to the airport in a car driven by an American major. An American military police jeep preceded them. They boarded a helicopter for Trang Bang district, fifty miles northwest of Saigon. Once there, they piled into a three-wheel Lambretta that took them into the jungle. At a certain point, they got out and walked for more than ten miles. Finally, a group of guerillas welcomed them and guided them to the Front's headquarters, located on the Mimot rubber plantation. Mimot was one of the Terres Rouges plantations, where my father used to work, along the Vietnamese and Cambodian border.

Recovered from his weakness and sickness at the Front's hospital, Tang went to work at NLF headquarters, where he met with his longtime friend, Dr. Duong Quynh Hoa, my former gynecologist. (The answer I got when I tried to make an appointment with her was that she had gone away "on a long trip and did not know when she would come back.")

These same intellectual activists, along with other opponents of Diem and Thieu, had established the Alliance of National, Democratic, and Peace Forces. The Alliance was headed by Trinh Dinh Thao, a wealthy and well-known lawyer. A couple of years later, Bong and I went to Thao's magnificent mansion to attend the wedding of his son, also a lawyer and a friend of Bong. The son had returned from Paris and married a close friend of my number seven sister, Thu Ha Bell. The bride's family was among the richest diamond dealers in Vietnam. All six bright, beautiful daughters had gone to Les Oiseaux school in Dalat.

The Alliance and the NLF were working in tandem out in the bush against the Thieu and Nixon governments. In June 1969, the NLF set up the Provisional Revolutionary Government, or PRG. Its proponents wanted the PRG to be recognized nationally and internationally as South

Vietnam's opposition government. Trinh Dinh Thao became the PRG's president. Dr. Hoa was named minister of health. Nguyen Thi Binh (who was the spokeswoman for the Communist delegation at the Paris Peace Talks with Henry Kissinger) was foreign minister. Tang became minister of justice.

At that very same time, Bong set up his own opposition party to the government, the Progressive Nationalist Movement. His was a genuine nationalist group with no link to the Northern Communists.

During these years, the Alliance and the NLF sent cadres to Saigon to arouse resistance among the populace, and one of their strategies was to recruit student leaders to incite unrest. Huynh Tan Mam, president of the University of Saigon Student Union, was arrested and tried for subversive activities. He denied any connection with the Front, and became a celebrity. Another of the student activists was Doan Van Toai, who was jailed by the Communists after the "liberation" and became disillusioned with them.

I came to know Toai after he migrated to France (his Vietnamese-born wife was a French citizen) and, in 1980, arrived in Washington. He presented himself as a dissident from the now Communist government of Vietnam, and urged the Vietnamese refugees in the United States to help him denounce the atrocities committed by the northern Communists. We were all willing to help Toai link up with American groups that could help him to travel around the country to condemn Communist repression.

Toai's complaint sprang from the fact that, once in power, the Communists had discarded their former allies, the southerners in the NLF, and had jailed hundreds of thousands of people. Toai and the Viet Cong in the South felt betrayed by their big Communist brothers, who gave them no role to play after Vietnam was unified. They felt that, as the Vietnamese saying goes, the new rulers of Vietnam had "used the lemon juice and thrown away the rind."

Cynical Vietnamese in the United States were glad to see that it was the Viet Cong's turn to suffer betrayal and serve their term of karma. They were aware of how much harm the Viet Cong had done to Vietnam in executing the orders of the North to carry out sabotage and terrorism in the South. The Viet Cong had deceived the whole world by portraying themselves as the only true nationalists, opposed to President Thieu's government in the South but with no connection with the Communists. So many Vietnamese wondered why my friends and I should want to help Toai, a former Viet Cong and a traitor himself.

I told them that I was not interested in judging; I was more concerned with seeing that human rights abuses were publicized and condemned. So I went on assisting Toai as much as I could.

The American Federation of Labor and Congress of Industrial Organizations sponsored a speaking tour for Toai, and he asked me to be his interpreter. Nguyen Huu Hieu, a former Buddhist monk and Toai's prison cellmate, came with us. We went to gatherings in New York and Miami. We discussed the NLF, the students' movement, religious repression, the Vietnamese reeducation camps and prisons, and other issues that related to the Vietnam War and its aftermath.

The next year, 1981, Toai arranged for Truong Nhu Tang, by then the highest-ranking defector from the NLF, to come from France to the United States. When he and his third wife, Marie Madeleine Huong, a classmate of mine from Les Oiseaux, came to the Washington area, my husband Lacy and I invited them over for dinner. Tang told me of his life in Saigon and in the jungle—stories he was to describe in *A Vietcong Memoir*, written with Toai and an American named David Chanoff and published in 1985. During Tang's visit, he asked me to help him meet Ambassador Ellsworth Bunker and other prominent Americans. I arranged for Tang and Toai to have lunch with the ambassador, who asked them, "Who among the Viet Cong gave the order to assassinate Bong, Jackie's husband?" They told me later that they told the ambassador they did not know. That might be the truth, since those responsible could have been under the direction of a different secret cell. Or did they know something but did not want to say?

Tang and his wife settled in the suburbs of Paris after fleeing Ho Chi Minh City by boat in late August 1978. Tang felt disillusioned and deceived by the northern Communists after Vietnam's unification. As for Toai, he went to California to live with his wife and three children. When

I was in Bangkok in 1987, I heard that Toai had been shot by a Vietnamese refugee, but had escaped death. I saw him briefly in 1991 in Washington at the Asia Society, where he had arranged a talk by one of the highest-ranking north Communist dissidents, Bui Tin. After that, I lost track of him again.

In the small circle of the Saigon elite, nearly everyone knew everyone else. Whether they were friends or foes, they were associated by an intricate web of personal and family bonds extending through generations. Through *tin,* "loyalty," they were ready to harm, even kill, their enemies to avenge their loved ones or achieve some other goal. They were even prepared to protect former friends turned enemies rather than denouncing them to the authorities, which would have been seen as betrayal. With *phuc duc,* good fortune, they were also apt to forget and pardon those who offended them. And with karma, inevitable cause and effect, they were aware that they could not escape fate, which would catch up with them in this life or the afterlife. It was the Confucian philosophy, and it ran in the Vietnamese blood.

Another intimate attachment I had with the Viet Cong was with Jeanne Tho, the daughter of National Liberation Front president Nguyen Huu Tho. I was not aware at first that her father was a top Viet Cong official, or that she and her younger sister, Genevieve, were protected by the Catholic nuns at Les Oiseaux when we were there in the 1950s. At one point, we had become so close that we gave each other nicknames, talked for hours, and generally behaved as best friends do in those years of girlhood. We studied and did our homework together in the last years of our senior high school at Les Oiseaux.

At night, I often heard her crying through the wall of my bedroom. Kim Hoa, another classmate, used to go with me to console her in the dark of night. Jeanne told us that her father had disappeared a few years earlier. I learned later that this was true. The Viet Minh had broken her father out of prison and taken him to the bush, where he was installed as leader of the National Liberation Front. He left her mother, a beautiful lady who, in her early thirties, had lost her memory after a shock, and had become like a child. Jeanne's mother needed to be taken care of and told what to do. She spent her days talking and singing to herself. She did not remember anything about her past, and said things that made no sense, Jeanne told us.

She also said that an attorney in Saigon kept a trust that provided financial support for her and her family. She had money to get by, but she missed her parents and felt lost and lonely. So Kim Hoa and I tried our best to cheer her up. Some nights, I heard Kim Hoa crying too. She told us that she had found out she was adopted, and did not know anything about her real parents. She resented the fact that her adopted parents had hidden the situation from her, and that she had had to find it out on her own. She, too, suffered a sense of loss.

Another night, it was my turn to cry. I learned that my father had had another stroke and died. So the three of us all shared miseries that involved our parents.

In our last year at Les Oiseaux, Jeanne told me who her father really was, the president of the National Liberation Front. Nguyen Huu Tho wanted her and the rest of his family to join him and live in the maquis. Jeanne refused. By then, she had converted to Catholicism and become a strong adherent. Besides, she told me, her father had another wife and set of children in the maquis living with him. Jeanne asked whether I still wanted to be her friend, or would turn away from her, since her father was outlawed by the government. I told her that I was not involved in politics, and that she was my friend and would remain my friend. I would not desert her.

Back in Saigon after we graduated from high school, I drove Jeanne around to look for an apartment to rent. She had only a limited budget. We found a one-bedroom place on the second floor of an apartment building. She and I went shopping together for all the furniture, kitchen utensils, and other items she needed to set up the small place she had found for her and her mother. She and I read cookbooks, and she learned how to cook so, as head of her household, she could feed her family. We saw each other practically every day.

Jeanne bought a motorbike. Now she could drive me around, or we could go in my car if we had bought things we needed to carry. We were happy doing things together. After a few weeks settling in, it was time for her to find work, and we went to different schools so she could apply for a job teaching primary school. She found one she liked.

I went back to Les Oiseaux in Dalat to teach middle school, then returned to Saigon when my mother told me that I could go to France to study. In preparation for my departure, there were days of paperwork to do. Jeanne would come to my bedroom every evening, and we would talk until past midnight. My mother heard the noise and caught us talking and drinking Coke. She forbade Jeanne to come at night, we could see one another only during the day.

When I left for Paris, Jeanne came to the airport to see me off, and she cried her heart out. I did too. She wrote me later that, riding back from the airport on her motorbike, she nearly had two accidents; she was crying so badly that she could hardly see the road or the cars.

When I came back from Europe to Saigon a couple of years later, Jeanne had moved to a smaller place, in an alley. She wanted to be an unknown entity. I went to visit her as often as I could. When I got married to Bong, well-known as an anti-Communist and therefore very much opposed to her father, our visits became rarer.

At one point, Jeanne was without work, so I helped her get another teaching job from a friend of mine who owned a primary school. I did not see her again for a few months. One day, she came to visit while I was feeding my children. She said she could not stay long, and did not want to be seen in my house or anywhere else with me. This was for my protection. She said she had been picked up a couple of months earlier on the street while she was on her way to work. The security police wanted to know whether she had contacted her father, or any other Viet Cong, or been involved in any subversive activities. She told me that they had subjected her to harsh interrogations, beaten her, chained her ankles, and thrown her into a small, filthy cell with a foul toilet bowl as her only companion. She was sometimes put in solitary confinement, and had to crawl on the floor like a dog to reach through the bars of the cell for a bowl of dark rice dotted with small pieces of dried fish. She did not see the light for weeks and became disoriented. She was told to write a full description of her whereabouts, her contacts, and her daily activities for the previous few years. The police showed her photos of herself and people she had been seen with, including me.

Poor Jeanne. I knew her only in the saddest periods of her life. She had had a childhood devoid of parental love and protection. Her mother could give her no help or support; on the contrary, Jeanne had to be *her* mother. She had few friends, since she could not confide in people about her past or present. The boys she cared about had all run from her as soon as they discovered who her father was. She had to support her sister, Genevieve, who was still in school. Jeanne lived a life of fear, like a fugitive.

Jeanne told me at one point that, in her darkest periods of despair, she had tried more than once to commit suicide. But she had not finished paying off her karma, and fate forced her to go on with a life with no hope or future. I asked myself when she would be able to relax and enjoy some moments of happiness. What had she done to deserve such a sorrowful fate?

Surprisingly enough, I later saw more of Genevieve, Jeanne's sister, who had grown into a beautiful young lady. She and her friends were frequent guests of Ambassador Jacques de Folin, the head of the French embassy in Saigon in the late 1960s. Bong and I used to be invited to his residence for dinner followed by dancing. Marie Laure, Jacques's wife, had remained in Paris to see to their children's education, so Genevieve became his sometime companion at social functions. Later, in 1975, she went to Paris, where Jacques and Marie Laure acted as her sponsors. She lived with them in their Paris apartment for a few years before marrying a French dentist.

As for Jeanne, after fleeing Vietnam in 1975, she, too, married a French-man. They opened a Vietnamese restaurant, and are retired now in a suburb of Paris. They had a son, a handsome boy named Kim, who became a blessed consolation for Jeanne.

Jeanne's life and mine drifted further apart. I had married an American government official, another person opposed to her father, and we lived now in different parts of the world, far from each other. But our friendship has survived time, distance, and politics. Our feelings and our memories are alive inside of us. We know that we will always be in one another's hearts and prayers.

In 1951, my number eight sister, Thu Cuc, also became a student activist. She joined the Viet Minh, or southern Communists, the same group that in 1960 would become the National Liberation Front, whose members were usually called the Viet Cong. I did not understand exactly where she had gone or why. My mother told me only that she had gone to a boarding school in the South, gotten married there, and had a daughter.

In early 1954, my mother entrusted me with an important mission. I was to go and visit Thu Cuc in the deep South, all by myself. It would take a day and a night to travel to that part of the country, and I was very excited at being given the responsibility for such an expedition.

My mother told me to be on my guard at all times, not to talk to any strangers, to keep silent as much as possible, and never to tell anyone where I was going or what I was doing. "Just say that you are visiting a relative, nothing else," she said. That, I thought, would be easy. I prepared myself to give that answer to anyone who asked.

My mother prepared a big basket of dried shrimp, beans, peas, sugar, condensed milk, and raisins. She had me wear black pajamas she had borrowed from the daughter of our maid so I would be dressed like everyone else in the countryside. She rolled big bills of money and a letter inside the belt of my black trousers and told me to hand them to Thu Cuc in person. I could hardly sleep that night, waiting for the morning to come.

At dawn, we took a taxi to Cholon, Saigon's Chinatown, where most of the Chinese lived who had migrated from China. Located half an hour from the center of the city, Cholon was bursting at the seams—noise, traffic jams, people jabbering in Chinese, and shops selling every kind of merchandise. It was like a fair all day, all night, all year around. If you were bored and had nothing to do, you could go to Chinatown. At night, whole blocks became large, open restaurants, with folding tables and chairs scattered in the middle of the streets, where you could eat for the equivalent of a dollar or two. Or you could go to huge, formal restaurants with up to 500 seats that catered to weddings and other such events. Or you could see modern shows in fancy nightclubs. I stared through the window of the taxi, amazed at the forest of fluorescent lights and the general bustle.

At the bus station in Chinatown, with me disguised as a country girl in my black pajamas, we met Co Ba, whom I had first seen three days before at our house. She had been introduced as the sister of Thu Cuc's husband, and had talked to my mother in private. Now, my mother held my hand and told me to obey Co Ba's instructions. She said that I would spend the weekend with my sister, Thu Cuc. I had never met her husband, or even seen photographs of him, and I was thrilled that I was finally going to see my sister's family.

Co Ba and I boarded a big bus—she with a sack of food and I with my small but heavy basket. At thirteen, I felt grown up and responsible, taking my first journey and going so far away from home. I drew a deep breath of pride and freedom, and my small frame swelled with satisfaction. I imagined a shiny medal pinned on the left side of my chest, gleaming in the sun.

I was witnessing an exciting scene. People filled the bus from front to rear, some sitting and some standing. A woman was breastfeeding her baby, and had another child on her lap whom she held down with her free hand to keep him from running around. She also had a talkative chicken and a pretentious duck attached to a basket of eels that undulated in place as two red-eyed fish lay immobile next to them. The sight of these creatures gave me goosebumps.

A bag of rice sat under the woman's feet. Co Ba sat next to her, and I sat next to Co Ba. We were all squeezed onto a bench meant for two. The little boy looked at me, started crying, and kicked me. His mother smacked him, and he kicked me again. I stared at him and stuck out my tongue, and he howled and buried his face in his mother's lap.

Late arrivals, standing in the middle of the bus, leaned into me when the bus turned corners too quickly. Three men hung out of the bus's open door, each balancing on one leg. They shouted at the driver to slow down so they would not be thrown off. Huge baskets of pigs, chickens, ducks, vegetables, and fruit were piled on top of the bus, held precariously in place by plastic cords that seemed about to break at any moment. Children were crying, people shouting, ducks quacking, chickens squawking, and, in the back, a dog was yelping. It was an incredible cacophony.

About an hour into this performance, the band seemed to reach a crescendo and then a grand finale. I lifted my two little hands to my ears and temples. A stone seemed to be falling on my head. The sweat of the people, mixed with the odor of urine and the stench of animals, permeated the whole stuffy bus. I was dizzy and carsick and started to vomit into my handkerchief.

Co Ba knew what to do. She drew a brown liquid from a small container and rubbed it on my temples and my nose. It was a lotion called *nhi thien duong*—"the second path to heaven"—a potent remedy that resurrected me from hell. My nose and eyes dilated under the anointing with that blessed medication. Instantly, I was revived, and was able to put up with the trip for another hour. Finally, tired out, I slept with my head against Co Ba's bony arm.

Co Ba finally shook me and said we were getting off. Sounding its last hurrah, the band trailed off in the distance as the bus disappeared.

We crossed the street to a tamarind tree where a man in his fifties, wearing a short-sleeved white shirt and long khaki trousers, was waiting for us. His name was Chu Hai. Co Ba recognized him and introduced me. He helped carry our two baskets.

I was thirsty and hungry. We stopped at the first corner and a young man, shirtless, sliced off the top of a coconut with one sharp slash of a big knife. The coconut milk was sweet and refreshing, and I drank it with delight, right out of the shell. We then followed Chu Hai to another street vendor two blocks away, where we bought French bread filled with *nem* (a Vietnamese ham), slices of cucumber mixed with parsley, and small plastic bags of crushed ice with red syrup tied with a rubber band.

Then we got onto another bus. It was a small, dirty van, but the ride was much more pleasant. Sitting quietly in the van's front row, I became so hungry that I devoured the bread and finished sipping the iced syrup within minutes. I was still hungry, but there was nothing left except the dry food in the basket. I wanted to eat some of Thu Cuc's raisins, but I did not dare take them. I had to deliver the whole package safe and sound, as my mother had told me. So I just looked at them with envy from time to time.

The van deposited us on a road with no houses or other signs of civilization. The scene was deserted except for a dog running toward us and barking furiously. I recoiled, imagining myself bitten by a wild dog and inflicted with rabies when all I wanted to do was see my sister. I stood still as a piece of wood. But Chu Hai whistled, threw the mongrel a piece of sandwich, and the dog wagged his tail and ate happily.

Chu Hai then pointed his finger to the east, and said we had to walk in that direction for about twenty minutes. It was late afternoon, and the sun was becoming less harsh. I walked behind Chu Hai and in front of Co Ba, Indian file, along a dirt road with rice fields on both sides.

Young, green rice plants leapt forward and back, following the command of the breeze. I smiled at them and they bowed to me, giggling in return. They caressed my fingers as I touched them. I shook hands with them and pulled their leaves. I courted them. I smelled their scent, the scent of life.

We passed some scattered houses, made a few turns, and finally arrived at a small, thatched-roof hut in the middle of nowhere. A couple in their sixties, in black pajamas, came out to greet us. I bowed to show respect. Their dark, thin faces showed deep lines, the effect of long hours every day in the sun. Chu Hai and Co Ba called them Uncle and Aunt Bay, and thanked them for their kind hospitality. Hot tea was ready for us to drink, and dinner would be served when we wished.

Inside was a big open space with two twin-size bamboo beds on each side, a square wooden table with three round stools in the middle, and a simple chest of drawers against the left wall. Two oil lamps shone feebly in the dark room. In the back was a bathroom with a large clay jar filled with rain water. Opposite was a very small kitchen, with a couple of dark pots and pans.

I asked to take a bath. Aunt Bay said I could either go to the river twenty yards at the rear or use the bathroom. I did not want the leeches to suck out my blood, or myself to be sucked underwater by an unseen current, so I chose the bathroom. I dipped half a dried coconut into the big clay jar, scooped out the cool water, and washed myself happily from head to toe. It felt good.

Placing the dishes on large pieces of newspaper on the dirt floor, I helped to serve the hot vegetable soup and three fresh fish that had been simmering in *nuoc mam*, pungent Vietnamese fish sauce. From the yard, I picked two cucumbers and cut them into bite-size pieces. All five of us squatted on the floor and ate in silence. I savored every bite with immense pleasure. Afterward, I helped to clean the dishes and asked to go outside.

Peasant life, I thought, was so simple. Everything was ready at one's fingertips. Rice, fish, vegetables, and fruit abounded. You just planted them and reaped the rich harvest when the time came. Everything was natural and fresh. There was no need for electricity or deluxe accommodations. People were uncomplicated and seemed to be happy with very little, I observed.

I gazed at the immensity of the velvet green rice fields and the lush vegetation outside. A huge, smiling red sun was sinking majestically into the firmament. While the god of the sun, Apollo, was descending, Diana, the goddess of the moon, appeared slowly on the opposite side, resplendent in her diamond cape. My own small being, a tiny cell lost in the infinity of the universe, stood in awe and wonder. My country was so beautiful and peaceful at that moment in time. I wished that everything would stop, that the moment would last forever.

But nothing lasts forever in this world. Sun and moon, day and night, black and white, life and death—each evolves into the other. The yin renews itself in the yang, war alternates with peace. Each phenomenon has its time to come and go. My father had explained all this to me.

Later I lay on a hammock, suspended between two mango trees, feeling overwhelmed by the mystery of nature. Why? Why? The more I asked, the more questions thundered inside my head. Soon I was swept into sleep by the cool north breeze—though not for long. Mosquitoes buzzed busily around my ears and awakened me. I went inside and lay on the bamboo bed next to Co Ba.

Then, in the middle of the night, Co Ba shook me and told me to get ready to leave; we had to continue our journey. Without a word, we assembled our things and bade farewell to our quiet hosts. Chu Hai, who had changed into black pajamas, guided us to a river nearby. A man deep in shadow waved us down to his small boat, and we jumped inside. Co Ba pushed me gently into the curved middle part of that tiny Noah's ark, where I felt as if I were embarking on a long journey. She had me lie down, while she sat erect next to me. The two men positioned themselves on each side and started to row.

Like a guardian angel, Lady Moon guided us along the river with her light. The curtains opened, and we were floating down the center of a long, vast stage, swaying with the smooth waves. Endless rows of tropical trees and bamboos protected us on each side. An orchestra, its conductor hidden in the deep darkness, struck up a nocturnal opera. The birds, sopranos, invisible in the trees, sang high, soft notes. The night owls were the baritones. Tree frogs blew their trumpets in the background, while the crickets whistled.

Music was everywhere. In my mind, a syncopated tap dance gave way to a romantic waltz, and the two boatmen became agile fireflies and rhythmic dancers. They turned into Fred Astaire and Ginger Rogers. Again I was enchanted. In the purity of the moment, I wafted up like a feather and lost myself in a dream.

Co Ba pulled at my foot; we had arrived. After thanking the boatman and Chu Hai and bidding farewell, we looked up and saw a faint oil lamp swinging slowly, like the pendulum of a clock. We climbed up a dirt path to meet the young man with the lamp. He grabbed Co Ba's bag and called her "sister," so I knew it was Anh Tam, my number eight brother-in-law. I bowed to him—the natural way to greet and show respect to older people. He led us inside a thatched-roof hut. An open space, with a bare wooden table and five stools, served as the living area.

My sister, Thu Cuc, came out from behind a partition in the back. She bowed to her sister-in-law, then grabbed my hand. She called me em, "little sister." She was so happy to see me. Anh Tam poured hot tea. We sat around the table and exchanged news about our family. When my sister rushed to the back to prepare breakfast, I excused myself and followed her.

She was squatting on the floor and fanning pieces of wood surrounded by grayish bricks that served as a burner, reheating a pot of rice porridge that had been cooked in the evening. I squatted next to her and looked at her face. She had gained weight, especially around her stomach. She wore black, faded pajamas, like everybody else in this part of the jungle. Her long, thick hair was tied into a big, messy bun behind her neck. Reflecting the fire, droplets of reddish tears ran down her cheeks. I wrapped my short arms around her shoulders. Holding each other, we cried in the silence of the night.

What had happened to the long, curly hair I had seen in her photograph in our family album? Where were her happy smile, her bright, vivacious eyes? What remained of that tall teenager, smartly attired in the Western dress and shoes my father had ordered from Paris? It was past midnight, and the splendid, eighteen-year-old Cinderella whose picture I remembered looked like a peasant. We held each other tightly and sobbed silently for fear the others would hear us. Then I gave her the letter and money my mother had rolled into the belt of my trousers.

After some sleep on the bamboo bed on the side of the living area I had shared with Co Ba, I awoke to daylight. I could see now that my brother-in-law was a handsome young man in his late twenties. After courtesies, his conversation turned into a passionate lecture as we ate our chao, "rice porridge," for breakfast.

"Do you know that Uncle Ho, our resistance leader, the great Ho Chi

Minh, is the one and only master of our beloved land? Do you know that it was he who drove away the cruel French colonizers, the pirates who bled us of our rich natural resources—our rubber, rice, sugar, coffee, and minerals?"

"But didn't the French also buy things from Vietnam? And didn't they build schools around the country?

"No. That's just what the French told you in school. Those are just lies to put you to sleep. The French are exploiting us."

"But at least," I said, "more girls are getting to go to school than when my mother was growing up, and when Vietnam was under the Chinese."

"But we want more. We want independence. Are you aware that a group of Vietnam's intellectual elite—professors, doctors, lawyers—is forming a front to liberate us from subjugation? Some upper-class South Vietnamese have already left their comfortable lives in the capital and are working for the destruction of the foreigners who came to wreck our country." Anh Tam pointed his finger in the air and said, "We have to stand up and fight for our survival, even if it means bloodshed. To do that, we need the support of our brothers, the Soviets and the Chinese. Only they can throw out the colonialists."

"How can the Soviets and Chinese help?"

"They advise us on guerilla war tactics and give us arms."

I was wide-eyed. "What else do you do?"

"We provoke arguments among the Vietnamese nationalists, the supporters of the puppet government of the South. They do nothing but abuse the workers and the poor. They are traitors and will have to bow to the will of the people."

"When do you think that day will come?"

"It may be soon, or it may take fifty more years. But we will defeat them. Marx and Lenin will help us bring the proletariat up to the level of their masters. Socialism is the only answer. That's what we need here."

This eloquent tirade served as the hors d'oeuvres to lunch, and it whetted my appetite.

Thu Cuc asked me to hold her daughter, Thu Tam, nearly a year old, and go outside with her to pick vegetables for lunch. A small garden in the rear contained peppers, squash, sweet potatoes, tomatoes, mint, and basil. She cut some of each and put it in a basket.

"I was fascinated by my husband's teaching in the school where I had gone to study," Thu Cuc explained. "It was in another part of the jungle. I thought I would be going to a real school, with courses like those I used to take in Saigon."

I asked Thu Cuc how the school in the jungle was different.

"I found only a few regular courses and a lot of grand theories," she said. "It was a kind of improvised school in a small, thatch-roofed house with no doors, only a few rows of benches. People had to listen every day to these big ideas. After a year, I met Anh Tam, who was my math teacher and the head of the People's Committee. He pressured me to marry him."

"Did you love him?"

"No, but I didn't dare resist. I had to do it for fear of being accused of being a spy sent by the Saigon police."

"You had no choice? Couldn't you go back to Saigon and stay with us?"

"No, I was afraid of the French, and of the Vietnamese police. If someone had reported me, I might have been on the government's blacklist."

"Why? What have you done?"

"When I was in Saigon, I helped my classmates distribute leaflets against the government."

"And what can you do now?"

"I have to stay out here in the bush. You see, I've graduated. This was my first certificate." Thu Cuc pointed at her daughter. "And now I am going to receive another diploma." She pressed the palm of her hand to her belly. "I'm pregnant again and sick a lot. If I had known what all this would be like, I never would have left our house. All I wanted was to study in a regular school."

I asked Thu Cuc how she had found out about the jungle school in the first place.

"You remember that in 1951 Saigon was full of students demonstrating

against the French and the government. One day, I was in the crowd at
the funeral of Tro On, a student killed by the police during a riot."

"Were you one of the demonstrators?"

"Yes, like most students at that time. All of a sudden, the police rushed
in behind me. I ran as fast as I could, along with all the other people.
But they caught up with us, and I felt myself being beaten with a *matraque*,
the iron baton used by the Vietnamese police. They hit me all over—my
head, my shoulders, my back."

"Couldn't anybody help you?"

"No, everybody else was running, too. I tripped and fell on the ground.
People ran over me, and I was left bleeding from my mouth on the street.
After a while, a student pulled me to my feet and helped me to get home."

"What happened after that?"

"Mother took me to a doctor, and he gave me injections and antibiotics.
Then I waited a couple of months, but it was still too dangerous to be seen
around. The police were interrogating my friends and putting students
in jail. I couldn't go to school anyway, because it was closed by the
authorities."

"Yes, I remember now. I couldn't go to school either."

"So I asked around about a school to attend that would be safe. One
of our cousins, Hai Buu, who was supervising the peasant-tenants at
Father's island, said there was a school farther south where they had
good, French-educated teachers. I was eager to go there, and our parents
gave their permission. It was the wife of Hai Buu who escorted me to
the liberated zone, deep in the forest. What I found was a makeshift
school taught by young resistance militants who had also fled from the
police. So I ended up here."

"What else did you do?" I asked.

"In 1952, I was sent to do secretarial work at the headquarters of the
Women's Committee. The head of it was Anh Tam. That's how I met
him. He fell in love with me and wanted to marry me, against my will."

"Couldn't anyone do anything to stop it?"

"No, I really loved a boy named Quan, another one of the cadres, and he had gotten written permission to marry me. He and our sister number five, Nam Ly, who was visiting me from another area of the jungle, tried to change the situation, but they couldn't. Anh Tam would not yield. And then, a few months later, he lost his position as the leader of the Committee and came to work in this area like any ordinary person."

"So you were pregnant right away?"

"Yes. And then Anh Tam started to beat me and sort of rape me. He felt that he was being punished by his superiors, and that I was rejecting him."

"Couldn't you go to anybody for help?"

"I did, and this was the reason I was sent back to Saigon in early 1953 to deliver the baby. I was afraid I would have a miscarriage. I decided to stay there and get away from him for good. But then Anh Tam sent a message asking for me and his daughter to come down to say goodbye to him one last time. He was to be sent to Hanoi after the Geneva Agreement."

"So why are you still here?"

"God was very hard on me. On that one fateful night with him, I became pregnant for a second time. And then Anh Tam received orders to stay in the South. That is why I am where I am."

The next day, I said my goodbyes to Thu Cuc and her family, and I started my trip home. In the boat, I heard no more philharmonic orchestras or Strauss waltzes. Instead, there were only grandiose words like Marxism, Leninism, Socialism, Revolution. Songs of the proletariat's struggle echoed inside my skull.

I was wide awake in the boat when I realized that I was in the middle of what the French called the *maquis,* or *khu,* the Vietnamese equivalent of the shrubby expanse where the French underground had fought the Nazis in World War II. Now, Anh Tam and my sister were part of an underground group fighting the French. I had heard often on the radio that the "maquisards" were the enemy of the nation.

Oh my God! I was among them, had become their friend, even their accomplice. Paradoxical thoughts jumped up and down in my mind, like an erratic fountain. One of my uncles, Cau Ba, had lied to me! How could he? He had told me that the *maquisards* were the devil personified—that they draped themselves in black, painted their faces like zebras, wore wigs made of leaves, disappeared into tunnels during the day, and popped up at night to kill disobedient children and bad adults.

These demons that had so frightened me were instead real, normal people—worse, they were my blood relatives. What should I do now? My mother had made me promise not to tell anyone about my trip and not to ask any questions. The trip was a secret between her and me.

The excitement I had experienced before my trip was gone. The truth was so disappointing. Life was actually very complicated. I was in a kind of limbo, not knowing what to do with myself. I could not make up my mind any more. I saw monkeys leaping from one branch to another in the trees above me. They encircled me and bound my hands, my feet, my mouth, my nose, my eyes. I was being choked to death. My dream had turned into a nightmare.

I came home disappointed. My trip was not what I had expected. For the first time, I was aware of grand theories and big ideologies my little brain could not comprehend. I started asking my father about Thu Cuc's situation and about war and peace. Although I do not remember, and could not understand, everything my father told me, I can imagine that our conversation might have gone something like the following.

"Why, Father, did you collaborate with the French instead of joining the resistance groups trying to regain Vietnam's independence?" "Well, after centuries of unrest and wars with the Chinese, some Vietnamese were attracted by the French and their culture. Vietname scholars favored the use of the western script the French brought to our country in the seventeenth century. Paradoxically, they were looking to fight the colonialist French with their own language. During that period, we learned about both Western technology and the revolutionary ideas of the promoters of the 1789 revolution in France. We wanted personal freedom and independence. We were looking for something different from armed rebellion to free our country. We were trying to find a poison that would fight poison."

"Was that why you learned French in school?" I asked.

"Yes. The French governor general of Indochina at that time, Albert Sarrault, abolished the Confucian examinations, and started a French and Franco-Annamite schools in the early 1900s. Even Phan Bo Chau, one of the most notorious radicals of my time, changed schools to be like the French schools, and he was among the few leaders who encouraged the nationalists to rebel."

"Did you like Chau and what he was doing?"

"He was one of my heroes at first, but, unfortunately, he later master-minded a series of assassinations and bombings. I hated violence. My idea of the thing to struggle for was the right for people to lead a peaceful life."

"Were there any other groups that thought like you did?"

"Not Bui Tuong Chieu who was at the other extreme and wanted to be like the French in everything. We were more in search of social development and economic prosperity—away from the uprisings and trouble and bad government that were going on when I was a child. The person I did like—who, I found, was moderate and willing to compro-mise—was Nguyen An Ninh. He had traveled in Europe, and got a law degree in Paris. He was more in tune with how the Europeans thought. He was critical of the lack of individual freedom under the French, and the poor way they governed their colonies. He also criticized some of the Confucian ideas we practiced. We needed new blood, new ideas, new values. He told us to seek a better future out in the world; to find the real 'Liberty, Equality, Fraternity.'"

"Did you find it, Father?"

"Yes, I did. You know that I left Go Cong and went to Saigon to earn enough money to bring up my family. I did not want to stay in a small town. It was hard and I had a lot of difficulties. But I thought it was important for me to become independent first before I started to try to make changes in the country. I thought it was wrong to resort to violence to make things better. That doesn't mean that I love my country less because I am not an extremist. I just never thought violence and terror were the answer."

"Didn't you agree with Communism?"

My father showed me his hand and asked me to look at it carefully. "See my five fingers. Can you describe them to me?"

"Well, let's see. The thumb is far apart and smaller than all the others, and the four others are of different shapes and lengths."

"Exactly. You see, all of you children were born each with a different body and mind. Although you all came from the same source, your mother and me, you have your own personality, your own character, and your own ideas about life. Even if you look like one another, none of you is the same. Each finger has a different fingerprint."

From that moment, I began to see that the Communist ideal of the "equal share" was utopian, not realistic. It was like the fingers of the hand. The more I looked at them, the more I saw that there was no way a person could be the same size, or enjoy the same talents, or feel the same needs, or have the same ideas as other people. People could have basic values in common, but after that they were very different. I could not see how Communism could work.

In a way, I was happy to have gone on the trip. It had opened my eyes to a lot of things. It made me think about political views and the condition of women. It started me thinking about what kind of family I wanted to have. I began to develop a compass that would shape my outlook and guide me in my future life.

I started thinking about marriage, too. My eldest sister's prearranged marriage, my number five sister's forced wedding to a Japanese, and my number eight sister's unwilling union with a Communist zealot made me resist marriage for a long time. My sisters were only sixteen at their weddings, and I did not want to be controlled like they were. I did not marry until I was twenty-three, and that was to a man I chose to live with.

A few months before Vietnam was divided in 1954, Thu Cuc and her family moved to Saigon. She and her husband had gone first to Phu Lam, thirty miles from the city, to work on a farm for a couple of years. Then they moved to Cholon, Saigon's Chinatown, to a rented house. She went to work as a secretary for Dr. Tao, my brother-in-law, while her husband sold paint, brushes, and hardware in the front of their house. They lived in the back until 1958, when Thu Cuc delivered her fourth child.

One evening in 1959 after the passing of my father, during a summer vacation from my school, Les Oiseaux in Dalat, Thu Cuc's neighbor rushed to our house. "Please come and save your daughter. She is in grave danger."

My mother and I found her, face down and unconscious on the floor of her living room. A wooden stick that served as a lock for the front door lay next to her. Her husband walked away from us. We took her to a nearby hospital. She told us later that her husband beat her regularly, but since she did not want to bring up her children as orphans, without a father, she had to endure his insults and beatings and stay with him.

Later in the year, Thu Cuc came to us, frightened. Her husband had disappeared three days earlier, without a trace. She had gone to the local police and to different hospitals to search for him, but in vain. Her husband's family, suspecting her of killing him, denounced her. She was brought to the police headquarters for investigation. She finally found out that her husband had been jailed for his secret activities.

In the end, Thu Cuc had to bring up her children all by herself. She had to be strong in the face of calamities. She worked for a doctor until 1963, when she became a distributor of pharmaceutical products to drugstores. She excelled in that trade. She became successful, and turned into a sophisticated city lady and businesswoman.

Forty-five years later, in May of 1996, at my mother's funeral in Houston, Texas, Thu Cuc told me that the place where I had visited on that unforgettable trip was actually on my father's island. While he had been trying to build up a farming community in one part of the island, the Viet Minh had been using the other part to foment revolution.

My youngest brother, Khanh, the last child in our family, or the eleventh in rank, was the first casualty of war. Two years my junior, born in the

Year of the Horse, he appears in retrospect to have spent his brief youth galloping to his death. Five feet seven inches tall, slim but muscular, he volunteered for the army after graduating from high school in 1962, at the age of nineteen. That alone would have set him apart from most of the boys we knew. The practice of well-off families was to buy their son's way out of military service, or to send them abroad to study.

There was another well-known system in Vietnam for evading the military. "Flower" or "ornamental" soldiers were those who paid their superiors so they did not have to be present at work or serve in action. King Tran Hung Dao, whose picture graced South Vietnam's five-hundred-piastre notes, traveled up the chain of command from the smallest villages. The King bought anything you needed or anyone you wanted.

Khanh and I were the youngest of the family and the last to live with our parents after our eight older brothers and sisters, already settled with their own families, had left the house. Perhaps as a result, our parents, who were in their late fifties while we were in our teens, protected and favored us. At one point, in fact, they made a will, complete with witnesses, and read it to us. It said they were leaving us all their belongings.

Khanh and I were always close. I do not remember us ever fighting, as most brothers and sisters do.

One day my mother gave me a tongue-lashing. She said that her friends had reported to her that I had been seen with a boy in restaurants, even at movies, all around town. When I denied this, my mother said that a friend of hers had seen me on the back of a motorcycle that very morning with my boyfriend. The lady said that it was shameful for a teenager like me to be running around town like that. She had been trying to match me with the son of one of her friends. I realized then that the boyfriend was no one else but my dear brother.

Before I went to study in France in 1960, Khanh brought home a friend of his to teach me ballroom dancing. He said that it would help me socialize when I went to France. That was his way of showing that he cared for me.

When Khanh went into the army as a young officer, he was sent often to combat zones in the Mekong Delta in the deep south. It was the part of the country where most of the war's killing occurred. He saw action a number of times and was wounded more than once. He used to tell me that he was so preoccupied with the war, he had given no thought to what he would do afterward.

After I returned home from studying abroad and got married, Khanh was shot. It was 1965. By that time, he had a wife, Lan, and a baby girl, Sondra. I remember seeing Khanh at my mother's house limping and on crutches. He was recuperating, but he swore that he would go back to the same place in the jungle to avenge the two soldiers in his platoon who had been killed while fighting next to him. He said that the calling of a true soldier was to show solidarity with his men.

Ten months later, my mother phoned and asked whether I had seen Khanh. She said she had dreamt that night that Khanh had come home wearing a white hat instead of his khaki lieutenant's hat. Khanh had not been seen for the past three days, and she had a premonition that something had happened to him.

I told her that when Khanh went to the battlefield, he sometimes stayed out for days before he returned. She should not be concerned; it was just a bad dream. But she was still worried and had gone to the altar in the living room and prayed to our ancestors to bless and protect him.

That very evening, a friend of Khanh, Tin, phoned and told me to hurry to the military morgue in Phu Lam. Something terrible had happened. Khanh had been shot. Tin came over to my house to help me find the way, and we went together.

I drove through the dark night, trembling and praying. The tortuous, narrow road seemed never to end. Worse, it started to rain, and I could hardly see where we were going—perhaps to eternal hell, I told Tin. Why was it so far? Tin said it was about ten more miles.

We turned onto a dark road and finally arrived at a structure that looked like an airplane hangar. Tin spoke to a man guarding the morgue, who told us to go in and search. We rushed inside. The filthy odor of the corpses caught me by surprise, and the nauseating stink nearly disabled me. I became dizzy and covered my nose with a handkerchief. I kept walking, looking for my brother in the freezing dark structure. Dim lightbulbs hung drearily from the ceiling. Bodies lying on narrow wooden pallets were lined up on both sides.

A mother was crying out for her son, telling his life story. She asked God why he had had to suffer such a miserable fate. Was it the beginning of bad luck for her whole family? Where was she going to find the money to bury him? In the aisle on my right, a young woman holding a baby was blowing her nose and weeping in silence.

I started to throw up. I hoped with all my might that my brother would not be among the dead. Tin must have been mistaken. My young, bright, handsome brother could not be reduced to a corpse on a piece of wood. He could not be like all these others.

I do not know why, but I passed a few pallets without looking, my eyes transfixed, while something pushed me toward one on the tenth left row. A man lay half-naked, his right leg severed above the knee, perhaps by a grenade, and sprayed with dark blue blood. Flies and mosquitoes buzzed around his open wound, sucking his flesh.

Next to him lay another man, a white bandage around his head with bloodstains at his ears. I felt my heart bleeding like a hose watering a tree. I ran to look at his face. His eyes were still wide open. I shouted, "Khanh!"

My two warm hands held his marble cheeks, and I shook him, trying to revive him. But he had already joined my father in the outer spaces beyond the reach of my power. My fingers touched his wide-open eyes and closed them so he could rest in peace. Suddenly, I found myself on his chest, sobbing with all my might. Tin pulled me up by the shoulders and carried me out. My feet were sinking into the ground, as if into quicksand. I felt as if my knees were shattered into a thousand small pieces.

Khanh's body was later transferred to the military morgue in Saigon. Lieutenant Khanh's funeral was held at the national cemetery, Mac Dinh Chi, in Saigon, in the hot sun of August 1966, with full ceremony. A medal of honor was added to two others of different colors on a velvet cushion in front of Khanh's coffin. I did not understand the meaning of these colorful pieces of metal and fabric; I only knew that they marked the end of a young patriot's life. Words like "heroism," "duty," and "nationalism" wafted through the thin air above us and blew away. I was proud of Khanh.

At the funeral, Colonel Thoi, his commanding officer, told how Khanh, commander of a squad, was on his way back to his base after a fight in which he and his men had been victorious. When he learned that some of his other troops were surrounded at Tan Binh in Vinh Loc, he immediately volunteered to go to the scene, saying it was an area he knew well. He and his troops, in fact, went on the attack and liberated the other men. But during the withdrawal, Khanh and a few of his troops were caught in a mass counterattack. The Viet Cong encircled him, and shot him in the temple, at point-blank range.

Ten of Khanh's men who had escaped were at the funeral, wearing on their heads the traditional white mourning bands signifying respect for their commander. They cried and said that he stayed behind and gave his life to save them. At the sad sound of the funeral trumpet, Colonel Thoi cried, too, the last words of his own farewell to Khanh broken by tears. Those of us in the family, and the many who were his friends, also wept. Later, a monument was erected in Khanh's name at the end of Tran Quoc Toan street in Phu Lam, a suburb of Saigon.

Khanh, immobile and strapped under the Vietnamese flag, was only twenty-three. He had not even had time to live out his youth, and had been robbed of his adulthood. His young widow and baby of sixteen months had lost their husband and father. Khanh had not yet fulfilled his wishes or his dreams, and he would never know the full cycle of life. He had only achieved battlefield victory and death.

The second fatality in our family was Trung, number six among us and the middle of my three brothers.

Trung had served for twelve years in the Vietnamese army. After his retirement, he spent six years in the United States, first teaching Vietnamese at Fort Bliss in El Paso, Texas, and then working in an import-export company in Washington, D.C. My mother missed him and urged him to come back to Vietnam to do business, get married, and settle down.

He missed Vietnam, too, and came back to Saigon in early 1974, nearly a year before it fell to the Communists.

Trung, his name, has a lot of meanings: loyalty, harmony, moderation, epicenter. He seemed to live in accordance with his name. None of his family and friends would say that he did otherwise. A gentle, self-effacing, honest man with curly hair and good manners, he had the same physical frame as Khanh. I always thought he looked like Charles Aznavour, the French singer.

Trung had a talent for drawing, and he was constantly using his pen or pencil to reproduce airplanes. All kinds flew out of his fertile head—large and small, passenger planes and fighter aircraft. His hands were never idle. As a child, I used to watch him with my mouth open drawing these admirable flying creatures on whatever piece of paper was at hand, finishing within minutes. I hated to see him ball up these pieces of paper and throw them into the wastebasket, and every day I pulled them out of the trash and looked at them, unable to figure out how he drew so artfully. It was not surprising that he chose to be a paratrooper in the army.

Trung's other memorable trait was his natural talent for music. Every night, before going to bed, for fifteen minutes to half an hour, he blew melodies—tunes he had composed or songs he had heard—on a short bamboo flute that had fewer than eight holes. He told me he had taught himself to do it, out of the blue.

His bright allegro notes enchanted me and lifted my spirits. Other times, his heart-melting adagio tunes filled my sleep with sweet dreams. At night from the dark of my bed, I could not wait to hear those melancholic hymns. They introduced my little heart to the delight of music.

On the other hand, Trung could be as strong as an aircraft, prompt to take off when need be. After my father's stroke, Trung quit day school, found a job, and helped to support the family. He was like a young father to me. He worked during the day and studied at night until the day he graduated, was drafted, and went to fulfill his military duty.

Nineteen hundred fifty-four was a fateful year. Ngo Dinh Diem, who had lived in the United States in a monastery, was installed as prime minister of South Vietnam in mid-June. His first years in office went very well. He welcomed to South Vietnam nearly a million Vietnamese Catholics who had fled the Communist North when Vietnam was divided into two at the May 1954 Geneva Conference. The refugees who came south brought nothing with them but their family members and tales of atrocities the Northern Communists had committed during the Land Reform campaign in 1953.

During the regrouping process, others moved in the opposite direction. Viet Minh troops from the South moved to the North, and they too, had violent tales to recount—stories of French and Vietnamese police brutality and killing. They too carried the seeds of hatred and revenge, and they wanted to get rid of the bad foreign elements at any price.

Not all the Viet Minh went North. Some ten thousand Communist operatives, who came to be called Viet Cong, remained hidden in remote areas in the South. Among them were my sister, Nam Ly, and Anh Tam, Thu Cuc's husband.

The Geneva Agreements also stipulated that general elections would be held in mid-1956, and the winner would rule a unified Vietnam. In October of 1955, however, Diem, wanting to stave off elections he feared the Communists might win, held a nationwide referendum in the South to turn the monarchy into a republic. Diem became the first president of the Republic of Vietnam. President Eisenhower backed Diem's regime and sent him military aid. Diem's troops subdued the threat to his authority, crushing the Binh Xuyen, a criminal force of forty thousand; then the Cao Dai and the Hoa Hao armed religious sects. He was keen, too, to fight the Communists in the North. Diem was consolidating his power.

In April 1956, the last French soldier left South Vietnam, and the French High Command for Indochina was dissolved. Diem had eliminated nearly ninety percent of the guerilla combatants in the South, and reduced the Communists there to near extinction.

The Geneva Accords had given Ho Chi Minh the North, and he was consolidating his power, as well. He eliminated the landlord class, executing thousands of people and imprisoning thousands of others. Angered that the promised general elections would not be held in 1956,

Ho and the northern Communists shifted their political struggle from "people's war" to "armed revolution." They were determined that South Vietnam would be theirs, too.

It was in 1955 that my brother Trung was called into the army, where he served the next twelve years as an officer. He used to tell me about his war experiences. He said he and his troops had to drink rainwater scooped from the muddy ground when they fought for weeks in the deep jungle. When they used up their provisions, they had to catch animals—insects, rabbits, monkeys, dogs, even snakes—to fill their stomachs. He told me how his unit went on patrol in search of Viet Cong hideouts, slept on the wet ground, fought in battles and skirmishes, took casualties.

Later, Trung became a paratrooper and dropped into areas where he could have been killed. Once, in fact, he was wounded, and I went to the hospital to visit him. He was in a ward with people who had their arms and legs in bandages, some suspended in the air. One of Trung's legs was wrapped in white gauze. He had been dropped near a Viet Cong nest. Fortunately, he had not been shot, but had caught his foot in a trap. Now he had excruciating pain in his swollen foot. Nothing serious, he said.

I devoured these stories as I had children's novels when I was younger. They seemed to me so heroic and romantic—Robin Hood and Peter Pan combined.

Trung retired in 1967, as a major. His war years were ones during which the Communist side grew in strength as the Diem government and its successors displayed ever worsening leadership. This was not the fault of Trung or his fellow officers. They made big sacrifices, and many acquitted themselves well, but they could not compensate for the bad performance of many of their superiors. Still unmarried when he left the army, Trung traveled to Europe to visit my sisters—Thu Ha in London and Thu Thuy in Paris—and then decided to go on and try his chances in the United States. There was a need there for Vietnamese-language instructors. He found such a job at Fort Bliss in El Paso, Texas, where he lived comfortably with a group of Vietnamese friends. In 1972, with the withdrawal of American troops, there was no more need for Vietnamese teachers, and he moved to Washington, D.C.

There he worked with a friend importing arts and crafts from Vietnam. He asked me to select and send him oil, watercolor, and lacquer paintings by well-known Vietnamese artists. It was easy for me. The Vietnamese artists, often talented and mostly poor, were only too happy to sell him their work.

I saw Trung in the capital in the summer of 1972. It was the year after Bong's assassination and I had gone to the University of Chicago for a summer seminar, bringing with me my oldest son, Victor. Trung offered to adopt Victor temporarily and bring him up as his own son. I accepted, and Victor stayed with Trung for a time before going on to live with a couple, Phuong and Hanh, who were Trung's friends. My brother was a father figure for me. I loved him dearly.

Back in Saigon, the government was encouraging trade and industrialization. It was also implementing a land reform program, and owners were being paid well to turn over their land to small farmers. My parents' island came under that program. My mother gave away small portions of acreage, and received compensation each time she did so. It was quite a contrast to the torture landowners had undergone in the North.

With the prospect of his going into business, Trung returned to Saigon in early 1974. He used some of my mother's land reform money to set up a company to export fish and shrimp to Japan. He also found foreign buyers for the skin of the crocodiles that crowded our island's swamps. He also did well with sugar cane, produced on the island in large quantities. But it soon became obvious that Trung had returned to Vietnam at the wrong time.

Trung's business ground to a halt as it became apparent, in early 1975, that Saigon would fall. Still, Trung thought he could go on when the Communists took over. He told me the day I left for the United States that he was sure he could continue his business under the new regime.

As an ordinary businessman, Trung was not among the first categories the Communists called up for "reeducation." But after a few months he was asked to pack a few belongings, enough for a couple of weeks, and register at one of the district centers. He never returned.

The fratricidal war had lasted ten years and claimed up to four million lives, fifty-eight thousand of them American, the rest Vietnamese, North and South. As if that were not terrible enough, a newly unified Communist Vietnam was now filled with reeducation camps and prisons, where the new rulers punished the "traitors" who had worked for the former regime. They also created "new economic zones," where people from the cities were sent to live in remote, desolate areas with no roads, water, or electricity.

The upper and middle classes were dispossessed. This was the Communists' policy of *danh tu san*, "strike the capitalists." Food was rationed. People had to line up to buy a couple of kilos of rice, which had to be eaten mixed with peas or manioc. At night, the police would come to take away people they wanted to punish. People's rights were worthless.

Under the "socialization" policy, the Communists became the new colonizers, and they were worse than the French. After long years of struggle and deprivation, they felt entitled to confiscate other people's money and properties, and to award themselves privileges and wealth. The religions were not spared, either. The Communists closed or confiscated the churches and Buddhist temples and arrested a number of religious leaders. The Northern Communists even dissolved the National Liberation Front, their South Vietnamese partners, betraying their own policy of national reconciliation and concord, and replacing it with revenge against southerners in general. It was a shock to the population of the South.

Frustrated, dejected, and sometimes in mortal danger, city dwellers and, increasingly, even poor farmers, did what they had not done during centuries of intermittent war—risked their lives to escape the country. Hundreds of thousands fled. These were not only the well-educated, but also workers, fishermen, and other common people.

Why did the liberators punish their own people—perhaps as many as three hundred thousand of them by 1976—and put them in "reeducation" camps? According to Truong Nhu Tang in his book, *A Vietcong Memoir*,

"These were acts of reprisal and discrimination." Much of the world watched these reprisals in silence. In comparison to the killing fields of the Khmer Rouge in Cambodia, the systematic detention of large numbers of people may have appeared mild. But to those affected, the results were anything but benign.

The consequences were dire for the nation, too. Unified Vietnam, rich in rice and other resources, became one of the poorest countries in the world, with a per capita income of about $200 per year.

I learned the news of Trung's death in 1980, shortly after my mother had left Vietnam and come to live with us in Virginia. My sister, Thu Cuc, wrote me that Trung had died in 1979, even before my mother left Vietnam. She asked me to keep it a secret from our mother, afraid to cause her any more pain.

Thu Cuc said that she had gone to visit Trung in prison in 1978 in North Vietnam, where he happened to be in the same cell as Thu Cuc's second husband, a former army officer. The prison was in a remote part of Vinh province, in a little town south of Hanoi. Thu Cuc wrote that, to move from one area to another, she had had to bribe Communist officials all along the way. She brought Trung and her husband food and medicine.

She did not recognize Trung at first. She saw a man with a long, white beard, half-bald, very thin, with a swollen stomach, and most of his teeth gone. His eyes were opaque and haggard. He looked like a dehydrated, hundred-year-old Santa Claus.

Trung was excited to see the sugar, condensed milk, and dried meat and shrimp Thu Cuc had brought him. He had not eaten this kind of food for the last three years. He opened the packages and sniffed them for a long while. He could not believe they were for him. When people were kept hungry for so long, Thu Cuc said, they yearned for food that most of us took for granted. These were Trung's last succulent meals before he became a spirit and needed food no longer.

Trung's normal day in prison was a terrible routine of hard labor and mistreatment. At 4:30 A.M., he and the other prisoners ate a breakfast of boiled cassava or sweet potato. At five, in the cold and humid morning, they marched under armed guard to clear the forests, dig canals, and plant rice, cassava, or sweet potato. They returned to their camp, walking in the punishing hot sun for an hour before being given their meager lunch. Then, back to work until four in the afternoon. Dinner was paltry, as well. The evenings were not free. From seven to nine, they had to study Marxist writings, memorize Communist propaganda, and make confessions and self-criticisms. Then they were ordered by their young wardens to make accusations against their fellow inmates.

Mail and gifts were withheld from the prisoners. Visits from outside were not permitted, unless someone in the family knew how to get around the regulations, usually through bribery.

The main punishment for all of them was hunger. The Communists believed the best way to govern people's brains was by controlling their stomachs. The results were chronic malaria and intestinal diseases, and these were among the highest causes of death.

Sick with little medicine, hungry with little food, ill-treated with no recourse to justice, the *nguy*, or "puppets," as the inmates were called, had to be punished, even though they were never formally judged or found guilty of any crime. If they did not die during the first five years, which were the hardest, they would remain victims of the Communists' revenge for up to fifteen years, when they would be said to be "reformed." Fortunately, Trung escaped that squalid treatment by joining the world beyond. He had to endure that purgatory for only four years.

There was no gas chamber, no bloodbath, no skeletons like those of Jews I had seen in the documentaries of Hitler's camps or the killing fields of the Khmer Rouge in Cambodia. The punishments in the reeducation camps and prisons of Vietnam were more subtle. In a way, it was worse than killing people once and for all.

Thu Cuc learned of Trung's death from another prisoner who smuggled out a message to her through someone in his family. Trung had died of a heart attack. In the morning, Trung had gone about his work as usual, carrying water on shoulder poles for the prison vegetable garden under the grilling sun. Exhausted, he fainted in the field, and that evening he died.

The night I received Thu Cuc's letter announcing Trung's death, I went inside the bedroom of our house in Falls Church, Virginia, and cried with Lacy. Late at night, without telling my mother, I set up an altar on top of a tall chest in the dining room, with two candlesticks, a vase of flowers, and a plate of fruit. I did not have a photo of Trung, so I placed a statue of Buddha in the center. Lacy, our three children, and I burned incense sticks and prayed for Trung's soul. I prayed that he would join my father; my husband, Bong; my brother, Khanh; and all our ancestors, and rest in peace.

Whenever I want to see Trung, I look at the picture of Charles Aznavour on a record jacket. When I want to hear him, I listen to Zamphir playing his flute, and I wrap myself in the soft, piercing melodies that Trung used to send me in the darkness of my room.

When my mother emigrated to the United States in 1980, Lacy, the children, and I went to pick her up at Dulles Airport. She looked like a peasant. She wore a dark *ao dai*, the traditional Vietnamese tunic, and her head was covered with a dirty, torn scarf, one of the thirty or so that my sister, Thu Thuy, had sent her from Paris over the years. When I asked her why she didn't wear a better *ao dai* or scarf, she told me she didn't want to look conspicuous for fear of being recognized in the United States by Northern Communist agents. She had only lived five years under the Communists, but she had become paranoid. She was afraid of being spied on by Vietnamese Communists in America!

On the way home from the airport, my mother asked me why there were so many lights along the streets and in the houses. It was a waste of electricity and money. The Americans could save by using oil lamps or candles instead. This was what she and the other Vietnamese had done for the past five years in Ho Chi Minh City.

Every night, she woke up at around two and went to eat ice cream and pound cake, the dessert I had served after her first dinner. She said she had not eaten in such luxury in years, so she longed for that dessert every time she went to bed. She asked whether I could buy enough of it to last a whole week, and she ate it for the next two weeks nonstop. It pained me to see my mother, a distinguished and Westernized lady in the 1920s, sunk to such a level, deprived of her dignity. She was so hungry for ice cream and pound cake that she gorged herself until she had enough of them.

In the spring of her first year with us in the United States, I took my mother to see the cherry trees blossoming along the Potomac River. We walked and talked as she gazed at the thousands of pink and white buds bordering the sidewalks and reflected in the water at the Jefferson Memorial. She stopped short, breathless.

"Now tell me frankly, you are sure that we are still on earth?"

"Of course. Where do you think we are?"

"Are you certain that you have not taken me to another planet? I've heard that Americans went to the moon. We are not on the moon in springtime?"

After I insisted that we were still on earth, and pointed to real people walking around us, she exclaimed, "This is too wonderful to be true."

She could not believe that there existed a place as breathtaking as Washington in the spring. She was confused. Having come from a Communist "paradise" where everything was so gloomy, she could not believe that such a bright and joyful scene, a real paradise on earth, was not a mirage.

She also found it strange that I did not serve my husband in the traditional Vietnamese way. One Sunday morning, while I was out grocery shopping with the children, she had a talk with Lacy.

"What do you think of Jackie going out to work every day?" she asked him.

"Oh, it's fine. She likes helping the refugees."

"But," she persisted, "doesn't it bother you that she doesn't get up in the morning and cook your breakfast before you go to work?"

"No, she doesn't need to. I wake up very early, at six. I just have a cup of coffee and a piece of toast, and I can make it myself."

"But you don't come home for lunch, either."

"No," said Lacy. "I eat at the State Department. There's not enough time to come home. Besides, a husband in this country today doesn't expect a wife to do all those things. Jackie works all day long, then cooks and cleans in the evening. She does more than her fair share."

"You know, in my day, if a Vietnamese wife behaved that way with her husband, he'd be very upset." My mother paused and shook her head. Finally, she said, "This is a wonderful country!"

Despite her affection for the United States, the generation gap between my mother and me widened every day, and there was a lot of unnecessary friction. I still saw her in her emancipated and sophisticated forties; I could not accept the fact that she had become old and tradition-bound. I found that my friends in the United States had the same frustrations when their parents came to live with them. It was too radical a change. We were not tolerant enough of them, and they did not understand our "untraditional" and Westernized ways of thinking, talking, and acting.

She also seemed to be confused about her boys. Sometimes she spoke about her "son," sometimes her "sons." Was it Trung, or Khanh, or both she was trying to remember? Her mind started to break down, little by little. She talked to herself during the day and in her sleep. At night, she used to sleepwalk, padding slowly around the house and scaring the children, especially Victor. He told me his grandmother used to come to his bed in the middle of the night and say things that did not make sense. She once said, "My son, I love you, don't leave me. Come and stay with me," and she pulled Victor out of his bed.

When I asked her the next morning to tell me more about her night conversation with Victor, she not only did not remember anything, she also denied that she could have done something so absurd. She deteriorated further, disclaiming things she had done or said. But she did it in such a rational and determined way that, foolishly, I argued back with her. Because she seemed strong and alert, I did not realize that her nerves were already frayed, and that she was already drifting slowly toward the Alzheimer's disease that would descend over her in her eighties. Time had stopped for her, and also for me.

She treated me like a five-year-old girl. She tried to tell me how to speak properly to my friends, how to stand, and where to sit. When I went out, she did not want me to wear clothes that were too colorful or too dark. She insisted on cooking Vietnamese food for all of us every day. I objected. I wanted to do the cooking myself—Vietnamese food on weekends, when I had more time, and American food during the week. I wanted to spare her the work of cooking an elaborate, time-consuming Vietnamese meal, standing over the counter and chopping the vegetables and the meat into little pieces.

I understand now that this was her way of expressing her love for me and for all of us. She wanted to cook for us, to tell us what to do, to tell us what not to do. But I did not see it that way then, and I was frustrated that she constantly seemed to be imposing on me her own backward, Confucian behavior.

At times she told me how much grief she had felt since she and my father were deported from Cambodia in 1945. After that fateful move, the turmoil in Vietnam had progressively taken her children from her and from each other. She was sorry to see us so far apart. She had heart palpitations and often asked me to take her to see the doctor.

My mother lived for sixteen years after coming to the United States, the last ten in Houston, Texas, where my brother, Anh Ba, and my sister, Thu Cuc, helped take care of her. I was out of the country much of that time, and saw her only on visits or talked to her on the phone. We did not understand each other fully, even though I had always been her favorite daughter, and she had always been my beloved mother. Now I understand her better. I understand how much she sacrificed to bring us up, and how much she suffered trying to keep all of us in harmony with one another. It was in vain. We were like the fingers of the hand.

THREE

Education in Vietnam and Europe

My father was still collecting rents from his peasant-tenants in 1946 when we first settled in Saigon. But with the prices for produce lowered and their living area less and less secure, some farmers started to move off the island, and my father's rents dropped. My parents were now living mostly on their savings.

Our house was small, so all of us were crammed into five partitioned sleeping areas. After a few months, several friends of my father who were heads of companies kindly asked him to do accounting for them at home. It was still not a steady job, and he worried a great deal. Although the political situation had stabilized, my father's blood pressure went up. He was unable to work, and others in the family had to take on new responsibilities.

Hai Duc, my eldest sister, had already moved to Saigon, where her husband, who still worked for the customs service, had been transferred. My eldest brother, Anh Ba, found a job at the Esso Oil Company in Nha Be, a suburb of Saigon, and lived there in the company's compound. Every month, he handed my mother a sealed envelope with his salary intact. My sister, Nam Ly, stayed in the *maquis,* and seven of us remained at home.

Little by little, my mother sold her antiques, then some of her diamonds. Perhaps that's what gave her the idea to start a diamond business. She would select, buy, and sell diamonds at a profit, or do it on behalf of others to earn a commission. My father continued with his part-time accounting and collected his rent income. Although our family did not live as well as before, we three youngest children were well cared for and protected. My parents enrolled us in French schools.

As a child living in Saigon for the first time, I enjoyed being near other children my age in the neighborhood. I came to know the girls who were my neighbours. One special friend was Marie Nguyet, who lived on the same block opposite my house. With eight brothers and sisters, she had nearly as large a family as mine. Another dear friend was Jeanne Thuy, daughter of Doctor George Tran, who lived ten blocks away. She and her six younger siblings were close to me too. Marie, Jeanne, and I went to Marie Curie and were in the same grade, although in different classrooms. I played dolls with them separately on different days of the week, and pretended to cook with tiny utensils in back of our houses.

Today, Marie is married to a former high school principal, Chau. They live in Canada with their four children and used to own a convenience store. Jeanne lives in Paris. She and her husband, Xe, a doctor, have two children. I visited them both in the early 1990s. We cooked for one another and shared stories about those innocent years.

Our stories brought back a rush of odd memories. I remembered the huge piles of trash our neighbors dumped early every morning in an empty lot near the corner of Frère Louis alley. A couple in their forties tended that mountain of garbage, keeping the area relatively clean in exchange for handouts from the thirty or so households in our neighborhood. There were no plastic trash bags back then, and the garbage trucks did not come until late morning. So each time we passed, we had to inhale that putrid odor, which perfumed our hair, our faces, and our clothes.

The dump was behind a small coffee shop on the corner of the alley. It had one rectangular table with long benches on each side and three small round tables. When we reached the shop, the aroma of the coffee canceled out the stench of the rubbish as patrons feasted on crisp French bread, fried eggs, or a hot bowl of *hu tieu*, the delicious rice noodle soup still found in Vietnamese restaurants today.

Outside, a dozen or so rickshaws, called cyclos, lined up at the corner of the alley, ready to take riders anywhere for a small fare. Fighting bicycles, cars, and ox carts, the cyclo peddlers could be seen day and night winding their way along narrow neighborhood streets. Driving was an art in Vietnam, and the trick was to avoid hitting jaywalkers and the other mobile objects that flitted across one's path.

What I enjoyed most in Vietnam was the Mid-Autumn Festival—*Tet Trung Thu*—the children's celebration that took place during the eighth month of the lunar year and lasted through the period of the full moon. I do not remember anything similar in Cambodia. Children poured into the streets of Saigon in the early evening holding colored lanterns with candles. We had to be careful that the candle held firm in the middle so it did not burn the lantern, which was made of transparent colored paper. The lanterns were covered with drawings of rabbits, fish, birds, moons, or stars. We could make them at home or buy them at neighborhood shops, and we badgered our parents to get the kind we wanted.

We then paraded around the streets of our neighborhood, chaperoned by our older brothers and sisters, singing songs and visiting friends until it was dark. If we were lucky, we would run into a troupe doing the Lion's Dance, which was like the Dragon's Dance performed every year at *Tet*, the lunar New Year. The Lion stopped in front of houses where money was hung from the roofbeams, and danced to booming drums and clanking cymbals.

The Lion had an undulating tail and five pairs of legs, long in front and short in back. He danced, tumbled, twisted, swung, and pirouetted to the loud, metallic sound of cymbals and the rhythmic pounding of drums. Then, with the help of a pole with steps attached to the sides, he climbed to the edge of the roof, weaving, nodding, and sniffing his prey, and finally devoured the money, which disappeared into his mouth. If the Lion did an outstanding job, people in the surrounding houses would hang more money from their houses. Everyone liked to watch the Lion, children and older people alike.

When I was six, my father enrolled me at the Lycée Marie Curie, Saigon's most prestigious French school for girls. Most of the teachers came from France, as did the textbooks. Because the school was subsidized by the French government, we had to pay only a minimal registration fee and the cost of renting books. There I began to use my French name, Jacqueline, given me by my father. I came to be called Jacqueline Thu Van.

My sister, Juliette Thu Thuy, three years older, attended another French school run by Catholic nuns, St. Paul's. My brother, René Khanh, two years younger, went to the Lycée Chasseloup Laubat, a French school for boys, also subsidized. Prince Sihanouk, who was to rule Cambodia intermittently for decades to come, had been a student there earlier. We went back and forth to school in a cyclo.

In my first history class, I had to memorize the phrase, *mes ancêtres, les Gaulois* (my ancestors, the Gauls). I showed the book to my father, and asked him whether it was true that my ancestors had yellow braided hair with blue eyes and a moustache, as the pictures showed. What, I wondered, had shrunk us and changed our features? Was it the snow that had kept them white, and the hot sun of the tropics that had turned our skin brown?

My father laughed and hinted that the French should have changed their history book when using it in the colonies. He showed me an illustration of emerald rice paddies lying between mountains and the sea, full of people with Asian faces. He explained that they were my ancestors, and that was my country.

He also said that, according to legend, the history of the Vietnamese began with a descendant of the God of Agriculture who married an immortal fairy of the mountains. They produced a dragon lord, who married a Chinese immortal.

This couple produced one hundred eggs, all sons. They separated, and Au Co, the wife, moved her fifty sons into the mountains, while Lac Long kept his fifty sons to help him rule over the lowlands. Their oldest son, King Hung Vuong, was the real founder of the Vietnamese dynasty, the Hong Bang. We were all descendants of *con rong, chau tien* (sons of dragons, daughters of fairies).

I realize now that this legend, passed on from generation to generation, describes how the people of the North and South became separated. It also reflects the divisions in the families and the country.

In China and Vietnam, the dragon was always regarded as the symbol of royalty, majesty, power, and authority, not the terrible monster perceived in the West. An ethereal, surreal creature, the immortal dragon commanded respect among average people. Emperors, kings, heads of state, and presidents used the same symbol to decorate their palaces and residences—dragons hand-engraved in jade, stone, or wood; hand-painted on furniture or ornaments; or embroidered on clothing.

My father explained that negritos were the earliest known inhabitants of Vietnam, some fifty thousand years ago. The Vietnamese of today are a fusion of different elements: from the south came Indonesian stock, probably between 600 and 400 B.C., the bronze age. From the west, we got the monotonic Mong-Khmer language, and the tonality and grammatical structures of the Thai people. Finally, from the north, between 200 B.C. and 200 A.D., came the Chinese, with their advanced civilization.

Even after a thousand years of intermittent rule over Vietnam, from 111 B.C. to 939 A.D., the Chinese failed to absorb the Vietnamese. That failure underscores the strength of our culture and national identity. The first major rebellion against the Chinese was led in 39 A.D. by Trung Trac, whose husband, a tribal lord, had been executed by the Chinese. Troops led by Trung Trac and her sister, Trung Nhi, attacked the Chinese and overwhelmed them. For three years, they ruled an independent Vietnamese kingdom. The Chinese Han emperor fought back, however, and defeated the Trung sisters, who drowned themselves in the river to avoid capture by their Chinese conquerors. This story and others from the Vietnamese resistance movements during the Chinese domination nurtured the Vietnamese spirit of independence from foreign domination.

Another legend was the exploit of Trieu Au, a sort of Vietnamese Joan of Arc, who launched a revolt against the Chinese in the year 248 and defeated them. She is pictured wearing armor and riding an elephant. At age twenty-three, she, too, committed suicide rather than surrender to her Chinese adversaries.

From legends like this, Vietnamese women inherited a unique status, achieving the right to share their husbands' property and to take over their husbands' lands and titles when they died. This meant that Vietnamese nationalism was alive among men and women alike.

In the thirteenth century, the Vietnamese defeated the Mongols, and thereafter took a more aggressive stance toward their neighbors. In the fifteenth century, the Vietnamese overran Champa, a kingdom in central Vietnam. They attacked the Chams in Indrapura, their capital, killing forty thousand and bringing their society to extinction. Starting in the sixteenth century, the Vietnamese expanded south, conquering the fertile Mekong Delta, then under Cambodian control.

At the same time, however, the Europeans started making inroads into Vietnam. Portuguese adventurers arrived in 1515. They established a trading center at Faifo, now called Hoi An, in central Vietnam near Danang, where Portuguese missionaries set up a mission. Spanish, Italian, and French missionaries followed. In 1615 French Jesuits, expelled from Japan, arrived, as well, and one of them, Alexandre de Rhodes from Avignon, France, came to Vietnam in 1627 at the age of twenty-eight. Under Portuguese tutelage, he mastered the Vietnamese language and transposed it into Western characters. That, as my father explained to me, was the reason we used the Roman alphabet.

In fact, our land offered a strategic position and rich resources that had always attracted foreigners. In 1637 the Dutch established a trading center in Hanoi, and the English did the same in 1672. Both did poorly and left Vietnam. The French replaced them, launching a trading center in Hanoi in 1680. But the Vietnamese mandarins, who had always resisted Christianity, persecuted the missionaries, who, by the nineteenth century, had converted nearly a tenth of the Vietnamese. In 1847 the French retaliated by bombing the port of Danang.

The French advance in Vietnam was part of a general European penetration of Asia. In the 1830s, the Portuguese and the British started the Opium War in China. The treaty of Nanking, signed in 1842, marked the opening of China to foreign traders and foreign powers. The so-called Open Door policy accorded most-favored-nation status to the Europeans, and the subjection of Asia continued.

Russia took over the mainland north of Manchuria and Korea; Britain conquered Nepal and Burma in the 1880s; Japan had control over Taiwan and Korea; and France, after invading and conquering Danang in 1858, and Saigon a year later, colonized Vietnam.

Napoleon III wanted to expand France's overseas markets. Vietnamese resistance groups tried to lead guerillas against the French, but in vain. In 1879 France appointed the first French civilian governor of Vietnam, and the Vietnamese governor hanged himself in protest. In 1883 Vietnam became a French protectorate, and in 1893 France annexed Laos and Cambodia. France called the three countries, "Indochina," and ruled the area for nearly seventy years.

Thus it was that my father's father, a man from a simple family with little education, was drafted into the French army. French domination was also why my father himself ended up working for the French during that period. Their association with the French did not mean that they loved their country less. Like most of us, they were subject to circumstances. My father used to tell me that something that is right today may be wrong tomorrow; and that I had to be flexible. But he also told me that endurance and excellence were qualities I should always pursue. "Whatever road you follow in your life," he used to say, "the most important thing is to try the best at what you do." These two admonitions, somewhat contradictory, still echo inside me.

I was fascinated by what my father told me. I promised him that I would go to school and further my education to show my love for my people and my country. And that is what I did.

At the Lycée Marie Curie, all subjects were taught in French. We were to speak French at all times, in all of our classes. If the French teachers caught us speaking Vietnamese among ourselves, we were sent to register our names at the administrative office. Punishment took place on Saturday mornings, and offenders were put together in the auditorium. Two French inspectors supervised us while we did our homework. We had to stay from one to four hours, depending on our level of guilt. Every time I broke the rule, I found a number of other offenders who had done the same thing.

At twelve, I passed my entrance exam to the sixth grade, entered middle school, and was rewarded with a bicycle. I was very proud to be able to ride to school like the other girls did. I chose to be with the *classiques*, where I studied Latin, English, and Vietnamese for two sessions of forty-five minutes each a week. Mathematics had never been my best friend; I had only passing grades.

In my middle-school class, I had a friend named Marie Ngoc, whose boarding house was on my way to school. Her mother was a well-known Vietnamese opera singer and actress, Miss Kim Thoa, and her father was a playwright and head of an opera troupe. She was one of twenty children who boarded with Madame Peyrou, a French widow who cared for them, tutored them, and taught them ballet. To please Marie, I offered to come and pick her up for school on my bicycle. She said that Madame Peyrou would not allow it, but we decided to do it anyway. It was more enticing to do something forbidden.

Holding her book satchel, she settled nicely on the back seat of my bicycle with her legs crossed and her feet pointed like a ballerina. We set off with me pedaling with all my force, inhaling and exhaling at every cycling movement. I did not know that Marie weighed much more than she looked, at least five pounds more than I did. She was also about three inches taller. After five minutes, I started to sweat, and my bicycle started to sway. I zigzagged my bicycle for another five minutes, trying my best to keep my balance. Before Marie and I knew it, we had crashed on the sidewalk.

Our hands and elbows were scratched, and our knees were bleeding. Worse, passersby were staring at us, and several boys on motorcycles even laughed at our misery. Embarrassed, we dared not go back to Madame Peyrou's house, where we were sure to get a piece of her mind. So we put our satchels on the seat and walked to school, each of us pushing one side of the bicycle, our bottoms and legs aching. We later went to the school infirmary to have our injuries cleaned and bandaged.

Marie and I used to do our homework together. Sometimes we escaped to the movies where we watched the likes of Debbie Reynolds, Jane Powell, Fred Astaire and Ginger Rogers, Gene Kelly, and Mario Lanza dance and sing.

After graduating, Marie became a teacher of French and married a

Filipino engineer, Lino de Leon. Today they have four handsome grown children and live in Houston, where Marie still teaches French in a high school in the downtown area. I used to see them when I went to Houston to visit my mother.

In general, I did well in school, and at fourteen passed my *brevet* exam and entered senior high school.

My fourth sister, Hue (meaning lily), was involved in political activities, from age eighteen. My mother told me that she and her husband, Thanh, had gotten to know one another in 1946 at secret meetings of the Dai Viet (Greater Vietnam) party. At that moment, the Dai Viet were one of the clandestine groups formed to fight both the French colonialists and the Viet Minh Communists. To avoid being spied on or killed by the French Sûreté or the Viet Minh, the Dai Viets met in small cells working underground.

When I was five, I considered Hue to be the hero in our family. She was my prettiest and smartest sister. Since I looked like her, I was called *Hue Deux*, Hue Number Two. She took care of me like her little pet. I became her child, her possession.

Working in secret, Hue helped to write and distribute pamphlets denouncing the French and the Viet Minh. To this day, my sisters, Thu Ha and Thu Cuc, remember that, in their teens, they helped Hue to mimeograph leaflets in our kitchen in the middle of the night. The leaflets would be distributed secretly with the help of other Dai Viet members in places where people gathered—the washrooms of schools, at the back of Buddhist temples or churches, in marketplaces, or at movie theaters.

The Dai Viet members were ardent followers of Truong Tu Anh, their leader. Anh was working underground in Hanoi, but he disappeared at the end of 1946 and was never heard of again. No one knew whether he was killed by the French—who had jailed him many times—or his rivals, the Viet Minh. He had founded the Dai Viet party in 1939 and preached independence and self-reliance. Students and academics followed his lead. Many believed that, this time, it was the Viet Minh who took him away and executed him.

Hue and Thanh had to go into hiding, too. Many of their friends had been eliminated; others had fled to Thailand, Cambodia, Laos, Hong Kong, or China. So the newly married couple decided to leave Vietnam, too. Their underground activities were thus short-lived because they had to run for their lives. In late 1947, they traveled to France to study and look for a brighter future. My parents paid their way.

Thanh registered to study law in Paris, while Hue helped my family expand its business. My mother was exporting rice, coffee, cinnamon, cooking ingredients, and other goods to France, where Vietnamese and other Asians abounded. Hue sent back French merchandise much in demand in Vietnam—cotton fabric, shirts, blouses, needles and thread, as well as apples and grapes. Although we did not live as well as we had on the rubber plantation, we were not doing poorly either.

Hue came back to Vietnam in 1949 with her daughter, Bibiche, who had been born in Paris in 1948. She had separated from her husband, Thanh, who remained in Paris to finish his law degree.

The following years were the turning point of many lives in our family and country.

In 1950, to prevent the expansion of Communism, President Harry Truman sent American troops to Korea, and the U.S. Seventh Fleet into the Taiwan Straits. He also increased aid to the Philippines, which was fighting a Communist insurgency. He built up U.S. forces in Western Europe and started giving military assistance to the French army and economic aid to the three Indochinese countries. This policy would determine the course of U.S. actions in Indochina for the next quarter-century.

Nineteen hundred fifty-one was the year Ho Chi Minh officially changed the Viet Minh Party into the Dang Lao Dong Vietnam, the Vietnam Workers' Party. The Cambodian Communists founded the Khmer Issarak, and the Laotian Communists, the Pathet Lao. These three Indochinese Communist blocs formed a common front to fight the French.

In South Vietnam, with the compliance of our Emperor, Bao Dai, the French began drafting young Vietnamese into the French National Army in 1951. The French also filled the important positions in the government with French-educated Vietnamese who had taken French citizenship. At the same time, the French showed hostility toward the Vietnamese nationalist parties that were demanding an independent South Vietnam and opposing both the French and Bao Dai.

One such group was an armed religious sect, the Cao Dai. It sent its troops into the *maquis* to fight the Communists while refusing to accept French financial aid or political control. Their main temple, the Cao Dai "Vatican," was in Tay Ninh, north of Saigon. Founded in 1919, the Cao Dai religion was a glorious, colorful mix of Buddhism, Christianity, Confucianism, and Taoism. The Cao Dai worshiped a pantheon of figures, ranging from Jesus and Buddha to Joan of Arc and Victor Hugo. In the late 1930s, the Cao Dai numbered three hundred thousand. They became political under the occupation and turned to the Japanese for protection.

It was said that a Cao Dai adherent who had joined the Dai Viet Youth Movement—another nationalist party—was alleged to have assassinated both the Vietnamese governor of South Vietnam and a French general in the 1940s. The Dai Viet Youth Movement was then disbanded, and its leaders reverted to clandestine activities. Youth groups from other nationalist parties were demonstrating, and students were put in jail. Schools were closing in the 1950s.

My father sighed with sadness at all this turbulent news. He wondered what kind of future lay ahead of us under these conditions, and what would become of his children. He watched helplessly as political currents beyond his control claimed three of his daughters, who left school to go off in different ideological directions. His number five daughter, Nam Ly, had gone with the Communists to the *maquis* in 1946. His number four, Hue, had joined the Dai Viets later the same year. And now in 1951, his number eight, Thu Cuc, had left to join the *maquis,* as well.

Father was also dejected that five years had passed without his being able to find a steady job in Saigon. He could not get the kind of responsible position he wished, and at his age he did not want to start on the bottom rung as an accountant. He felt unwanted and powerless, and sank into depression, withdrawing ever more deeply into his own silent world. He slowly stopped talking to us, even to me.

One morning, in late 1951, as he rose from his breakfast, my father fell to the ground unconscious. A stroke on the left side of his brain had paralyzed his right arm and leg. He would lie in bed for years to come. I was just ten.

We were in a difficult period, emotionally and financially, focusing all our efforts on our sick father, and watching our income dwindle. Others now had to help. My number three brother had a family of his own to care for, so my sixth brother, Trung, volunteered to drop out of his last year of high school to take care of my father and help to support the family. At seventeen, he helped to clean and bathe my father early every morning, and carried him anywhere he needed to go. Then at eight o'clock, Trung went to work for the French shipping company, *Messageries Maritimes,* in the administrative section. He also attended evening classes so he could take his final baccalaureate exams and finish high school.

A few months passed. One day, on my way to school, I saw a funeral cortege followed by women and children, crying. It dawned on me that the dead person could have been my father. At lunchtime, in the empty yard in back of the classrooms, I sat all by myself, leaning against the trunk of a beautiful tree known as "Flamboyant" in French. Flaming slivers of sun shone through the immense umbrella of scarlet flowers above me, and seemed to set me on fire. My face blushed with fever in the boiling heat. My sandwich was in my hand, but I was not hungry. My mind was aburst with morbid thoughts. What would happen if my father died?

Suddenly, I heard piercing shrieks coming from high over my head. My eyes fixed on a flock of five large passerine birds with black, glossy plumage. They were gliding, their pointed wings outstretched, harsh "caw caw" calls coming from their heavy black bills. They tilted slightly and rapidly descended. Two of the crows flapped their wings swiftly, and, just as abruptly, folded them. The two landed on a branch at the top of the flamboyant tree, while their companions continued their journey, shrieking a last good-bye.

Curious, I kept my eyes fixed on them, my neck craned upward as I sank into a lying position, my head resting on one of the tree's huge roots. Breathless, I squeezed my eyes almost shut under the harsh sun. A friend of my mother had told me that crows were a bad omen. They were members of the vulture family, creatures that could smell death. That macabre description did not help me feel at ease in their presence.

One of the crows hopped toward the other, its sharp, curved claws holding it firm on its perch. This could be the aggressive female, I thought, trying to court her mate.

My thoughts went back to my father. What would his fate be, and ours? As if answering my question, the crow uttered a loud, harsh cackling sound. She seemed to be saying, "He is in a very bad shape."

"Can he survive?" I muttered. "He can hardly talk or move."

"He has to be strong. He has to overcome his torments," the crow countered.

"We are giving him all the help we can," I pleaded. "I am scared."

At that point, a soft, familiar "croo kuk-croo" joined the conversation. A pigeon flew straight down from a nearby fence. "Don't worry. He just needs a lot of love and care," said the pigeon, adding another "croo-oo." He advanced toward me, pecking for seeds on the ground and begging for food, remarkably tame. Pigeons are part of the dove family, and this new arrival was bringing me a happier message. I sat straight up and sang back to him, "Cruu, cruu, cruu. Come closer and cheer me up, please." I threw him pieces of my bread.

"Caw, caw, caw, it will take a long time for your father to recover," the aggressive crow jabbered.

"Croo, croo," my friend approached slowly, looking straight at his feed, his light gray bill ready to snap it up. He had a small, plump body covered with a dark, gray mantle and a broad tail with even darker tips. His transparent white eyes, ringed with red, looked at me without fear. He repeated several times, "Croo, croo, crooo, don't worry, he'll be better."

I smiled at him as he ate. "Oh, thank you. I feel so secure with you here. Cruu, cruu, cruu," I said to him gratefully.

My attention was then diverted by the high-pitched voice of a tiny, exquisitely colored bird with iridescent plumage. He hovered around a hibiscus bush a few feet in front of me, splendid in the sunlight. He dipped his long, slender bill into an open pink bloom and sucked its nectar. His narrow, metallic green wings vibrated incredibly fast, producing a humming sound. Then, like a buzzing bee, his minute mate, duller in color, her white underpart spotted with green, zoomed down aggressively, tail tilted upward. Both of them twittered happily and rose face-to-face to a great height, clutching each other by the feet. Descending, they flew backward, tumbling head over feet, then parted, falling away in an arc in different directions. Their prolonged, distinct titter trailed away behind them.

I was shaking with excitement. The world, I thought, was filled with such marvelous creatures. They had souls like we did. They could breathe and talk and bring us joy and peace. I had to learn how to sit still with them, speak to them, and make friends with them.

That evening, I came home and told my father what had happened. He was in bed, still unable to speak clearly. I took his hand in my two hands, and tried to revive it by massaging it and communicating my energy to him. I told him that I had had a conversation with a crow and a pigeon, and had seen the happy union of a hummingbird couple. There was hope and happiness everywhere. "I know you will be fine soon. We love you and are going to take good care of you, Father. Don't worry about anything."

He lay immobile. Looking into his eyes, I saw his irises contract until they became dim lights. Faint tears fell one by one, sliding down onto his temple. I swept away the wet droplets with my fingers. Then I placed my own watery cheeks next to him, below his pillow, stroking his hand gently. It was the second and last time I saw my father cry.

My mother and my sister, Hue, took my father to a Dr. Tao, who had been introduced to us by my eldest brother-in-law, Phuoc. He and Dr. Tao had gone to school together in the Delta. Dr. Tao had graduated from medical school in Bordeaux, France, and had just returned to Vietnam. My father's health improved under Dr. Tao's care and that of a nurse who came to give him physical therapy. Gradually, he was able to move and to walk around with a cane. We all felt relieved with his progress.

Dr. Tao's practice prospered, and he was soon looking for someone to run his office. His patients had become too numerous for his current staff, a secretary and a nurse, to handle. He asked whether my sister,

Hue, would be willing to help him manage his office. She accepted, went to work for Dr. Tao, and left Bibiche in my mother's care. My mother was still engaged in her diamond business so I became Bibiche's nanny and second mother.

She was nearly two when my mother entrusted her to me. Minuscule, with deep, dark, round eyes, Bibiche had a favorite French doll that was nearly as big as she was. Bibiche's hair was cut straight down on both sides, stopping at neck length in back, with fringe on her forehead, a common style for children in those days.

Well prepared for motherhood after years of playing dolls with my friends, this time I did it for real. I bathed Bibiche, fed her, carried her, and played with her. I taught her as much as I could, and she often came to me with her problems. We slept in the same big bed and became inseparable companions. A special bond developed between us. She was less my niece than my daughter. Because of her, I knew the joy of mothering when I was only ten.

A few years later, very much in love with each other, Hue and Dr. Tao married. Bibiche would still stay with my mother and me. When she was five, her mother enrolled her at Marie Curie, so Bibiche and I went to school together. She was too small to ride with me on my bicycle, so her mother's driver took her in the car. But she did not want to be separated from me, so the driver drove slowly enough for me, struggling and breathing hard on my bicycle, to stay up with him. I refused his offer to ride inside the car with Bibiche; I felt much freer driving my own vehicle.

Bibiche was a gifted pianist, too. At six, she attended the Conservatory of Music in Saigon. Every year she had to perform a piece of classical music, as a final exam, in front of an audience. She and I did everything together, so I studied the piano, as well, but with a private teacher. I was too old and too lacking in talent for the Conservatory. We often practiced on a piano Hue bought for us.

By the time my parents moved to the house on Paul Bert street, Bibiche had also moved—to Dr. Tao's newly built house on Pasteur street. There, in the back of his villa, he had a twenty-room clinic for his patients. He was reputed to be among Vietnam's most skilled surgeons in the field of tuberculosis. The more his patients' health worsened, the more money he made. He bought a conservative French Renault, then two Elvis Presley-style American cars, in red and green, for my sister to drive. My brother-in-law was so busy with his work and his research that he hardly went out at all. It was my sister who managed his business—handling his public relations and maintaining contacts with top government officials and the diplomatic corps—and she was excellent at it.

She came in her flashy cars to visit my parents two or three times a week, after work hours. One day, she discovered that, at fourteen, I had a *petite amourette*—a small romance—with De, my math tutor. My mother had hired him to go over my algebra and geometry exercises with me twice a week in the livingroom of our house. De was three years older than I was, went to the exclusive Chasseloup Laubat high school for boys, and excelled in math and science. I was awful in those areas, my mind being more at home in literature and the liberal arts. So I needed help in my weak subjects to pass my *brevet*, the mandatory exam that was the gateway to senior high school.

De's family lived in Vung Tau, then called Cap St. Jacques, a beach resort two hours southeast of Saigon where many people went on weekends and in the summer. He and his older brother boarded with an aunt in a narrow house right across from ours. His family owned a small fabric store in the Vung Tau central market. De was a serious, methodical teacher who treated me with respect. I considered him to be more like a brother. He never said an improper word or made a gesture that went beyond his teaching responsibilities.

After a few months, my math grades had improved, and my parents were happy with my progress. But I observed that De was also progressing—looking at me with more tender eyes. His face become redder and redder as he talked to me, and at times his hands shook. He buried his sentiments under his usual polite exterior, but I could perceive the changes in his comportment toward me. As a young girl, I was not supposed to show my feelings toward a boy, and I went on as if nothing had happened. But I was also attracted to his good manners and his intelligence.

De and his brother used to organize parties on birthdays and holidays, and they invited a dozen or so friends, including me. Their house was too small for these festivities, so they held them in front of the veranda next to the street. My mother let me attend these get-togethers. Usually, after dinner, someone played the guitar, and people sang and sometimes performed folk dances.

One evening, one of De's friends invited me to a birthday that was held not at his house but at a restaurant. We left quite late, and I then went with a couple of the guests over to De's house for tea. I finally emerged from my tutor's house by myself at eleven—and my mother and sister, Nam Ly, were waiting for me at the door of our home, where they greeted me with some choice words.

After that, my tutoring was canceled, and I was not allowed to go to parties unless I was chaperoned. De started waiting every night until all the lights in our house were extinguished, then leapt like a leopard in the dark up to my bedroom window, where he threw notes through the window bars. Feeling guilty, De sent me little apologies for having gotten me into trouble. During the day we were forbidden to talk to each other, and we had to ignore one another if we happened to meet on the street, walking right on by. At night, the little notes became bigger notes, telling me how much De loved me and missed me.

De wrote that, every evening, he listened to me practice the piano and looked forward to the soft music, especially my romantic Chopin or Debussy's *Clair de Lune*. They helped him sleep well and dream of me. He wrote that every night, before he could go to his bedroom, he waited in the front corner of his house to see the lamp in my bedroom go off, and my "little jade hand" close the window. So I knew that he was always there, looking at me in the dark, every time I closed the window.

I never answered any of his notes. I tore them up as soon as I received them—except one, which I forgot and left on my desk.

My mother got hold of it and showed it to Hue (Madame Tao). Although she was only number four in the family, my sister was by then the richest and most powerful of us all. My father was incapacitated, and my mother was half-retired from her diamond and other businesses. Madame Tao was generous with her gifts and provided us with anything we needed. She took us to her huge weekend house next to the official presidential hideaway at Long Hai, an exclusive beach resort twenty miles from Cap St. Jacques. We rode in her speedboat at the yacht club. She knew all the big shots in Saigon society. So we all looked up to Madame Tao for advice and guidance; she had become the master of the family clan. And her decision was final: I was not to talk to De or see any more of him. My family, I was told, did not want to see me end up selling fabric in the market like his family. The judge's gavel had come down hard.

To give force to the decision, I had to be sent far away from De. As soon as I passed my *brevet* exam, Madame Tao and my parents found a solution that seemed to accommodate everyone.

Bibiche had been having bouts of asthma since she was small. To improve her health, Hue decided to send Bibiche, and me, to a Catholic boarding school in Dalat, *Le Couvent des Oiseaux*, or *Les Oiseaux*, the "Convent of the Birds." It was twenty degrees cooler in Dalat than in Saigon, and more secure and peaceful. Located in the central highlands two hundred fifty miles from Saigon, an hour by plane, Dalat was known as the Switzerland of Vietnam. The Vietnamese Emperor, Bao Dai, and the upper crust of society, both French and Vietnamese, spent their vacations hunting and relaxing in this resort city. The Empress, wife of Bao Dai, had been a student there.

By the time I went to Les Oiseaux, my father was doing much better than in previous years. He could walk with a cane and speak intelligibly. Our family worried less for his safety.

The imposing two-story school at Les Oiseaux, French in architecture with polished wood and glass windows, sat majestically on top of a hill. The structure was surrounded by huge pine trees and well-tailored gardens with multicolored flowers. Les Oiseaux was among the best religious schools for girls anywhere, including France. It was run by a branch of French Catholic nuns, *les Chanoinesses de St. Augustin*, with headquarters in the Paris suburb of Verneuil. French nuns, and a few Vietnamese nuns who had studied in France, taught us and prepared us to the highest levels of education. The school changed my outlook on life.

Bibiche was sent to board with *Les Petites* in the primary section of the school. After a few weeks, she began to enjoy the companionship of the other girls and the nuns who acted as their mothers. Today, after thirty years of living abroad, Bibiche attends school reunions at Les Oiseaux in Verneuil. And, six of her middle-school classmates from Les Oiseaux, who have been living in Paris since their graduation, are still her best friends.

After graduating from Les Oixeaux, Bibiche went to England to study at the London School of Economics for three years. Later, she received a master's degree in business administration in Paris. Married, with three children, she is now a career woman in Paris working in computers and publishing.

For my part, at sixteen, I went with *Les Grandes,* the big girls in the senior high section of Les Oiseaux. We all wore the same uniform: a light blue or white blouse and dark blue skirt. An apron, with small blue and white square designs—vichy style—ran up to our chest and our back, protecting our uniform.

Twenty nuns and novices, eighty percent of them French, managed the school and taught us. We were about four hundred students, from third to twelfth grade. The nuns were covered from top to toe in thick black cotton robes, a black belt tied around each waist. A black cape ran straight from their heads down to half the length of their shoulders. Attached to the cape in the front, a piece of white cloth covered the forehead, temples, and ears, going around the chin and falling down under the chest. You could only see their faces and hands. They inspired seriousness and respect.

Early every morning, the nuns, whom we called *Mère,* Mother, walked in a single line under a covered walkway from their quarters to mass. They prayed in a separate area, on the side of the altar, and none of us could see or go near them. We could only hear their prayers and songs. We students went to chapel along a route parallel to the nuns' walkway, with a courtyard separating us, walking silently under a covered corridor alongside the spacious classrooms.

We studied Catholicism in theory and practice. I went to mass as regularly as I could. A French priest came at 6:30 every morning to say mass in Latin. I was fascinated by the allegories in the Bible, and made a special effort to learn more. At the end of the year, for the final exam in Catechism, Mère St. François d'Assise, a Vietnamese nun, gave me the highest score, higher than anyone had ever gotten in that course: We had been given two hours to write a paper demonstrating the existence of God.

I was told that it was not only for my knowledge of the subject, but also for the unique style of my dissertation that I got the highest grade. I gave names to everything—stones, rivers, flowers, animals, and stars. They all embodied Creation, and in my paper I had them strike up a conversation among themselves to demonstrate that there was a Supreme Being who had created them. Existence was not just an accidental encounter of cells and chemicals: I did not believe that it was just pure coincidence.

There was something more than the naked eye or the most sophisticated science laboratories could perceive, and believing in that "something more" made the difference. Belief could not be totally demonstrated or experienced, as in physics. In the end, there would always be questions. We reached a point where we asked ourselves the simplest question, one that only we could answer. The next step was to choose a way to live life to the fullest, a philosophy, or a religion. The matter had nothing to do with coincidences or chance.

One evening, Mère St. François asked me to arrange flowers at the altar. She went to her evening prayers with the other nuns. From the altar, I could see, for the first time, the imposing engraved wooden pews where the nuns were praying and singing. The soft Gregorian chant so elevated my spirit that I stayed there for the whole hour listening to the music and watching the nuns. I forgot completely that I had a class to go to at that time.

One Christmas, I was chosen to play the part of the Virgin Mary in the school auditorium. The next Christmas, at midnight, in the cathedral of the city of Dalat, I had the honor again. Mère Thành, my Vietnamese philosophy teacher, dressed me in a white Vietnamese *ao dai* and crowned with a golden turban. I played the Mother of Jesus. I knelt, my hands to my chest, and stared down at a life-size baby doll lying in a manger, near the altar. Three hundred people crowded into the gothic cathedral for the two-hour Christmas liturgy.

After mass, some of the worshippers came up to me and said they had never seen the Virgin Mary dressed as a Vietnamese. They had known her only as a lady with Western features, the one we had always seen in pictures. For me, it was another small awakening.

Leadership had been unknown to me, since I was the smallest girl in my family and the most spoiled. I learned it at Les Oiseaux. The nuns divided us into *equipes,* or teams, composed of *Les Moyennes* (middle school) and *Les Grandes* (high school) students. I was chosen to head a team of eight girls. Dominique Faure and Marie Pujos, two French classmates, were among them. It must have been funny to see the three of us together, I, reaching up to their armpits, and they on both sides of me, walking or running. They were my best French friends until we graduated. Afterward, for forty years, we lost track of each other. Then, suddenly, at the end of the year 2000, I received a letter from Marie Pujos. Through a friend in Paris who had my address, Marie wrote that she was still single and about to retire after working as a human resources career counselor. She had lived in Switzerland and Canada, and was now settled near Paris. She gave me the bad news Dominique Faure had died of a disease.

Our team would line up together, eat our meals together, and do the chores assigned to us together. I would supervise my team, wash the dishes with them after meals, and counsel them like a big sister. At breaks between classes, we played ball and other games. This was to teach us how to live together in harmony with others, and to know how to communicate with one another.

We also had to make our own beds and clean our rooms, including waxing the wooden parquet by ourselves. All that helped me organize myself better and become more disciplined.

Students came to the convent from all over the region. One teenager from Thailand could not speak a word of French when she arrived. She was away from her country for the first time, and she cried often the first week she was there. She was put on my team, and I tried to communicate with her in broken English. On her second evening, she went to the bathroom after dinner. The big door to the toilet area was locked at a certain hour, and the nun did not know that she was inside. Locked in, she panicked, then shouted and banged on the big door. After yelling a long time for someone to come, but afraid no one could understand her, she suddenly remembered what she thought was a French word from mass the previous Sunday. So she gathered all her force and shouted, "Alleluia, Alleluia." Finally, the nun—who was doing the regular night round—unlocked the door and rescued her.

The school also gave me a deeper appreciation of the fine arts. Every evening after dinner, I would go back to my classroom to play games with my classmates or listen to classical music. We also acted out parts in the plays of the French immortals—Corneille, Racine, and Molière. The most famous paintings and monuments of Europe were shown to us in pictures or slides, and we discussed them. At 8:00, we went to our bedrooms to study.

At 9:30 every night, I had to say aloud to the twenty-four bedrooms (called boxes) of *Les Grandes* on my side of the wing, "It's time to sleep." All lights had to be extinguished immediately.

We studied philosophy and logical reasoning. My psychology and philosophy instructors, Mère St. François and Mère Thành, both Vietnamese, were my best and most beloved teachers. They had taken their master's degrees in France. They instilled in me strong principles, entrusted me with responsible tasks, and fortified my self-confidence. They refined and polished my character. I was one of their favorite students.

Mère Thành also taught me Vietnamese history. I remember her first class. She started with a battle that had taken place in the eighteenth century between two Vietnamese armies. Five minutes into the battle, I stopped paying attention, figuring that I would learn the chapter in the history book later. Instead, I took out a novel, hiding my head behind a classmate sitting in front of me. But Mère Thanh was not blind. She called my name: "Jacqueline, tell me what happened during the battle."

Red-faced, I stood up. "Well, it was a fight between the Nguyen dynasty and the Le dynasty," I mumbled.

"Yes?" She wanted to know more.

"I think that the Nguyens chased the Les back to their territory with their swords and sticks and shouted at them to give up." I tried to remember more of what I had heard her saying, but I ran out of words. My classmates looked at me with pity. I played with my fingers, straightening them out one by one.

"And then?" She pressed me to go on.

"Seeing that they were losing the battle, the Les did not know where to go, so they ran onto a farm and got behind a huge stack of hay. Some of them hid inside the hay, too." My classmates were starting to put their hands in front of their mouths, to keep from laughing. But Mère Thanh insisted. "Finally, what happened?"

Scratching my head, I kept inventing. "The Nguyens burned the farm, the haystack, and the whole area. The Les ran out from everywhere and surrendered." At that, my classmates burst out laughing, some curling themselves up on their desks.

Half-smiling, half-embarrassed, I bit my fingers hard and waited for the verdict. Mère Thanh suppressed a laugh, composed herself, and said in a serious tone, "Nonsense! None of that happened. Where did you get that from? You will stay an hour extra this afternoon to learn that lesson, and you will recite it to me at the break tomorrow morning." I learned quickly that Mère Thanh was not to be trifled with.

Another of our teachers, a Vietnamese man in his sixties who lived in Dalat, taught us Vietnam's most famous literary work, *Kim Van Kieu* (*The Tale of Kieu*). The author, Nguyen Du, was a Vietnamese mandarin born in the late 1700s, and his classical poem of 3,250 verses has influenced generations of Vietnamese to this day. Nguyen Du was born of an aristocratic family in Ha Tinh province in central Vietnam. At nineteen, he was made a *Tu Tai*, or "esquire," and in 1812 he attained the rank of High Chancellor of the Empire, and was sent as ambassador to China.

Kim Van Kieu is about a Vietnamese woman named Kieu, modeled on the heroine of a Chinese novel, who lived in Peking under the Ming dynasty in the sixteenth century. This beautiful girl fell in love with the young Kim Trong and vowed her loyalty to him.

Then, Kieu's father and brother became victims of a slanderous accusation and were arrested and thrown in jail. In complete poverty, Kieu sold herself to Ma Giam Sinh for three hundred pieces of gold to free her father and brother. But Ma handed her over to a brothel and she became the concubine of three other men. After fifteen years, Kieu was finally reunited with Kim Trong, who had married Kieu's sister at Kieu's pleading. The two former lovers, having satisfied their karma by atoning for the sins of their previous lives, became chaste and loyal friends.

Nguyen Du had this to say about Kim Trong's progression through his previous life, his reincarnation, and his karma:

Vi chang duyen no ba sinh
Lām chi nhung thoi khuynh thanh trēu nguoi

"He had to pay debts from three previous lives
How, otherwise, could his heart have suffered so much for a woman
Whose beauty could bring a town or citadel crumbling down?"

Here is how the author described Kieu's beauty:

Ro rang trong ngoc trong ngā
Day day san duc mot toa thien nhien

"Transparent as jade, white as ivory
Perfect, sculptural beauty, a masterpiece of heaven ... "

Although she was forced into a life of shame, Kieu's soul remained as pure as the rainwater that fell from the sky. The heroine was like the symbolic lotus that keeps all its freshness and perfume above the mire that covers its roots. Her patriotism and her fidelity to her first love never faltered, and they filled Kim Trong with respect and admiration for Kieu's Confucian virtue:

Guong trong chang chut buoi tran
Mot loi quyet han muon phan kinh them

"The limpid mirror of your soul remains in my eyes pure of all stain
My esteem for you has increased ten thousand-fold."

For Nguyen Du, *bac menh*, "unhappy fate," was an inseparable part of human destiny. An Oriental reader of faces had examined Kieu's features when she was young and foretold her sorrowful future:

Anh hoa phat tiet ra ngoai
Ngan thu bac mang mot doi tai hoa

"When charm and talent shine from a girl's face
She'll lead a life of woes, an artist's life."

Many Vietnamese saw in *The Tale of Kieu*, with its various interpretations, the story of Vietnam herself. The separation of Kieu and her family on the one hand, and her and her lover on the other, not only depicted the disintegration of a family, but also represented the destruction of society and even human civilization.

The tale has a variant interpretation, as well. Kieu was the concubine of four men, but always remained true to herself, struggling until the end to rid herself of what was bad and to safeguard her identity and her purity of heart. In the same way, Vietnam had been the victim of foreign intruders, but she struggled again and again to take back her own freedom and independence.

Vietnamese men and women tend to find aspects of *The Tale of Kieu* that apply to them personally. The story seemed relevant to my own life, as well. When I was in the grip of some tragedy, my mother and her friends often consoled me in my pain by comparing my fate to that of

Kieu. They said that I had to go through years of trial to purify and rid myself of the karmic debts accumulated in my previous lives. No one could escape them. They often reminded me of the verse:

Troi xanh quen thoi ma hong danh ghen

"Casting hatred upon rosy cheeks is a habit of the Blue Sky . . ."

They told me that it was the law of compensation: If you were rich in one thing, you would be poor in another. There were cycles of *yin* and *yang*, of reward and penalty, in the span of one's existence. I had to serve my sentence before I could be happy and free. All I knew was that the purgatory I suffered in my thirties nearly destroyed me physically and mentally. That period "compensated" for my happy youth, but it also was to pave the way for a brighter future, they predicted.

As in Nguyen Du's story, where the heroine had to be separated from her relatives, my brothers, sisters, and I were like constellations. We often could not find a common understanding, with our differences in ideology and character.

Nguyen Du used astrology to illustrate the disharmony of siblings. When Kieu was kidnapped and mistreated by the number one wife of her second master, Thúc Sinh, Kieu explained to Thúc Sinh that the two of them had to be separated:

Sam thuong chang ven chu tong
Tai ai ha dam phu long co nhan

"Like the constellations Orion and Scorpion, we could not remain united
You understand why, yet I cannot forget all your kindnesses."

For us Asians, the reference to Orion and Scorpion has a special meaning. The three stars of Orion's belt, called in Asia the *Sao Cay*, the "Plough," are part of the constellation, *Sam*, that always appeared in the east. Three stars of the Scorpion, on the other hand, called the *Thiên Long*, "Celestial Dragon," are part of the constellation, *Thuong*, that resided in the west. From these constellations comes the legend of the two children of King Cao Ton Nhi of China who were constantly bickering and quarreling with each other. Distressed at such dissension in his family, the king exiled one child to govern Orion and the other to govern Scorpio so they would not meet and fight. History came to know the two sons as *Sam Thuong*. It pained me to see that the legend brought to mind our own family, divided by our differences.

As my mother had often said to me, "You and your brothers and sisters should try first to reconcile with one another. If you cannot, you should treat each other with civility."

So I had plenty of occasions to recall the professor in Dalat who came to us each week to sing by heart several dozen verses of *The Tale of Kieu*. Classical literary Vietnamese, with its Chinese roots, was an incomprehensible language for most of us, filled with double or multiple meanings—like Latin to an American student. Each word had to be explained in ordinary Vietnamese and interpreted for us. The professor spent the whole year on the book, and even then did not finish it all. He dissected every tone, rhyme, and symbol; interpreted the feelings of each character; and explained the plot and subplots. His passion for that great work was absolute. For him, it was all of Shakespeare in one volume. It was thrilling to learn so much about a work that had so many interpretations and was such a lasting legacy for the Vietnamese people.

Through the author's writing, Chinese culture, philosophy, religion, and science also influenced the Vietnamese people deeply. The legend, riddled with paraphrases and metaphors, is regarded as the most beautiful poetry ever written in Vietnam.

At Les Oiseaux, we were not only bookworms; I also learned the joy of helping others. I volunteered to go to slum areas on weekends with a friend to teach poor children to read and write. One week, one of the boys, Nam, missed my class; the following week, he missed another. I was told that he had been sick, so I decided to visit him. I somehow got inside the wooden house where the boy lived, and saw a man in his fifties, staring out the window, his protruding eyes lit red like a flame. I asked for Nam. The man turned and gave me a ferocious look, as if he were ready to attack me. He was holding a big bottle, half-filled with a white liquid. He was breathing hard, and smelled of rice alcohol.

I heard a faint cry and a strange noise above my head. I looked up and saw Nam dangling upside-down, his feet bound by a rope tied to a wooden beam that supported the house. The horrible scene, mingled with the cold weather, sent chills up my spine. A strong wind came through the door and seemed to push me to my knees. I found myself kneeling and praying, begging the man to release his boy. I was alone and helpless with a demented wretch who was torturing his own son. He could have turned on me, as well, I thought. But I stayed there, on the dirt floor, weeping and holding up my hands to plead for the life of an innocent boy.

I do not know by what miracle of God it happened, but the drunken man slowly went over and untied the rope. I ran to catch Nam as he fell, gliding down like one of those acrobats in a circus. I untied his feet. His tiny hands were holding me tight, and his body, swollen and purple, was shaking. I held him in my arms, warming his cold body to revive him. I had saved a life and knew now that I could make a difference. Nam was eight, and I was seventeen.

I became aware that I could do a lot for others. Caring for those underprivileged children in Dalat marked me for life and provided me with inspiration that would extend far into the future.

The big event every year at the convent was the *kermesse*, an annual charity fair. It was the only time we invited the public in to visit us, particularly the boys from the other schools, like the French Lycée Yersin. We all dressed up in our long tunics, trying to look our best. The boys came, played games, and spent money on the drinks and cakes we served. It was an exciting day for them and for us.

After each *kermesse*, a few twelfth-grade girls were caught *nhay rao*, "climbing the fence" to go out at night with boys they had met during the day. The boys slipped them notes at the fair naming a time and place to rendez-vous. Some were caught and reprimanded, and could even be dismissed. I was warned not to get involved in such action.

Protected within the convent's walls, we girls were shielded from the terrorist attacks and Communist assassinations that were taking place in the remote parts of the southern countryside. We were safe, too, from the fighting to the west. I remember reading in the papers, in 1958, that the Vietnamese Communists had sent troops to reinforce the Pathet Lao, who had taken over the area of Laos that bordered Vietnam.

After the *kermesse* of 1959, my mother phoned to tell me that my father had died, and that I should return to Saigon the next day for his funeral. Two years earlier, we had moved from Paul Bert to a large villa on Cach Mang street, the main street leading to the airport. This was where my father's funeral took place. After three days of wake, all of us in the family accompanied his body to the family cemetery plot on the outskirts of Go Cong, where my grandparents and their family had been buried, too.

I had known my father as a gentle man who had always given me good advice and wanted me to have a higher education. Standing next to his coffin, I promised him that I would go on to university and would not disappoint him. I also remembered him confessing to me that the only regrets in his life were his escapade with Miss Ba Tra, the beauty queen who later became a good friend of both my parents, and his opium smoking. He knew he had made his wife and children suffer during that turbulent period. He repented and became a good deal wiser in his later years, but he had already broken my mother's heart.

During that mourning period in Saigon in 1959, I learned through the murmurs of some of the guests that Ho Chi Minh had established the Central Office in South Vietnam to be his command organ in the South. It was known thereafter as COSVN in the memoranda and reports that recorded the war's progress, and would be pursued, mostly in vain, by the Americans and South Vietnamese until the war's end. He also dispatched some four thousand Communist cadres to the South to join the Viet Cong forces, and deployed support troops to open a supply route that would run from North Vietnam through northern Laos, down the east side of Cambodia, and, finally, into South Vietnam.

This mammoth task became known as the Ho Chi Minh Trail, an

incredible, 12,500-mile-long road over which men and women traveling by bicycle, truck, and elephant transported Chinese and Russian arms and equipment to the South. The Communists also conquered deep rivers and tall mountains to construct three thousand miles of pipeline to bring fuel to the southern battlefields. At the peak of the war, more than a hundred thousand North Vietnamese transport and engineer troops and infantry forces were working and dying along the Trail.

I was spared the fighting and turmoil of these faraway places. For my classmates and me, life went on as usual. At nineteen, in the summer of 1960, I graduated and received my French Baccalaureate II. It had not been easy. The exam process required that our papers be sent to Paris to be corrected. If a student failed even one of the six subjects, she had to redo the entire year and then retake the whole exam, not just the subject failed. No one could go to the university without a baccalaureate degree.

The disclosure of the exams' results, which came by cable from the Ministry of Education in France, was an excruciating experience for us students. My classmates and I waited in our classroom in total suspense and anxiety. Finally, the French Reverend Mère Enfant Jesus strode solemnly onto the platform and, in a serious tone, announced that not one of us had failed. Then she displayed a broad smile. We jumped, screamed, and kissed each other like wild birds twirling inside a cage. It was a euphoric moment.

Our success showed how well the nuns had educated us. We received not only an education at Les Oiseaux, but a revelation, as well. Now it was time to leave behind the innocent, secluded life we had known and face the world. Some of us would marry, some would continue our education, some would go to work. At that moment, none of us knew what awaited us.

After my graduation, my number four sister, Madame Tao, organized a national beauty contest at a big theater in Saigon. When the show was over and we were leaving, I had the thrill of being mistaken, in all the excitement, for one of the beauty queens. Later, when I had the chance to stand next to a real beauty queen at a reception at our house, I could see that I did not measure up to her. She was trained to walk and talk with sophistication, and her body was well sculpted. But I did not want to compete with her. I was determined to compete in the field of education instead.

I was enthusiastic about school and ready to go to the university in France, as my mother had promised before I passed the baccalaureate. But that summer in Saigon, she changed her mind. We had gone to some weddings, and the wedding of Modeste Kim, a classmate at Les Oiseaux, to Mai Tho Tuyen, the son of my mother's friends, gave her a new outlook. She decided that it was time for me to get married, and that there were a lot of well-educated young men of good families available to me.

Most girls back then got married by arrangement, through matchmakers. The parents of potential grooms would set up a date and bring their sons to visit and "look at the girl's eyes" (*coi mat*). The prospective bride and her family would receive them.

In my case, my mother dressed me up in a soft-colored Vietnamese *ao dai* while my seventh sister, Thu Ha, painted my face, fixed my long, curly hair that ran halfway down my back, and readied me to receive the guests. I did not need any rouge because the cool climate in Dalat had kept my skin light and pinkish.

The young man and his party would come at the appointed hour for tea and talk to my mother. After fifteen minutes, I would appear in the living room and answer a few questions from the boy's parents concerning my schooling and my studies. The young man would glance at me from time to time without uttering a word. I was not supposed to look straight into the guests' eyes; I was to lower my gaze while answering their questions softly. Then I was to retire from the scene.

This was the time when the parents would inquire into each other's religious inclinations, ferret out their respective social and family status, and get to know each other better. They would spend up to an hour sipping tea and chatting. The ladies usually chewed betel nut, a universal custom in Asia over two thousand years old.

Betel chewing was not only a sign of hospitality, but had medicinal and supernatural connotations, as well. It was conducive to communication and helped to bond relationships. It could constitute a ceremonial act of allegiance, sealing alliances and bringing good luck. Even more, the chewing of the betel nut imparted an aroma to the mouth, thus correcting bad breath, and was thought to dispel diseases by strengthening the teeth and gums. Finally, it was an aid to beauty in that it reddened women's lips, serving as a kind of lipstick.

A Vietnamese folk tale tells the story of twin brothers, Tan and Lang, who fell in love with the same girl. One agreed to let the other marry her. But one day the wife touched the hand of the brother-in-law by accident. Ashamed, he ran away and died of grief near the bank of a stream, and his body turned to limestone. The husband looked in vain for his brother. Stricken by grief, he died in the same place, and turned into an areca palm. The wife went to look for the both of them, and died at the same spot. She turned into a betel vine that grew beside the rock and entwined itself around the palm tree.

The king heard about the matter and chewed the three ingredients: lime, betel, and nut. He felt euphoric and was filled with well-being. Thus it was that the betel nut came to be chewed in Vietnam, a practice starting in the early centuries of the Christian era. At weddings, the groom gives betel leaves and nuts to the bride's family as symbols of alliance and loyalty.

My mother started to chew betel nut in her early forties and continued to do so until she left Vietnam to come to the United States in her late seventies. Storing, preparing, and presenting the betel nut is a distinctive art. I remember the round, open, engraved silver box bought in Cambodia that stored all the components needed. From age ten, I used to replenish all the freshly bought ingredients and present them to my mother as a daily ritual.

I prepared the betel nut as follows: I removed a piece of white lime paste from a small bird-shaped silver container with a tiny spatula and spread it on a half-ripe, yellowish-green betel leaf. I cut a thin slice of soft, unripe areca nut and folded it inside the leaf as if I were wrapping a small gift and gave it to her to chew. To complete the performance, I pulled a small roll of fresh tobacco from another silver container, this one in the shape of a rabbit. My mother clipped it tightly in between her gum and her lips and inhaled the smell of tobacco during the whole chewing procedure, which took fifteen minutes to a half-hour. Helping my mother with this ceremony allowed us children to show her that we cared for her. When my mother was in her sixties, to relieve her teeth from biting into the hard quid, I pulverized the nut in its shell with a mortar and pestle before wrapping it.

Chewing betel nut turned a person's saliva red, and the chewer spit out the red liquid into a small ceramic or copper spittoon. Seeing what looked like red blood coming out of people's mouths, some European visitors thought they had tuberculosis. Betel nut chewing was addictive, and was even considered to be an aphrodisiac. Largely replaced by cigarette smoking starting in the 1950s, it remains a widespread practice in Vietnam among old people.

Soon I began to act smarter. After each dreadful tea and betel nut ceremony, I changed into my jeans and climbed onto a low branch of the mango tree near the gate of our house. I waved and made sure that all of the potential in-laws saw me before they drove away. They were so shocked at my comportment that they did not come back to ask for my hand. I had succeeded in scaring them off, and I was waving good-bye to them for good.

A few persisted and came back anyway. But I was determined not to marry, and I rewarded my mother's efforts with a big no and a long face. She was not pleased, having given me a good education and gotten only disobedience in return. But I was nearly exactly like she was: I inherited not only her height, weight, and stature, but her strong character, as well.

She often said that I was not as obedient as my eldest sister, who acquiesced in nearly everything she was asked to do. Hai Duc only addressed my parents as, "Yes, respectable mother," or "respectable father." In fact, I never heard her say no to them.

Unable to go to France to study, I decided to go back to Les Oiseaux to teach at the convent and study at the University of Dalat, under the pretext that I could not stand the heat of Saigon. The Mother Superior, Mère Enfant Jesus, kindly boarded me in a spacious room in the teachers' quarters, and asked me to teach French and history to the sixth graders. This way I got to teach Bibiche and her classmates a few days a week, and I went to the university in my spare time. It was the best arrangement for me, and I began to think that I might spend the rest of my life cloistered inside those walls and end up an old maid. But I refused to get married under the absurd orchestration of my mother's friends.

Two classmates, Madeleine and Bach, the best students in my senior high school class, came from Saigon to bid farewell to the nuns and to me before going to France to study. Seeing them, I burst into tears. They said that they would go back to Saigon and try to persuade my mother to let me go to France with them. They did, and my mother finally relented and agreed that I could go.

Along with Madeleine, Bach, and a few of my classmates, I registered with the Ministry of Education to study at La Sorbonne in Paris. Only with the consent of the Ministry would we be allowed to get a student's exit visa from the Ministry of the Interior and a limited amount of foreign exchange at the official rate from the National Bank. Only with the Ministry's imprimatur could my mother send me money to study and live in Paris. That year, the new policy was to require all the girls to take political science. It was explained to us, off the record, that it was an order from Madame Nhu, the first lady of Vietnam. She wanted to see more girls trained and involved in national politics.

None of the twenty-five of us who were to be allowed to study abroad that year had any desire to study politics, nor did we want to make it a career—particularly after we had seen how Madame Nhu and her authoritarian husband, the infamous brother of President Diem, managed our country. The couple wanted to mobilize the masses after the examples of Hitler's brown-shirted storm troopers and Chiang Kai-Shek's blue-shirted youth organization.

In Vietnam, Nhu set up the Republican Youth, a group of militant young civil servants, dressed in blue shirts with blue trousers and berets. For her part, Madame Nhu established the Women's Solidarity Movement, a female militia armed with U.S. army carbines and dressed in blue uniforms and bush hats. The two aroused resentment when they forced these youth groups to parade on the streets and to pledge allegiance to the republic and to them.

The twenty-five of us selected to study in France were also their victims. We had no recourse but to register for political science. However, once in France, we took another major, the one we wanted, and studied both. I chose liberal arts. The second year, we all changed to our favorite subject and dropped political science.

I was excited about going to France and told my mother than I planned to stay in Europe for at least ten years. I would graduate and work there before I came home. My dreams were so intense that I could hardly sleep the week before I left. I stayed in my mother's bed the whole night before I went to Paris. I simply wanted to be with her.

Finally, the Paris I had longed for so much was there. I arrived in the dark of the winter months and breathed the cold air. The darkened Eiffel Tower, gloomy Notre Dame, and all the majestic monuments sat stone-faced. I was disappointed by the reality of their impassivity and indifference, but I was determined to explore all the treasures buried behind those inscrutable exteriors. I hoped the city of my dreams would come alive in the spring.

Longtime friends of my parents from Go Cong, the Nguyen Huu Haus sponsored me in France. They had retired as French citizens and settled in Paris. I stayed in their apartment on the *rue Vaugirard*, fifteenth district, when I first arrived. I registered at La Sorbonne. After I had attended a few classes, however, my mother ordered me to change to the University of Bordeaux, in the south of France. An aunt in Vietnam Di Sau, had influenced her, saying that a young girl alone in Paris would be exposed to too many temptations. They had heard stories of girls who had ruined their family's reputation.

So, in the middle of a somber winter, I moved to Bordeaux where two of my cousins, the children of Di Sau, and a French family acted as my new sponsors and chaperones. My sister and her husband, Dr. Tao, arranged for me to live with a French doctor, Dr. Moreau, and his wife in a large house on the *rue Turenne*. With its dark, engraved paneled wood, tall columns, velvet drapery, and museum-like paintings, the place overwhelmed me. It looked like one of those mansions I had seen in an album at Les Oiseaux. I felt like Alice lost in Wonderland.

Doctor Moreau, in his sixties, had his office on one side of the house. He received his patients with the help of a nurse, whom I rarely met. His gentle smile reminded me of my father. His wife, a pious lady, took me to church sometimes on weekends. They had fourteen children, most of them doctors or married to doctors. One of them, Dr. Roux, had known Dr. Tao when they studied medicine together in Bordeaux in the early 1940s. My brother-in-law was the bridge that linked me to that aristocratic family.

The Moreaus' maid, who had a very strong Mediterranean accent, cleaned my room and cooked breakfast for me every morning. She and her three-year-old daughter lived on the third floor, which she called the pigeons' dungeon. She gave me a tour of the house and took me down to the basement, where hundreds of wine bottles were stored in the cave.

The Moreaus; the Rous; my cousins, Dr. Chanh, a research physicist, and his brother, Dr. Trung, a heart specialist, took turns hosting me on weekends. They all insisted that I drink Bordeaux wine. One sip of that potent red liquid and my insides burned like a torch. I would stare at the crystal glass and see a witch making a potion as I slid into the inferno. My heart would beat strongly, my eyes dilate and my mind waltz. I used to think I was going to black out.

The following summer, the Moreaus drove me to their *château*, a huge country property in the Gironde, two hours from the city. Acres of grapes, green on one side and red on the other, adorned their country-style castle. They made wine for their family's consumption and to give as gifts to their friends. They were celebrating the christening of a great-grandchild, and at least forty members of the family had gathered for the occasion.

I was seated at the long table with the adults, on Dr. Moreau's right side. The hors d'oeuvre was caviar, served in abundance. Next came oysters set on silver plates kept fresh by crushed ice underneath. They had to be accompanied by the right white wine, and Sauvignon blanc was chosen. Homemade red wine accompanied the filet mignon.

I ate in a state of tension. There was no water, because no adult drank that bland liquid. I had to drink all the white and red potions when they toasted; and they did often. I felt as if I were about to explode, like a volcano. I excused myself and rushed to the bathroom. The chef would have fainted had he seen the masterpieces he had prepared so carefully splattered all over the sink. So ended my efforts to appreciate French wine.

I took my first-year exams at the faculties of Political Science and the Arts in Bordeaux. I studied political science with Dr. Robert Escarpit, who each day wrote a small satirical piece, "Au Jour Le Jour" for the front page of the newspaper, Le Monde. He was an outstanding professor, and I started to like the subject. I learned a great deal by reading political books and participating in open discussions in class. But I did not want a career in politics, like the one Madame Nhu had in Vietnam. I did not see myself as a politician.

I focused my studies more on the French literature I loved. I had studied the sixteenth- through nineteenth-century French authors in high school. Now, at the University of Bordeaux, I continued with the mid-nineteenth- and twentieth-century writers. I took a special literature course for a semester with a well-known professor who taught only Charles Baudelaire, the morbid poet who died in 1867. We examined Les Fleurs du Mal (The Flowers of Evil), a collection of 157 poems published in 1855. Like my professor of Vietnamese poetry and The Tale of Kieu, M. Flottes, a Frenchman in his late fifties, recited two or three of Baudelaire's most famous poems by heart in each class, always winning our applause.

M. Flottes was totally absorbed. When he recited "La Chevelure" ("Hair"), for instance, he made us smell the strong odors Baudelaire had put into the heroine of his poem. He shook his head in delirium in describing Baudelaire's sensuous, exotic passion for his creole mistress, Jeanne Duval, a "black Venus" and "dancing snake." He wanted us to drink in the perfume of her flesh, hear the music of her walk, see the colors of her skin, and "harvest" the jewelry in her hair.

Baudelaire was considered a revolutionary and a libertine, torn between his immortal excesses—opium, hashish, unrestrained sex (he contracted syphillis)—and his devoted adoration for Mme. Sabatier, an angel he adorned with virtues and unearthly charms. His secret love for this untouchable married woman was a divine yearning for a friend, a supernatural sister, an ideal mother. He longed in vain to find peace in the kind of platonic love that he had always had for his own mother.

The poet, strongly influenced by Edgar Allan Poe, found himself beset by loneliness, misery, and misunderstanding. He became manic-depressive. He expressed the paradox of these contrasting and repressed feelings in poems on the themes of *Spleen*, a state of malaise, a feeling of boredom and absurdity, and *Ideal*, an elevation to pure spirituality, which he failed to reach.

I was so impressed with Baudelaire's poetic inspiration and his tragic life that I volunteered to give a presentation on him to my class in Bordeaux. I remember explaining how he used romantic words over and over in his poems to burn them into the reader's mind. The word, "heart," appears more than one hundred times; "soul," seventy times; "sky," sixty times. Words like "love," "body," "perfume," and "beauty" appear about sixty times each. "Voluptuous," "pleasure," "hell," "remorse," and "God" play prominently, as well, appearing thirty times. I told my classmates how Baudelaire used that limited vocabulary to express not only his familiar themes of anguish, nostalgia, and sin, but also peace and hope. Through a slow erosion of his heart and soul, he reached poignant platonic and satanic states at the same time.

Despite his talent, the poet was fined by the courts, and six of his poems, judged indecent and decadent, were suspended from publication in 1857. He had scandalized and horrified his fellow citizens, even his mother, by combining both God and Satan, and the "unethics" and the esthetics.

It was not his blasphemy or his character that I admired. He dared to reveal his deepest feelings and beliefs in an age when society was restricted and severe in its thinking. He shocked his family, his society, even the church. Baudelaire was one against all. He was on the same cross that Jesus had carried. But the more deeply he dug into his own private vision, the more desperately he failed. Instead of the sublime, he found absurdity. I saw in that revolutionary writer an avant-garde architect of freedom of expression, a precursor of modern poetry obsessed by an enormous appetite for the *yin* and the *yang*.

There would be times in my life when I would take solace from Baudelaire and his lonely struggle. When I was involved in the controversial work of advocating family planning in Vietnam, it was Baudelaire who inspired me. Like Baudelaire, I was condemned by society for doing something it considered outrageous—in my case, informing other women that they had the right to make their own decisions about their reproductive lives. Like the infamous writer, I was swimming upstream against the values of the time: Confucian total obedience to the family and society, an outdated French legal code, and the teachings of religion. I began to know what Baudelaire must have felt like.

Later, on my first Foreign Service post with Lacy, I fell into a state of malaise and absurdity that Baudelaire would have recognized. In Milan, less than two years after the fall of Saigon to the Communists, I found myself in a state of crisis, haunted by the loss of my country and of myself, unable to understand why I had to subject myself to what was expected of me by society, religion, and convention. I suffered profoundly and was in rebellion. Unable to find harmony in myself, I became inwardly, then outwardly, depressed. Fortunately, rediscovering the consciousness of the good and bad in myself and in the universe, I tried to find a cure for my traumatic experience.

Right after my final exams in Bordeaux in 1962, I spent a month of my summer vacation in London with Doan Thu, a classmate from Les Oiseaux. She found a British family for me to board with and practice my English.

Tired from my exams and my trip, I spent my first two days sleeping. The English words I heard most often were "tea time." The lady of the house awakened me regularly in what was for me the middle of the night—10 A.M. and 4 P.M.—to give me biscuits and hot tea with milk and sugar. Strange manners, I thought.

I used to watch TV with Mamom, my English mother, her husband, and their teenage daughter after dinner. Mamom broke into tears of pride when the queen or the royal family appeared. Whether they were shown inside Buckingham Palace or on the streets waving to the public, they provoked her enthusiasm. "How marvelous! Wonderful! Splendid!" She was full of reverence for the royals.

After a week of settling in and growing more used to the daily tea practices, I asked Mamom to show me the post office. I wanted to mail letters to my mother and my friends to tell them my first impressions of England. This was my first time by myself outside the house. The sun was out, the velvety green lawns were well tended, and the people were smiling. But after four turns, I got lost and could not find my way to the post office. Stricken by fear, I did not dare talk to strangers.

I went into a shop under the pretext of buying a box of chocolates, gathered up my courage, and asked the cashier for directions to the post office. A kind, elderly lady, a client, took me outside, curious to see a little Oriental girl. She asked me all sorts of questions I did not understand, since I had never confronted a British accent in Vietnam. She talked awhile, pointing up the street. I said yes, yes, thank you very much. Then I went home. I did not understand her at all. It was my first real encounter with spoken English.

Doan Thu and I went to museums, to the theater, and to Hyde Park for picnics. We attended concerts. On weekends, we took trips to Oxford, Cambridge, and Stratford-upon-Avon, Shakespeare's home. I observed that the people on the streets were most polite. They never started a sentence without uttering a "please," or ended without a "thank you." They were very cordial and nice. I wanted to live there and learn English. When people asked us to repeat our names, too difficult to pronounce or remember, we told them simply to call us "One Two," for Doan Thu; and "Two One" for Thu Van.

Doan Thu told me that, at the French Lycée, there was a university-level course where French professors from Paris and Lille commuted regularly to teach liberal arts. All the exams were sent to France to be corrected, and the results were equivalent to a French degree. It was like attending a French university in the heart of London. What more could I ask for? I decided to stay and study there.

My mother was not happy with my sudden move to London; nor were my sister or her husband, Dr. Tao. They felt I had somehow deserted the respectable French families that had agreed to look after me, as well as my Vietnamese cousins, who had sponsored me. Again the stubborn littlest child of the family was going her own way. Were they sorry to have given me a rational Cartesian education so that I could think and make up my own mind?

But I had support, too. The nuns from Les Oiseaux in Verneuil, France, kindly introduced me to a religious order that had a school in London. It had ten rooms on the top floor where students boarded. I applied and was allowed to share a room with a student from Leeds, in northeastern England. The four-story building was located on Cromwell Road, oppo-site the Natural History Museum, in South Kensington—just a block away from the French Lycée, and three blocks away from the underground. I was very lucky.

On the first day of the academic year, I went to the Lycée to register. I asked for the registration office, and a French teacher told me to join a line in a courtyard. I fell into conversation with a teenage girl, Kate, in line in front of me. She was an American who had come to live in London for two years. Her father, Dr. Hugh Chaplin, from St. Louis, Missouri, had received a fellowship to do research at a London hospital. She hardly spoke French, and I hardly spoke English, but we understood each other.

Kate told me that she was queuing up to attend high school. I realized then that I was in the wrong line. Seeing my petite size, the French teacher thought that I was going to high school. Kate and I exchanged names and phone numbers. From that brief encounter, I was to develop acquain-tances that would be profoundly significant, and fifteen years later, I would be reunited with Kate's family after I had fled Vietnam.

During the day, I went to the British Council to learn English. At night I attended university, where the French professors were teaching the same French history, literature, and other courses I would have taken at La Sorbonne or in Bordeaux. Dr. Chaplin called and asked whether I would like to babysit Kate and her brother, David. I came to see him and his wife, Alice. Alice's mother was French, her father American. They asked me to tutor their children in French, too.

I also enlarged my social circle. The British Council organized programs at night and on weekends where I could meet people and practice my English. Doan Thu introduced me to Vietnamese embassy officials, Vietnamese BBC radio broadcasters, and others. (Later, Doan Thu married a Vietnamese BBC broadcaster, Ton That Ky. They had two children and now live in Los Angeles, where Doan Thu, good at heart as usual, works as a social worker.)

At the British Council in London, I met Chi Tuyet, "Snow White," who led me to the man who would become the cornerstone of my life. Chi Tuyet, three years older than I, had been in her senior year at Les Oiseaux when I entered the school. She later went to France, and had recently come to London to study English. She was to return to Paris at Christmas to get married. She asked me to be her bridesmaid. I accepted, and we went back together. By day, Paris in winter was dark and cold, but nighttime was exciting, with bright lights. I shared Chi Tuyet's apartment.

On the morning of the wedding, a group of us went to the Vietnamese embassy with Chi Tuyet and her fiance, Liem, an engineer, to sign the required papers, then to the Paris City Hall to sign some more. Finally, we arrived at the church. No one from Liem's family was there; they were all in Vietnam. Chi Tuyet, radiant in her white gown, waited at the altar for the groom. I was at the entrance of the church, helping the little flower girl. Liem waited to walk up the aisle to the altar.

The organ struck up the solemn wedding march. Liem suddenly told me he was panicking. His knees were failing him, and he could not walk. He grabbed me and said, "Help me please." He leaned on me, held on tight, and we both walked into the church. The more I pushed him forward, the more he said he was going to fall if I let go. He was breathing hard. I could see the guests staring at us. Some raised their eyebrows, wondering why the groom was in the arms of a young girl. This was not, I thought, the traditional role of the bridesmaid. But we made it.

The wedding lunch was at a well-known Vietnamese restaurant, La Table du Mandarin. Relaxed, we laughed about what had happened. I observed that Anh Muoi, the restaurant owner, had placed me between two young bachelors. Tan, the dean of the School of Pedagogy in Vietnam, had been sent by the government a few months before to finish his doctorate. Bong, who had gone to high school and university in Paris, had recently presented his doctoral thesis at the law school.

Both Tan and Bong were in their early thirties and were devoting their full attention to me. They took turns feeding me, pouring drinks for me, and talking to me, without a moment of respite. In the evening, at the reception in another restaurant, we danced until past midnight. I did not even have the chance to sit, because either Tan or Bong invited me to dance continually. Chi Tuyet finally came to my rescue and pulled me away from Tan. Laughing, she said that two sharks had been attacking me from all sides.

The next afternoon, Bong called me. He was going back to Vietnam the following week to teach at the Law School, and he asked whether I would like to buy a few presents to give to my family. I certainly did. He came by with a small, beat-up car and we drove to the *grand magasin*, La Fayette, to buy the gifts. He invited me to dinner in a small cafè restaurant, and we talked about Vietnam. Bong had spent more than ten years in Paris, and his only desire was to return home and help his country. I told him that my only desire was to study in Europe, and then stay for ten more years. Both of us had come to one decision in common: we wanted to spend our careers teaching.

The next day, Bong asked me to help him select some classical music he wanted to take home. At the music store, we met Jacqueline Duc, who had been at the Lycée Marie Curie with me before going on, as I had, to Les Oiseaux. She, too, went to La Sorbonne, then to the university in Bordeaux. Her father, my family doctor, graduated from the medical school in Bordeaux. Jacqueline reminded me of the music the nuns taught us at Les Oiseaux.

Bong chose a few records and said that he wanted to give me a souvenir: an adagio by Albinoni. We went into a booth, where I put on earphones. I was laughing, happy to meet Jacqueline Duc again. Suddenly, the music overpowered me; the slow steps of the march, like a funeral, penetrated my brain, ground into my chest, and twisted my abdomen with the deepest and saddest notes I had ever heard. Unexpected tears ran down my face like a waterfall. Bong, surprised, extended his hand to me. Were they tears of distress, ecstasy, or nostalgia? Were they a presentiment of what was to come?

Bong and I met a few more times in Paris, always in the company of friends. The night before he was to return to Vietnam and I to London, we said goodbye over dinner in a small restaurant. Again, he expressed his wish to serve his country and, through his law students, to make it more democratic. When I asked if he would dare to confront an authoritarian government, he said that he would, and he would try to improve the situation. I told myself that he was like all the other inexperienced, hot-headed idealists just out of school.

Anh Muoi told me that he had known Bong for many years, and that he was self-reliant and a self-made man. He had worked as a waiter so he could buy books and had done all kinds of odd jobs to finance his education. Bong came from a simple family in Go Cong, my mother's hometown, Anh Muoi continued. I felt closer to Bong.

But I was not physically attracted to Bong at first. He was six inches taller than I was, with strong bones. He wore white glasses with thick lenses, and his small eyes did not look at girls in a romantic way. Also, he had no flair for the sophisticated language of courtship. He said very little, but when he did speak, he was direct and precise. In fact, he was rather shy, quite unlike the boastful Vietnamese men who often exaggerated their own exploits.

Bong had a sincere smile, a frank laugh, and an easy-going manner. I was mostly drawn to him by his strong character: here was a young man who, by virtue of hard work, determination and resilience, had realized the dream of earning his degree in Paris. He was a self-made man. I held him in high regard.

On the drive back to my apartment, he held my hand for the first time. I did not resist; it was a good and warm feeling. I felt protected and attracted to him for the first time. Behind his cool pragmatism, I sensed his strength and sincerity, and I was drawn to him. In the silence of that night, he suddenly communicated his feelings to me, and I responded.

We did not say a word until we reached my apartment. I shook hands with him and said goodbye. He held my shoulders and kissed me softly on one cheek, then the other. I flushed and returned his kisses. Then, I quickly pushed him away, not wanting to commit myself further.

Once back in Saigon, Bong went to see my mother to give her my gifts. He then started visiting her several times a week, and, finally, nearly every evening. My mother wrote me that he usually stayed twenty minutes to half-an-hour, perched on the sofa, and confined himself to answering her questions. He did not seem to know how to conduct a lively conversation. She wrote that he was "too quiet," but also a "mature and sound man," and that he seemed to miss me and be very much in love with me.

Bong also wrote to me every week, no more than a page each time. In his tiny handwriting, he gave short, exact replies to the questions I asked him about his teaching and the situation in Saigon, nothing more. I felt a little frustrated by his short, curt letters, but we became loyal pen pals.

Although we steered away from personal feelings in our letters—writing instead about our daily lives—we gradually closed both the physical and emotional distance between us by using more personal language. His first letters began with "Miss Thu Van," then switched to "dear." His first letters ended with "cordially," escalated to "affection-ately," and finally, "lovingly yours." Slowly, I responded in the same style. We never expressed our love to one another in plain language, but our deep feelings could be read between the lines.

It was six months after our first meeting that Bong asked my mother if he could marry me. Ours had been a platonic love that deepened and grew with time and distance until our two destinies were sealed. The Vietnamese say that predestination binds people thousands of miles apart, and that, without it, even people who are face to face cannot be united (*Huu duyen thien ly nang tuong ngo, vo duyen doi dien bat tuong phung*). Bong also proposed to me in a letter. He said that he loved me and wanted to marry me.

But did I really want to give up my schooling and return to Vietnam to marry Bong? I was getting the education I had always dreamed of. Was I ready to be tied to the strict responsibilities of a family? I felt I should stay in London through the summer until I finished my studies, and think more about it. But my mother thought it was time for me to settle down, and Bong assured me I could finish my degree at the University of Saigon.

The end of the school year was approaching. During exams, I received a proposal from another quarter. De, my first boyfriend, whom I had not seen for seven years, sent me a fifteen-page letter saying that he had just graduated from medical school and wanted to marry me. His love for me, he said, had helped him carry on and succeed. He would do anything for me. He included two poems he had written to me, and said his diary contained many more.

Now I found myself in a real dilemma, and had to make the most important decision of my life: choosing between Bong and De. Bong was a poor professor, ten years my senior. In contrast, De, only three years older than I, would become a wealthy doctor. I chose Bong. My love for him crowded everything else out of my mind.

I packed up and headed home. On the way, I stopped for week in Rome and for another in Athens sightseeing. I did not know if I would ever be able to travel again.

FOUR

ASSASSINATION AND WIDOWHOOD

Than so lam noi bat bang,
Lieu nhu Cung Quang, a Hang nghi sao?

Why is my life so full of unjust misfortunes,
Must I resign myself to loneliness and sadness like Hang Nga in her
cold moon palace?

Nguyen Du

I arrived back in Vietnam in the summer of 1963, after nearly three years in Europe. I found things had changed, not physically, but psychologically. Most people feared the iron fist with which the Ngo family managed the country. They had spies everywhere and people dared to speak their minds only among their intimates. I remember the slanted jokes and the allusions to legends and historical events that featured the downfall of royal families. These stories raced through Saigon's upper middle class society.

Although I was happy to be back among my own people, I felt confined in that tense political environment. And I missed the cultural and social outings in Paris and London. I had grown attached to the spirit of the western world, where I could express my feelings without restraint. I missed this freedom so intensely that both my dreams and my nightmares transported me back to Europe. Vietnam now seemed dull and provincial by comparison. Still, this was my country, and I wanted to be there.

And I was busy preparing myself for passage into the new life that would start with my wedding. In the fall, Bong's mother came up from

Camau, a provincial town at the southernmost tip of the Mekong Delta, to ask for my hand. It is a Vietnamese tradition that the marriage process starts with a visit from the groom's parents to the bride's home. Since Bong's father had separated from his mother and remarried, Bong did not ask his father to come. He figured our two mothers would understand each other and work out the complicated details of the wedding ceremonies.

Bong's mother had already consulted a fortune-teller in the deep South, another custom, and knew the best dates for our engagement and wedding ceremonies. My mother had also seen an astrologer in Saigon. The two of them told Bong and me that both fortune-tellers feared that our horoscopes were not compatible. We were doomed to part, or one of us would die.

With our western education and attitudes, we tossed aside such superstitions. We told our mothers that we were determined to be united both in marriage and in death, and went on with our plans. Bong now came to visit me every day after work. We were able to talk and get to know each other better.

Bong had returned to Vietnam with a Ph.D. in both Constitutional Law and Political Science. Since early 1963, he had been part of the University of Saigon Law faculty. Only a few months after he began teaching, while I was still in Europe, he gave a commencement speech on "Political Parties and the Opposition." Widely reported on in the newspapers, it electrified the country.

In his talk, Bong used metaphor to criticize the government. To build a good house, he said, one needed a strong foundation. Otherwise, rats would eat holes in it, and the walls, beams, and ceiling would crumble. The "foundation" was a democratic system in which opposition parties were allowed to operate. The "rats" were corrupt government officials. The "walls, beams, and ceiling" were the legislative, judicial, and executive bodies. His point was that, without a constructive opposition, there were no checks and balances, no freedom, no democracy.

Bong also used history, showing how a Vietnamese dynasty of the fifteenth century had declined due to abuse of power. He urged the government not only to permit opposition parties, but also to nurture and institutionalize them.

Bong's friends told me that he received a standing ovation from the crowd of over two hundred, and accolades from his colleagues and students. People were surprised by Bong's grasp of ancient Vietnamese history, since he had left Vietnam in his teens. And they were impressed by his mastery of the Vietnamese language and his precise use of technical Vietnamese terms. Bong told me later that he had learned much of what he knew from Vietnamese dictionaries, histories, and literature books borrowed from the French libraries and from friends. He was, in large measure, self-taught.

That speech risked the wrath of the ruling Ngo family, which had banned opposition parties. Harvard Law School Professor Ta Van Tai recalled in 1997 that this speech made Bong "a rising star . . . It was the turning point." Bong "put himself on the Vietnamese map, and put Vietnam on the map of the world," Tai explained.

Teachers, intellectuals, and students started to gather around Bong. They wanted to take political action, but did not have the resources or the freedom to organize themselves. They did not want the dictatorship of the Northern Communists, but did not want to live under the dictatorship of the Ngo family, either.

Ngo Dinh Diem, South Vietnam's president, had spent the early 1950s in the United States. Living at the Maryknoll seminary in Ossining, New York, Diem was supported by Francis Cardinal Spellman, archbishop of New York and the unofficial leader of the American Catholic hierarchy. Spellman helped Diem lobby U.S. government officials and congressmen for a non-communist Vietnam. In June of 1954, following the Geneva Accords, which partitioned Vietnam into North and South, the Emperor Bao Dai recalled Diem to Vietnam and installed him as South Vietnam's Prime Minister. The next year Diem became president, by referendum. In October of 1956, Diem proclaimed the Constitution of the Republic of Vietnam, ousting Emperor Bao Dai for good.

With his own family, Diem exhibited the virtue of *tin*—loyalty—to a fault, putting his brothers into high positions. Nhu became his political advisor; Monsignor Thuc, archbishop of Vietnam; Can, governor of Hue; and Luyen, ambassador to Great Britain. It was rumored, then known openly, that Thuc and Can had acquired huge real estate and business holdings. Nhu's wife, Madame Nhu, became the regime's First Lady (Diem never married). She was soon a public figure, delivering speeches and acting as spokesperson for the Ngo family.

The paternalistic Diem ruled the country with "all or nothing" policies and an absolutist style of leadership. Brave and stubborn, Diem out-smarted his enemies with intricate manipulations and generous American aid. The Americans gave Diem his own personal strategist, Colonel Edward Lansdale, a former OSS officer. Lansdale was depicted in *The Ugly American* as Colonel Edwin Hillendale, and portrayed in Graham Greene's *The Quiet American* as Alden Pyle, a naïve U.S. official. Lansdale set up the Saigon Military Mission, funded by the CIA, and advised Diem on such matters as psychological warfare techniques to counter Communist guerilla tactics.

The Ngo brothers, Diem and Nhu, however, had their own agenda— to eradicate all domestic opposition to their regime. In 1956, with Lansdale's men and money, they had crushed the leaders of the religious sects. The Cao Dai Pope fled to Cambodia, and the Hoa Hao sect leader and warlord, Ba Cut, was guillotined in the town of Can Tho in the Delta. The Binh Xuyen crime organization was, rightly, suppressed.

By 1960, the Ngos were alienating the independent-minded national-ists and running the country like an oppressive oligarchy. They jailed a group of non-communist intellectuals who had written the so-called *Caravelle Manifesto*, which urged the Ngo brothers to recognize other political parties. Also imprisoned was former Minister of Foreign Affairs Tran Van Do, Madame Nhu's own uncle.

Bong, therefore, had reason to be concerned, but he delivered his opposition speech without fear of reprisal. He did exactly what he told me he would do before he left Paris. He never wrote me about the speech that gained him such notoriety; I learned of it from friends who took turns letting Bong stay with them because they were afraid he would be seized during the night.

One evening, Bong told me he thought we should postpone our wedding until the tense political situation had improved. My mother was disappointed to the point of alarm. "The situation has not changed for the last ten years. Only a miracle could change it. My poor girl, you are going to rot like an old maid." I told her to be patient. I trusted Bong and was willing to wait until things simmered down. But my mother was not placated. "If I had known this was going to happen, I would not have sent you a return ticket. What a waste of time and money!" she complained. "And you are stuck now with no prospects, either for a wedding or for an education, because I am not going to send you back to Europe."

I, too, was concerned about my future and what I would do next, but I was more worried about the dangerous political atmosphere. My brothers and sisters and their friends all saw the same depressing situation: abuse of power by a Catholic family backed by U.S. dollars, oppression of Buddhist leaders, repression of political parties and youth groups, cruelty from the government's secret police, assassinations of innocent people. These were the sources of fear that people whispered to their friends.

President Diem had given full power to his brother Nhu to imprison, torture, and murder not only the Vietnamese Communists but also noncommunist nationalists suspected of opposing their regime. Insulated from the bad news while I was in Europe, I was shocked to hear about all this turmoil and repression.

Nhu had established the Can Lao party, a secret society designed to penetrate and manipulate the armed forces, the government bureaucracy and intellectual circles. (He also oversaw more than a dozen security agencies that imprisoned or executed people without trial.) Party members vowed absolute loyalty, and spied on their own friends. The party's five-man cells were spread throughout the government structure and the army. They viewed adherence to Catholicism as important to deciding which civil servants and which officers would be promoted and which would not.

For the countryside, Nhu had a program of "strategic hamlets," also

known as *agrovilles*. These were communities of peasants inside compounds, enclosed by bamboo fences, meant to protect them from Communist attack. But the peasants, uprooted from their villages, instead felt
harassed and alienated.

Meanwhile, there was a pronounced rift between the *Nam Ky*, South
Vietnam's native southerners, who were traditionally considered easy-
going and a bit lazy; and the *Bac Ky*, the more aggressive, mostly Catholic
northerners, who had fled to the South in 1954 to escape the Communists.
The Ngos, Catholics themselves, favored the northern Catholics and gave
them the most prestigious government jobs. This produced a fissure along
religious lines between the Catholics, ten percent of the population, and
the Buddhists, eighty percent. The Buddhists saw themselves as victims
of official discrimination, a situation that deteriorated as demonstrations,
arrests, and killings mounted.

At one flash point, a venerable monk set himself on fire. In a radio
address, which I heard, Madame Nhu demeaned the monk's action by
saying he had "barbecued himself to death." Madame Nhu had emerged,
in the words of Robert McNamara, as "diabolical and scheming—a true
sorceress." Martial law was declared, and Nhu used it to raid pagodas
and jail hundreds of Buddhist monks. More violence erupted.

Bong started meeting clandestinely with other intellectuals to try to
deal with the crisis. When he did not show up some evenings to visit
me, I was afraid that he had been jailed or killed. He never told me where
he went during the day or slept at night. He only said that he had to go
to important meetings. Bong told me that we had to find a solution, but
without provoking an uprising that would end in a bloodbath.

There was speculation that certain top military officials, supported
by the Americans, were plotting against the government. They were only
waiting for American Embassy officials to give them the green light.
Everyone agreed that it would be impossible to do anything without
the Americans' consent. Diem was commonly considered an American
product, processed in the U.S. and exported back to Vietnam.

In November of 1963, a group of generals, those Diem trusted most,
turned against him and his brother. Like Julius Caesar, Diem was

murdered by his most loyal disciples. On the streets, there was euphoria. Overjoyed, people went on a rampage, destroying the presidential palace and the last vestiges of the Ngo family. The pressure cooker containing the Vietnamese people had exploded.

Thirty-five years later, General Ton That Dinh told me his side of the story. Dinh was one of the five principal generals (Don, Dinh, Kim, Khiem, and Minh) who masterminded the coup. Coming from the central part of Vietnam, like the Ngos, he was the most trusted and loyal of the Ngos' allies. He had served them since his early thirties. In 1958, he took over the military branch of the powerful Can Lao party. Two years later, he was promoted to commanding general of Region III, the area around Saigon, as well as commander in chief of the Saigon area itself—the most crucial part of the country. He was among the youngest and most decorated generals, and proudly called himself *ngan tang*, "fearless and arrogant." Dinh considered himself the adopted son of Diem.

Seeing how the situation had deteriorated with the jailing and self-immolation of the Buddhist monk, General Dinh and another general Diem trusted, Tran Van Don, tried to persuade the president to expand the cabinet, include some generals to unify the divided armed forces, and give people more religious freedom. It was in vain; Diem did not move.

At the same time that the internal political situation was worsening, so was the Ngos' relationship with the U.S. Diem thought that the CIA had conspired with the Buddhists to provoke unrest in Vietnam. The American media, on the other hand, were very critical of the repression of the Buddhists and strongly condemned it. Also, the American administration was displeased to learn that, in February 1963, Nhu had secretly made an agreement with Pham Hung, a high ranking North Vietnamese Communist official. They negotiated to build railroads from Saigon to Hanoi to promote reunification of Vietnamese families divided in the North and South by the 1954 Geneva Accords, and to improve trade between the two regions. They'd also agreed that the Communists who were caught in the South would not be eliminated but rehabilitated under an "Open Arms" agreement, whereby they would be pardoned and could live freely.

The U.S. found this overall situation intolerable but was apparently confused about what to do. Nonetheless, on August 24, 1963, President Kennedy and his senior advisors sent a cable to Ambassador Henry Cabot Lodge, who had just arrived in Saigon. The cable instructed Lodge to tell Vietnam's "key military leaders" that the U.S. would not continue to support the current government if steps were not taken immediately to change the oppressive situation ". . . which we recognize requires removal of the Ngos from the scene." The cable also said, "If, in spite of all your efforts, Diem remains obdurate and refuses, then we must face the possibility that Diem himself cannot be preserved."

Lucien Conein, a CIA officer in Saigon, told General Don about U.S. support for the coup. Don then persuaded Dinh to go along. Dinh told me that without his consent the coup would have failed; he controlled all the armed forces in Saigon and the surrounding military region—the most crucial area in the country.

In his book, *Vietnam: A Witness*, General Don recounted that ten generals gathered at the Joint General Staff Headquarters on November 1, 1963, at 1:30 P.M. Lucien Conein was invited to join them. Conein brought with him a radio to contact the American embassy and a bag of three million piastres to help finance the coup.

Outside, General Dinh and his troops took over the radio station, police headquarters, the airport, and the prison—releasing hundreds of political prisoners, among them the monks and students who had participated in the demonstrations against the Ngos. By late evening, the military controlled most key posts.

Then, according to his own account, General Dinh took charge of leading the attack on the presidential palace. He recalled that he faced strong resistance from Diem's guards, and did not take over the palace until six o'clock the next morning.

The plan was to capture Diem and Nhu and his family and fly them out of the country in a plane Ambassador Lodge agreed to charter. But during the late afternoon of the coup, Diem and Nhu had fled the palace and taken refuge in a Catholic church in Cholon. Learning that the palace had fallen, Diem telephoned the generals and surrendered. But he refused to leave the country, and he and Nhu were taken prisoner in the church.

Diem and Nhu, hands tied behind their backs, were driven in an armored personnel carrier to military headquarters, accompanied by Captain Nguyen Van Nhung, an aide-de-camp of General Big Minh, who had been proclaimed president. When the carrier arrived at headquarters, both Diem and his brother, Nhu, were dead—knifed and shot several times. Their death came as a shock to most of the generals. President Kennedy was said to be shaken when he heard the news.

In mid-September, Mme. Nhu, as a member of Congress, had gone to a conference in Belgrade with her eldest daughter. They also went to the U.S., where Mme. Nhu spoke wherever she could about the Buddhist situation in Vietnam, defending the Diem regime against those who thought it had badly overreacted—which meant most Americans. When the coup took place, she was in Los Angeles. She called General Don and told him she wanted to go back to Vietnam to take care of her other three children, who had taken refuge in her summer residence in Dalat. But the generals did not allow her to return.

Ambassador Lodge himself had to intercede on the children's behalf. He had them flown to Rome, where their mother joined them. She has remained there ever since.

Years later, in the spring of 1998, General Dinh told me that he felt guilt and remorse at the part he'd played in the coup. He regretted deeply the death of Diem. Still, he thought that Diem was wrong to have favored the Catholics over the Buddhists, trusted his own Can Lao party over other political parties, and governed the country with an iron fist. That was why Diem had lost the mandate of Heaven, and, consequently, of the people. Dinh, who was a senator from 1970 to 1975, thought that, in retrospect, the coup had led to political chaos, and left Vietnam without strong leadership. The long-term result, he said, was that the country fell to the Communists.

With hindsight, I recognize that President Diem was a true nationalist and that he did a great deal to rebuild South Vietnam with the seven billion dollars in economic and military aid that the U.S. pumped into our country from 1955 to 1961. A man of integrity and our first elected president, he used the early years of his rule to bring order, hope, and some prosperity to our people. Had he been more flexible, and had he not allowed his family for an entire decade to abuse their power, things would have been different.

My mother was thrilled. Now I would not become an old maid. She immediately called Bong's mother, and both of them resumed preparations for the wedding.

As for me, I was happy that Bong was now safe, and that the political nightmare was over. A bright future lay ahead for us. I applied to teach French at Regina Mundi, a branch of Les Oiseaux, in Saigon. I also registered for classes at the University of Saigon.

Bong and I got married in January 1964, after stability had been restored following the coup. Our wedding was a mixture of East and West. In the morning, we followed the traditional rituals, paying respect to Buddha, our ancestors and the elderly, and giving gifts, with family and old friends in attendance. Bong gave me only a gold wedding ring, being unable to afford more. My mother understood the situation and had a well-known jeweler design earrings for me, with four rows of cascading diamonds. They were, she told me, the symbol of beauty and virginity that any bride should have at her marriage.

That night, we invited two hundred guests for a reception and Western-style dance in the beautifully lit garden of our house. I was attended by six bridesmaids.

Two months later, we invited Bong's mother and her two daughters to come and live with us. They had to flee Camau, at that time overrun with Communist guerrillas and subject to government attacks.

Our twins, a boy and a girl, were born at the end of the year. Friends wondered how such a petite woman could have twins. I told them I carried one in front and one in back.

Bong had wanted a son and I had dreamed of a daughter. Thu Anh— Autumn Light—was the more aggressive at birth, pushing herself out into the light of day five minutes before Le Viet, her brother, named for Vietnam. They weighed very little, five-and-a-half pounds each. I had to breastfeed them every two hours, day and night. I got little sleep and found the regimen exhausting.

The new babies would wake up exactly at the same time to cry for milk. Although they were not identical twins, they were sick at the same time, with the same ailment. But it was a delight to watch them in their cradles babbling like birds. They kept my mother-in-law, their two nannies, and myself occupied around the clock.

My mother-in-law, in a very traditional gesture, celebrated the twins' first birthday by symbolically marrying them in a ceremony at home. It was believed that boy and girl twins were born together because they could not get married in their previous life. So my mother-in-law dressed the boy in a traditional blue brocade tunic, and the girl in red. We burned incense and prayed that their wishes in their former life would be fulfilled, and that, from now on, they would live as brother and sister.

Our youngest son, Le Quoc, meaning "patriotism," was born two years later, at the end of 1966. The twins ran around and pulled their brother's legs or hands through the crib so they could kiss him every morning and evening. Le Quoc was much easier for me to handle, since I now had twice the experience and half the work.

Three children. Our ideal family. I was twenty-five and felt fulfilled. I had spent a quarter of a century well protected from the storm. Autumn Cloud was radiant under the sun.

After the 1963 coup, Bong became the head of the National Institute of Administration, or NIA, the government-run academy that trained South Vietnam's top civil servants. Graduates became the chiefs and deputy chiefs of South Vietnam's forty-five provinces, and were appointed to diplomatic posts overseas. Gradually, the NIA began to train mid- and lower-level employees in all government agencies.

The NIA was thus a platform from which Bong thought he could bring about reform. His job gave him the unique opportunity to influence those who would run the Vietnamese government. Bong believed that this was the way to build the "firm foundation" upon which Vietnam's democracy could be erected. He had little trouble earning the respect and trust of his students. He was in a job he loved.

Bong and I were both happy teaching. He taught courses in law, political science, and government, while I continued with French at Regina Mundi. I also went to the University of Saigon to finish my B.A. degree. I wanted to learn more about my roots, as well, and took courses in oriental philosophy. Bong and I made a pact. Hooking our right index fingers together, we agreed that he would not take a cabinet post, which he'd been offered by each new government. The bright lights and notoriety were not worth it.

Bong's high school teacher, Mr. Huynh Cam Chuong, came with his wife to visit me one day. He had been headmaster of his own primary and secondary school, located near the Thai Binh market, in a suburb of Saigon. They told me about Bong's childhood and adolescence. They recounted how one evening Bong, at fourteen, had come to Mr. Chuong's school and asked for work. He said he had no financial support from his parents, nor from anyone else in his family, but he was willing to clean the classrooms and do odd jobs in return for an education.

Bong's parents had divorced when he was a small child. His father, a goldsmith, remarried and had four other children. Bong's mother, then twenty-nine, took her daughter, Bong's older sister, and another son, only a year old, to the country's southernmost province, Camau, where she opened a dress-making store, married a boat pilot, and had two more daughters. She did not take Bong to Camau, but left him, then only three, in Go Cong, in the care of his father's parents.

So Bong lived with his grandparents in Kien Phuoc village, five miles from the sleepy town of Go Cong. At six every morning he left for school, crossing the rice fields on foot. Since his grandparents, who had owned a fish sauce factory, had retired, they did not have money for school uniforms or books. Bong was such a good student, however, that he won enough supplies to be able to stay in school. He even won an umbrella, an aunt of his told me, that kept him dry in the rain.

At twelve, Bong went to Go Cong to live with his father so he could go to middle school. There was none in the small village of Kien Phuoc.

His father gave him an old bicycle that often broke down. He learned how to fix it, then started repairing bikes for others, one of the odd jobs he did to earn pocket money.

After two years in Go Cong, Bong went to Saigon to attend high school, and boarded with a poor uncle. He slept on a cot in the kitchen. Needing a school but having no money, he went out looking for a place which would take him, and eventually found Mr. Chuong's school.

The Chuongs had five children of their own, but they gave Bong a job and allowed him to live in their home in back of the school. There, Bong woke up early every day to help clean the school. He went to classes in the morning and studied in the afternoon. Evenings, he learned how to type, earning a diploma in typing, then helping Mr. Chuong teach it. He gave some of his wages to Mrs. Chuong. She put his money in a savings account where it earned interest.

After four years of hard work, Bong had earned enough money for a third-class boat ticket and went off to Paris to study, the culmination of his dreams. In Paris, a friend of Mr. Chuong's took in Bong as a boarder. Bong earned enough to get by, typing and doing other odd jobs. He enrolled in a French high school to prepare for his baccalaureate exams. French lycées and universities were all free; students needed only pay a small registration fee and rent for books. Bong passed his two baccalaureates and went on to the University of Paris. There, he studied political science and law, earning his two Ph.Ds. Two years later, he presented a post-doctoral thesis in public law, and received the prestigious title of "agrege," achieved only by a handful of professors in all of Vietnam.

Now, back home, he saw that a door was opening for democratic reforms. The 1963 coup d'etat had ended a decade of autocratic rule. But there was much that was still wrong. Anarchy followed in the wake of the coup—six cabinets in two years. Military and civilian factions, unprepared to take up the reins of leadership or to manage the country, fought with each other instead of the real enemy—the Communists and their more than 100,000 well-trained guerrillas in the South.

The administration of President Lyndon Johnson, trying to pursue a policy of Communist containment, was caught in that swirl of domestic upheaval. In early 1965, the U.S. government, with the urging of Defense Secretary McNamara and the Joint Chiefs of Staff, started B–52 attacks against the North. The operation was called "Rolling Thunder," and targeted the Ho Chi Minh Trail along the Cambodian and Laotian borders, where North Vietnamese troops infiltrated into South Vietnam.

American advisors to South Vietnam had increased from a few hundred under the Ngos to 23,000 in 1964, the year Bong and I were married. The following year, in March, President Johnson sent the first American Marines, who landed at Danang. American troops swelled to 200,000 by the end of 1966.

In the midst of all this turmoil, Bong told me that he wanted to form a national political party. He thought that was the way to rebuild a country torn by the terrorism, corruption and political despair of the mid-1960s. His ultimate goal was to hold power, one day leading a united, democratic Vietnam, with broad support from the people. He wanted to dedicate his life and talents to the service of the country.

I agreed entirely with his political views. But I was worried about Bong's safety. And where would he find the resources to finance his political plan? He said that, with determination, he and his friends would find a way.

Although Bong wanted to set up a system of democratic procedures, he knew that it would take years to achieve. He was well aware that, for a country where truly free elections had never been held, democracy was a long way off.

So, with the collaboration of the Tan Dai Viet party (Neo Great Viet), headed by a former fellow student from Paris, Professor Nguyen Ngoc Huy, Bong started the Progressive Nationalist Movement, or PNM. (The Tan Dai Viet party was the South Vietnamese offshoot of the North Vietnamese Dai Viet [Great Viet] party, which opposed both the Communists and colonialists.)

After several years of recruiting and other preparation, the PNM was officially inaugurated in the spring of 1969. It became, almost immediately, South Vietnam's premier non-communist opposition party.

Bong and Huy had been friends in Paris, where Huy, too, had earned a Ph.D. in political science. As students, they worked in laundromats and restaurants to pay for their schooling, Huy's wife told me. She said that Bong had led a hard life in Paris. One year, he contracted tuberculosis. "He was studying too late at night, and getting up at dawn to go to work at *Les Halles*, the Paris market. He had to carry heavy containers and help the merchants set up their stalls, and he earned very little." My respect and admiration for Bong grew even greater.

Bong never told me about these hardships. Vietnamese men hesitate to express their emotions or recount bad experiences, perhaps because they do not want to be pitied. Like all men everywhere, they want to show only their strong side, to stay in control. Bong did tell me that he'd gone to a French hospital and even showed me the release form from the sanitorium where he had been treated.

In those early days of the party, Bong and Huy traveled throughout South Vietnam to teach, talk, and recruit members for the PNM. Their former students, many now in key positions at the province level, welcomed them. These alumni supported the movement and quietly encouraged people to attend PNM meetings.

Young professionals, teachers, businessmen, old people, politicians, intellectuals, and women formed PNM branches, joining the students and old Tan Dai Viet members who were the party's mainstay. Members of the army, police officers, and government officials joined, too, but did not register. The government might consider them disloyal. Their bosses, the colonels who by then were the province chiefs throughout South Vietnam, would not be happy to see their subordinates supporting an opposition party.

In 1970 and 1971, local PNM inauguration ceremonies were occurring nearly every weekend in various parts of the country, the result of the hard work of a growing network of PNM political cadres. Huy and Bong, for their part, stayed close to their supporters, visiting people in their homes, eating with them, and even sleeping on their floors at night. They came to be seen as true practitioners of "liberty, fraternity, and democracy."

Family rubber plantation in Cambodia, 1931. From left to right: Second row –
housekeeper, nanny holding Nam Ly, Le Van Gia, Le Van Thong, Nguyen Thi
Hanh. First row – Hai Duc holding Trung, Hue, Hoai Lang.

Family portrait in Cambodia, 1939. From left to right: Second row – Trung,
Hue, Hoai Lang, Hai Duc, Nam Ly. First row – Thu Cuc, Le Van Thong, Thu
Thuy, Nguyen Thi Hanh, Thu Ha.

Couvent Des Oiseaux in Dalat, Vietnam, 1957. Author is last person in the first row.

Saigon, Vietnam, 1964. Jackie and Nguyen Van Bong. Twins Le Viet (Victor) and Thu Anh (Annie).

Saigon, Vietnam, 1973. Dedication of Nguyen Van Bong's bust at the National Institute of Administration.

Jodjarkarta, Indonesia, 1973. United Nations' Conference on the Status of Women in Indonesia. Jackie is representing the Republic of Vietnam.

Georgetown, Washington DC, 1976. Jackie weds Lacy Wright.

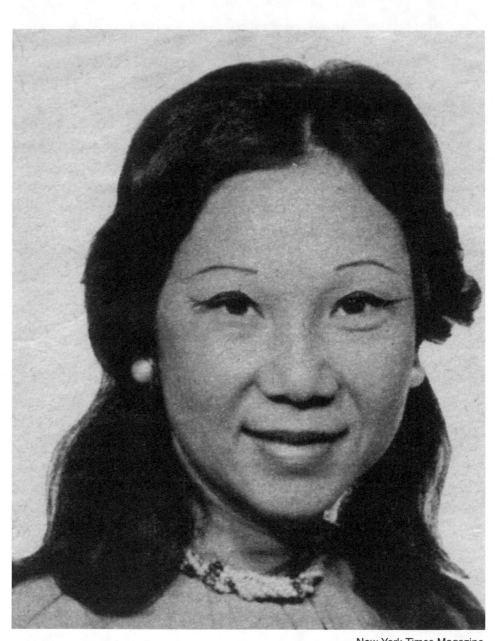

New York Times Magazine article, 1981. Jackie received National Award from the US-Asia Institute.

White House, Washington DC, 1981. Jackie and First Lady Nancy Reagan.

Official Photograph, The White House, Washington D.C.

Trinidad, 1990. Jackie meeting General Colin Powell. From left to right: Jackie, Lacy Wright, General Colin Powell, Ambassador to Trinidad Charles Gargano.

Jamaica, 1994. Jackie presenting Martin Luther King Award to Jamaican Prime Minister's wife, Lady Bustamente.

Brazil, 1995. From left to right: Jackie, President Jimmy Carter, Rosalyn Carter, Lacy Wright.

Bong did tell me about incidents of harassment, where the police used red tape to delay inauguration ceremonies. Before approving a request for the party to hold a meeting, the police insisted on checking not only with the province chief but also with police headquarters in Saigon. Since meetings were held mostly on weekends, higher-ups were sometimes hard to locate. But the PNM branches overcame this petty harassment, and succeeded in enlisting more and more supporters.

The result was a rebirth of hope for Vietnam. In September 1971, the PNM started running candidates in elections. Using the motto "anti-communism and anti-corruption," the PNM won nineteen seats in the Chamber of Deputies. When two other deputies joined them, the PNM had a bloc of twenty-one. This impressive showing was the result of hard work, not bribery or the buying of votes, common in Vietnam. The PNM achieved its gains by fighting on two fronts: first, against the infiltrators from the North and the Viet Cong; second, against corrupt elements in the South Vietnamese government itself. It was not easy.

In 1969, there was speculation that Bong would represent South Vietnam in Paris at the negotiations with the North. We both would have been pleased to go to Paris, since we'd met there. But there were rumors that sending Bong to Paris was a scheme to remove him from the domestic scene and weaken his links with his party. Was the government trying to get rid of him?

Bong decided that it was more important for him to stay in Vietnam at that crucial moment and to nurture his party. I was disappointed, but I supported Bong in his position. His political stand was more important than any personal considerations. So Bong proposed that Prof. Huy be part of the delegation instead, and Huy went.

It was not long after that, in late 1969, that the first attempt on Bong's life occurred. It was around noontime and I had just come home from teaching French at the Alliance Française when a friend phoned to say that Bong had had an accident. I jumped into my car and rushed to the French Grall hospital. Bong was just coming out of intensive care; his head and arms were bandaged. NIA students and professors had formed a security cordon around him.

Professor Le Cong Truyen, one of Bong's assistants, quickly told me what had happened. In mid-morning, Bong had been in his office at the NIA talking to one of his students. After the student left, Truyen heard an explosion and ran out of his office towards the noise. From the ground floor, he saw smoke coming out of Bong's office. He dashed upstairs, passing the entire second-floor staff, who were all running the other way to get away from the blast.

Rushing in, Truyen saw a huge hole in the wall behind Bong's desk. The desk was covered in concrete from the wall and glass from the windows. All that could be seen of Bong were his hands, still holding the desk's edge. Truyen and the student unearthed him and pulled him out. Bong was unconscious. They carried him downstairs to his car and then to the emergency room at the hospital. After nearly an hour in intensive care, Bong regained consciousness.

Truyen told me what Bong had said when he opened his eyes. "Was anyone else hurt? Is everybody okay?" Bong always thought about other people first. "He was really cut out to be a great leader."

The bomb that almost killed Bong had been planted in the corner of the conference room adjoining his NIA office. The explosion had pushed him under his desk, and it was that thick piece of rosewood furniture that saved his life. There was speculation that the Viet Cong had planted the bomb, but no one was ever caught.

Our children, then five and three, were too small to understand their father's close call with death. Fortunately, my mother-in-law was always at home to take care of them. She and I did our best to protect them from the dreadful sight of their bandaged father lying in the hospital bed, and we took them to visit only after Bong looked much better. I did not want their memories tainted with that sad scene.

Although the cuts to Bong's head, back and arms were only superficial, the shock kept him in bed for several weeks. Hundreds of friends and well-wishers came to the hospital in hopes of visiting him, but only a few were allowed in. Bong could hardly sit up in bed, and could eat little except fruit and the few spoonfuls of soup I fed him every other hour.

Before the attempt on his life, Bong had been scheduled to go to Tunis for a conference three weeks hence. When Minister of Education Tang Kim Dong came to visit Bong, I suggested that he find a replacement. Three days later, the minister replied that the people he had asked to sit in for Bong thought that it would be best for Bong to go to Tunis as originally planned. They felt he would be safer out of the country. Bong and I debated, then agreed.

With Bong's pay and some income from his teaching, we had only enough money to get by from month to month. I had to sell our car in order to buy my ticket so I could travel with him. On the flight to Tunis, I was his nurse and escort. At the stopover in Athens, passengers were asked to disembark. I helped Bong to stand. It was early December and cold. As soon as I put Bong's heavy winter coat over his shoulders, he sank down, too weak to walk. So we stayed in our seats for the hour that it took to clean and refuel the plane.

Once we arrived at our hotel room in Tunisia, Bong dictated an editorial to me; he did not have enough strength to write. Each night of our stay, I transcribed his editorials and sent them back home to be published in his newspaper, *Cap Tien (Progress)*, the official voice of the PNM party. Bong was the publisher, and every day he wrote a front-page editorial giving his views on national issues. In Saigon, Bong wrote at six every morning. His friends told me that they waited every day to read Bong's political messages. It was like eating a full breakfast before going to the office. Bong did not want to disappoint them, and have them start their day on an empty stomach.

Bong needed a lot of special assistance during the five-day conference. I helped dress him, and even tied his shoes. I sat next to him during the entire conference, holding him so he would not fall over. I cut his meat into small pieces so he could eat. We tried to act as if nothing had happened, and took part in all events. Although still in pain, Bong never complained once. What a stoic man, I told my sister later.

After Tunis, we went to Paris to stay with my ninth sister, Thu Thuy, a nurse who worked in a Paris hospital. Bong convalesced at her apartment, and I tried to recuperate from the whole frightening experience. I had time to take a training course in the new audio-visual method for teaching French, a technique developed by the St. Cloud Institute outside Paris, near where Thu Thuy lived. Her husband, Christian Mennessier, a French IBM engineer, gave us a tour of the Paris suburbs.

After two weeks in Paris, a dozen of Bong's Vietnamese friends invited us to dinner. They were professors at the Paris Law School, doctors, and other professionals who had been active with Bong when he was the head of the Vietnamese Students' Association in Paris in the 1950s. Huy, who was attending the Paris Peace Talks, planned the gathering. The purpose soon became evident: they did not want us to return to Vietnam. One couple told us that they had made arrangements for us to live in Paris and share their apartment. The group had also talked to Bong's thesis advisor, a professor at the Paris Law School. He had agreed to hire Bong as his assistant. Eventually, Bong would become an associate law professor.

They went on to say that they and other friends would raise funds to bring our children to France. They would take care of everything. It was a tempting offer. Paris was Bong's second home.

He thanked them for their kindness but said he would return to his home in Vietnam, regardless of the risk. He asked these friends for one favor: "That all of you make a sacrifice and go back to Vietnam to help rebuild our country." A few of them did. I had not only married Bong but espoused his ideals. He became my hero, the person to whom I would devote my whole life. My love for him grew deeper each passing day.

Back in Vietnam, Bong was provided with security protection. We had guards at our house twenty-four hours a day, and Bong had bodyguards whenever he went out—two units of three men each who rotated every other day. Although I strongly believed that every person has an inescapable fate, I felt more secure with these men protecting Bong and our house.

Gen. Nguyen Van Thieu, then forty-two, had been president of South Vietnam since 1966, and had an enormous job on his hands. The North Vietnamese repeatedly demanded that he step down as part of the price for progress in the Peace Talks. They were gaining momentum, fighting a conventional war in addition to their guerrilla warfare. On the home front, Thieu had to satisfy both the divided South Vietnamese military and a fractious mélange of nationalist politicians. Thieu was under siege, his time running out.

By the fall of 1971, Thieu saw that to shore up support at home and effectively fight the North Vietnamese Communists, he had to put together a strong coalition government. Bong had the same idea; in fact, he had put together a broad-based opposition agenda for the PNM around which he hoped anti-communist forces could coalesce.

The PNM platform provided for reunification of the country under a democratic regime, participation of every citizen in political activities, respect for human rights, administrative reform, and the eradication of corruption. On the economic front, the PNM platform encouraged economic development, land reform to make farmers independent, a stronger tax system, and a plan for foreign investment. The PNM also backed a social security system for the underprivileged to include job training, employment assistance, and unemployment benefits. The PNM called for an equitable military draft that would affect the rich and poor equally. The platform was strongly pro-education, calling for compulsory schooling, the elimination of illiteracy and the restoration of the prestige and authority of teachers. The PNM platform also welcomed international assistance.

What the PNM really wanted, of course, was to find a way to defeat the Communists, offering an alternative to the corruption and excesses of the succession of military governments that had ruled since the assassination of President Diem.

On November 9th, Thieu sent an emissary, his own brother, Nguyen Van Kieu, ambassador to Taiwan, to our house to talk. Bong guessed what he wanted, and invited him to stay for lunch. After lunch, Bong told me that he had agreed to become Thieu's prime minister. I remember our conversation vividly.

Bong explained his reasons for accepting the position. He felt that, with the PNM party solidly in place and with support in most parts of the country it was the right time to join forces to fight the Communists.

Bong believed that despite Thieu's personal shortcomings—he was recalcitrant, secretive, suspicious, and authoritarian—he was by far the lesser of two evils.

Bong saw Thieu as moving toward democracy. He had demonstrated this by allowing Bong's PNM party and others to openly oppose him. Bong was willing to join with the Thieu government as prime minister because he thought he could achieve his goals better by working from the inside than from the outside.

Bong explained that Thieu had surrounded himself with a lot of corrupt and incompetent "yes" men, both military and civilian. "He values *tin*—loyalty—above ability." Like Diem toward his end, Thieu had antagonized a great many groups: religious, political, intellectual, leftists, and rightists. He had no popular power base. Worse, hundreds of thousands of antiwar protestors kept pressing Nixon to get out of the war. Thieu's only option was to enlarge his base of support. Inviting Bong to join his government would accomplish this.

Thieu would benefit not only from Bong's political support, but also Bong's impeccable reputation. Bong had always been known as "Mr. Clean." People who had tried to bribe him had always failed. Sometimes they tried to bribe Bong through me. People would bring me boxes of gold pieces, U.S. dollars or Vietnamese piastres. When I refused to take them, some thought that they had not brought enough. One came back the next day to double his offer.

Some people tried bribery out of concern for their children. If a student did not pass his exams at the end of the year, he was automatically drafted into the army. This meant the end of his education, his career and, possibly, his life. Bong taught hundreds of students, both at the Law School and at the NIA. So, he and I frequently received appeals—by letter or through acquaintances—to give a particular student a passing grade.

One evening a lady who claimed to be a distant relative from the Mekong Delta came to see me. She told me about her family. Two of her boys had died as soldiers in the Delta, in two successive years. Her only remaining son was studying law with Bong. She wondered whether I could ask my husband to give her third son a passing grade.

I said that I could not interfere with Bong's work, and that he graded strictly according to the papers the students wrote. The lady, in her sixties, held my right hand tightly and suddenly slipped a big diamond ring on one of my fingers. Still holding my hand firmly, she said, "Please accept this family ring as a small token to tie our relationship together." I pulled my hand away and gave her back the ring. She cried, "You know that your refusal will mean the end of my son's life." She fell to the ground and held my knees, begging. I knelt down, too, and we both found ourselves on the floor. "You are my last chance. I beg you to come to my rescue." Later, she sent us a message saying that her son had failed the exam. She blamed Bong and me.

On another day, I heard a commotion outside the gate to our house. Bong had come home from work, and a man was shouting and gesturing to him. The children and I rushed out. The man was making a confession. "I have been following you for the last two months now. I have tried everything I could to get something on you or your wife, to dig up some dirt on you, but I have not come up with a thing." Bong's bodyguard helped push the man out the gate.

I recognized him. He had called on me once, pretending to know a relative of Bong's. I had received him, and he handed me a box of *Petit Beurre Lu*, French biscuits "for the children." When I opened it, I saw that the box was packed with money, along with a list of names—students whose grades he wanted Bong to raise on their final exam. When I refused and returned the box of money to him, he said that he would be back. I refused to let him in again, and did not see him any more, until the day he forced himself inside our gate.

Within fifteen minutes of Thieu's brother's departure from our house, journalists, tipped off by leaks, started calling Bong to confirm his appointment as prime minister. He declined to take the calls, and had me talk instead, telling me it would be better for President Thieu to announce the appointment officially to the Vietnamese media and public. But when Francois Nivolon, correspondent for *France Soir* and a good friend, called, I handed the phone to Bong. Pressed by Nivolon, Bong confirmed his acceptance.

Thieu's offer to Bong took me by surprise. "I am Thieu's solution," Bong explained. "My opposition stands are moderate and constructive, not extremist. It is in his own interest to collaborate with me. I have with me the best technocrats and the best professionals in the country, ready to support me and work with me as a team."

That was Bong's last political statement to me.

The next day, November 10, 1971, at lunchtime, Bong was murdered. A bomb was thrown under his car as it stopped at a traffic light on Cao Thang street, a few blocks from his office. Bong died instantly in the blast. His driver and a bodyguard were thrown out of the car on either side, unconscious. Another bodyguard, sitting between the driver and the other bodyguard, was consumed in the blaze that devoured the car, including Bong who was in the back seat. The car and its occupants burned like a huge torch.

The second bodyguard should have been riding behind the car on his motorcycle, doing surveillance. But he had said he did not feel well, and asked that day if he could sit inside, next to the driver. I heard later that the real reason was that he had just withdrawn some money from his savings to put a down payment on a new house, and did not want to ride his motorbike with the stack of money in his pocket. Outside, he might have saved Bong's life; inside, he became another victim.

I was thirty years old. Our twin boy and girl were seven and our youngest boy was five. That midnight, in a corner of our house, the grandfather clock struck. But time had stopped. My soul bled. I burned with fever, yet felt ice cold. My eyes stared all night into the darkness. Dawn would not return for years to come.

The night of Bong's assassination, the National Institute of Administration students organized a vigil. The next day, wearing black arm bands, the students took to the streets to proclaim their love and express their sadness at the loss of their beloved master. Students from other faculties joined in. During the four days of the wake, thousands of people from all over the country poured into the headquarters of the Progressive Nationalist Movement where Bong's body lay. Government officials, diplomats, journalists, politicians, the rich, the poor, the uneducated came to pay their respects.

The next day, Francois Nivolon, the correspondent for *France Soir*, came to the house and sat next to my bed. I told him that he was the only correspondent to whom Bong had confirmed his appointment. How had the news gotten out so fast? It had not been officially announced. Nivolon told me that after speaking to Bong, he'd cabled his paper in Paris. He covered his face, feeling very sad. I said that sources of leaks might have come from many quarters. Anything was possible in that war-torn environment.

On the third day of the wake, around nine in the morning, a thin man in his late forties, wearing a frayed brown shirt and blue shorts, was waiting for me at PNM headquarters. My children and I had just arrived by car, clad in our white mourning tunics. The man approached me with two oranges in his hands. He said he was a rickshaw peddler and did not have enough money to feed his five young children, so he could afford only two oranges to pay homage to a great man. He hoped that I would not feel offended. He asked to be let inside to pray in front of Bong's funeral altar.

I lit three incense sticks and gave them to him. He bowed to the floor four times and prayed aloud for Bong's soul. The children and I bowed back to him four times to return his gesture.

During the period of the wake, Buddhist monks came in busloads from the outskirts of Saigon. They prayed day and night. The PNM headquarters and surrounding streets were decorated with hundreds of wreaths.

I did not see anything, hear anything, or know anything. I had lost all feelings; I was completely empty and numb. I could not cry, eat, or sleep for nearly a month. Day and night were the same for me. My heart was like petrified stone. I did not even feel pain. A part of me was dead. I shrank to under eighty pounds.

Some people wanted an official funeral and honors for Bong. I refused. Others wanted the American-built highway from Saigon to the Delta to be called "Nguyen Van Bong Highway." Again I refused. Bong's name was alive in the hearts of the Vietnamese people. That was enough.

The newspaper reported that three thousand to five thousand people came to the funeral. Police blocked whole streets as row after row of mourners, ten abreast, walked in cadence to the chants of Buddhist monks. A long line of rickshaws, two dozen or more, pedaled the monks from the funeral to the burial place. When they reached the gate of the cemetery, friends told me that the line of mourners was so long that they could not see the end of the funeral procession.

Afterward, Madame Nguyen Van Thieu, wife of the president, invited me to tea at the Presidential Palace. She told me that she had never before seen such a huge funeral. She wondered whether any Vietnamese king had been loved and respected as much as Bong.

After the funeral, I remained in a state of shock, not able to believe that Bong had really been erased from this earth. It was a Buddhist custom to go to the temple every seventh day of the week, for seven weeks, to pray. This was to enable the dead person to be reincarnated as a better being on the forty-ninth day following his death. My mother-in-law made sure that I adhered to this ritual. I had a hard time even leaving my bed. I just wanted to stay there contemplating the emptiness, and escape into my own, inner world, thinking of a thousand things and nothing.

The second week, after returning from the temple, I went to Bong's library, a room on the ground floor of our house. I saw one of Bong's articles on a pile of papers, and started to read it. After ten minutes, I said aloud, "Bong, do you remember where I left my book, Le Petit Prince?" Silence. So I called out: "Bong, do you hear me?" A silence echoed back to me. I looked around, and realized that Bong was gone forever.

I lost track of time, space, and memory. I climbed the stairs to my room holding the railing tightly, my whole body feeling light and weak. Then I lay on my bed, staring at the ceiling for another four weeks. No longer would I have Bong to kiss me on the forehead as he had done every morning before going to work. Bong would not reappear and wake me up from this terrible trance. Autumn Cloud now felt deep and dark, dangling alone beyond the horizon.

At Bong's death, friends contributed money to pay for his funeral expenses as well as his coffin and marble tomb. They also erected, on top of his tomb, a fifteen-foot monument. As an epitaph, a poet wrote a "cau doi," two parallel verses praising Bong's integrity and patriotism. The following summer, the students taking the national baccalaureate exam in Vietnam were given Bong's life story to translate into a second language.

A couple of months later, two young Viet Cong were caught and charged with Bong's murder. One of them, Nguyen Huu Thai, was the head of the student body at the School of Architecture at the University of Saigon.

The following summer, I went to the United States to attend a summer workshop on "Population and Family Planning" at the University of Chicago. On the way home, I stopped in Washington, D.C., to visit my brother Trung. I got in touch with Ambassador Martin Herz, who had been counselor for political affairs at the American Embassy in Saigon until 1970. He had known Bong and me well. He had left Vietnam about a year before Bong was killed, and later became Ambassador to Bulgaria.

He immediately invited me to dinner at a Chinese restaurant in Virginia. It was less than seven months after Bong's death, and I asked him to tell me honestly who had killed my husband.

"Do you still have doubts?" he asked.

I said that while the government had caught and charged two young men with the murder, rumors and hearsay were rampant. Many people did not believe that the two Viet Cong were the actual killers, or, if they were the assassins, they'd been hired to do the killing. There was speculation that the Vietnamese Army; Bong's political partner, Huy; the Communists; even the CIA were responsible for Bong's death.

Martin asked whether I had proof of any of these alternatives.

"That," I said, "is what I want to know from you. Tell me truthfully. Who killed Bong?"

Martin said that Bong had been dear to his heart and he had admired him greatly. So he had followed the aftermath of Bong's assassination very closely. As soon as Ambassador Bunker came back to Washington for consultations after the killing, he'd talked to him in person. Martin said that Bunker had confirmed that the Vietnamese government had proof that the two young Viet Cong they had caught were the killers.

Still dubious, I asked for some proof.

"I trust the Ambassador, and our intelligence," was Martin's answer.

I was not satisfied. "The Vietnamese," I told him, "are great fans of *Mission Impossible*, and I am, too." I related some of the scenarios my friends had suggested.

Many people suspected that the military had killed Bong, who had always advocated honest, competent government, headed by civilians. In his editorials, he discredited the army as corrupt and unqualified. So the military officers who were in power might have felt threatened if Bong became prime minister. They might have had good reason to kill him.

I told Martin that others believed that Professor Huy, Bong's political partner, wanted Bong out of the way because their political party was now strong and ready for the next move into the government. Huy no longer needed Bong and wanted to replace him. He wanted to form a coalition with the military, or with other groups that Bong opposed, behind Bong's back. Some politicians said Huy had his own hidden agenda: to be in power, at any price.

Martin asked me whether I believed that Huy was involved in Bong's death.

"No," I answered. I did not believe that Huy could have done such an awful thing. Martin asked why I thought the CIA would have wanted to remove Bong.

I said there was speculation that Nixon, in order to get reelected, desperately wanted a policy of disengagement—to withdraw American troops from Vietnam and end the war. If Bong had become prime minister, a strong cohesive government might have preferred to keep on fighting rather than sign a peace agreement. Bong would have been a stumbling block to U.S. disengagement.

Martin dismissed the CIA scenario. "I do not think that our government could even have thought of such a scheme. On the contrary, we wanted Thieu to form a coalition government with Bong a long time ago. It is a pity that he did not do it until it was too late."

I related my last scenario, that the Vietnamese Communists had murdered Bong. This would have allowed them to accomplish two objectives: to kill Bong, and to destroy President Thieu's reputation. People knew that Thieu feared Bong's popularity, and resented him for criticizing his government. According to this scenario, the Communists could cast blame on Thieu, saying that he'd directed the army to kill Bong after asking him to join the government. "It's a set-up right out of *Mission Impossible*," I admitted. "I don't know whether Thieu is capable of such a thing, but I know that the Communists are. They have assassinated so many political leaders already."

"All I know is that the Viet Cong killed him and that I have lost a great and valuable friend," Martin said, after I'd recounted all of the possibilities.

I believed the Viet Cong killed Bong, too. This was confirmed in 1976, in *Giai Phong (Liberation)*, a book by Tiziano Terzani, a leftist Italian journalist, who was in Saigon during the Communist takeover. He had interviewed his Vietnamese Communist soul brothers, who proudly admitted that they had ordered their cadres, including Nguyen Huu Thai, to kill Bong.

When my mother was living with us in Virginia in 1980, she told me that Nam Ly had confessed to her that the North Communists had ordered Bong killed. My Communist sister said, wrongly, "Bong was considered the enemy because he had strong connections and support from the CIA." She added, "Besides, his party had become too popular and powerful." Bong's assassination by the Communists was confirmed by General Nguyen Van Tay, the older brother of my brother-in-law, Dr. Nguyen Van Tao. General Tay had joined the *maquis*, became a Communist, and resurfaced in Saigon in 1975 as most *maquisards* did. In 1985, my sister Mme. Tao from Paris and I visited our mother in Houston, Texas. She said that she had asked Gen. Tay in person whether the Viet Cong had killed Bong. He said that they had indeed masterminded that scheme, and that the two Viet Cong students who executed their plan had been freed from prison and received awards and decorations after Saigon was liberated from the American "imperialists."

At the first anniversary of Bong's death, I was invited to attend a memorial service at the Xa Loi pagoda organized by hundreds of his friends. The PNM, now headed by Huy, also organized a bicycle marathon from Camau to Saigon. A torch was lit to honor Bong's patriotism and leadership. Men on bicycle, riding night and day, relayed the torch through all the towns in the Delta. In each locality, the PNM branch organized a memorial ceremony to pray for Bong's soul, attended by hundreds of ordinary people and PNM sympathizers. When, after several weeks, the torch finally reached Saigon, a huge rally was organized to welcome the torch, which was placed on a large, impressive altar with Bong's photograph.

On the second anniversary of Bong's death, a number of students at the NIA and Law School commissioned a bronze bust of Bong, four times life-size. I was invited to unveil the bust, which stood in front of the National Institute of Administration. A memorial ceremony followed, attended by hundreds of professors, students and friends. On that occasion, I donated all of Bong's cherished books to the NIA library. I felt honored to have inherited Bong's good reputation.

To Bong's supporters, he had represented hope for a democratic and united Vietnam. Had he lived, would the fate of Vietnam have been different? A lot of his students and colleagues think so. Dr. Hoang Xuan Hao, a former senator and NIA professor, wrote to me in early 1998: "Dr. Bong had extraordinary leadership virtues—not only integrity, talent, and generosity, but also the gift of being able to analyze Vietnam's situation accurately. With his God-given vision and his inner strength, he would have brought Vietnam the support not only of the Americans and the French, but also the other countries of the free world."

Hao thought that Bong would have given legitimacy to the government. He would not have been seen as the puppet of the Americans, which is how the Communists were able to characterize all South Vietnamese governments. Bong would have regained the trust of a demoralized people and enabled them to fight the Communists from a position of strength.

Dr. Hao thought that Bong would have been able to reform the South Vietnamese administration from the top down to all the governmental outposts in the countryside. His disciples, the NIA graduates and party members, would have kept the civil service running properly. With good policies in place, he would have been able to make wise decisions on military and economic reforms.

Others thought this assessment was too optimistic. Dr. Truong Hoang Lem, minister of Civil Service reform and the highest-ranking woman in Thieu's cabinet, has told me, "Even if Bong, with his charisma, his organization, and his ideology, was the best man to lead our country, would he have had the guts to fight, to imprison, and to kill to preserve his own survival? Neither the South's corrupt elements, nor its interest groups, nor the Communists would have let him govern in peace. He would have been a strong target for elimination. How could he have won over those evil forces? How long could he have lasted?"

My children pulled me out of my stupor at Christmas, six weeks after Bong's death. They jumped into my bed, put shoes on my feet, and told me that it was time to buy them Christmas chocolates and presents. They also wanted Santa Claus to give each one of them a special gift.

I finally got up of my own will. I went to the bathroom and looked into the mirror. I saw a gaunt, lined face, tinged an unappealing green, and opaque eyes. I looked like an old, dehydrated apple. How long had I been in that awful state? As I stared at my image in the mirror, I told myself that it was time to come to my senses and live for my children. "They are the most precious parts of your life. You must not lose them."

I put each of the children into my king-size bed, and one of them slept with me every night. We kept each other company in order not to feel lost and empty. Thu Anh, Autumn Light, seven years old, kept asking me to marry the same husband again. She could not figure out how she could have lost her father forever. She said that there must be another Bong exactly like him somewhere. I must find him, she insisted. Of course

I could not, and Thu Anh became sad and withdrawn. Le Viet and Le Quoc, the two boys, promised me that they would grow up very quickly and would study hard like their father. They would protect me and take care of me in my old age.

My children missed evenings strolling in the yard with their father. He always patiently answered their many questions. They remembered that we often sat on the marble entrance steps leading to our living room, surrounded by beautiful pots of flowers, as we taught them words in Vietnamese and French, and drilled them on what they'd learned previously. We told them legends of the moon and stars, and the names of the trees and flowers. We answered their questions about animals. These vivid memories of their father were gone forever with the blast of a bomb.

We spent Christmas Eve with Dr. Bach, the children's pediatrician, and her husband, Dr. Than, an economist and former minister of Finance. They had invited us and Bong's circle of friends to a Christmas party to cheer up the children and me. Than and Bach had no children of their own—only five huge dogs they adored. After dinner, the parents helped their children open the presents. Bong was not there to open our children's presents, and they asked for him. I did not know what to do. I drifted toward the bathroom, closed myself in, and wept for half an hour. These were my first real tears.

On New Year's eve, the American Ambassador Ellsworth Bunker and his wife Carol Laise, herself ambassador to Katmandu, Nepal, invited us to a party at their residence. They held the children's hands as they moved around among their American guests, or held the children on their laps. We were their only Vietnamese guests. The Bunkers became our guardian angels in Vietnam after we lost Bong. And they were our mentors in the U.S. after we lost Vietnam.

With the Vietnamese, Ambassador Bunker had the nickname of "the Old Refrigerator" (ong gia tu lanh). He was a tall, distinguished, gray-haired diplomat, in his late sixties, who appeared phlegmatic and cold to the Vietnamese who dealt with him. He had a reputation for talking little—just enough to relay and reply to official messages. His stance was upright; he listened with patience, without arguing. Poker-faced, it was hard to read whether he agreed or disagreed with your position. He had a reputation for doing his job well, and conveying the policy of his government clearly.

But I had a different impression of Bunker. Our relationship was personal and warm. He often joked, smiled, and talked to me at length. He called me "Jackie," a shortened version of my French name, which Nancy Bennett, the Chinese-born spouse of the American minister for Political Affairs, had first called me.

Ambassador Bunker had often invited Bong and me to official functions at his residence. He and his political officers regarded Bong highly, and consulted with him frequently. An American political officer, Richard Thompson, often attended Bong's political rallies, and followed the progress of his party. He reported to Bunker and the Department of State in Washington about the politics and positions of the PNM. Bong had nothing to hide, and gladly cooperated with them and invited them to his official functions.

After Bong died, Ambassador Bunker continued to invite me to dinners and receptions. Other ambassadors did, too. But I was timid; I felt uncomfortable going out alone, without Bong. After a few refusals, I made an effort to go out, stand on my own feet and mix with people. I tried not to withdraw inward, away from others.

I had been teaching French part-time for the past four years at the Alliance Française. The French Cultural Attaché, whose Vietnamese wife was a friend from the French Marie Curie school, proposed that I become a full-time teacher. That way, I could get the same salary and benefits as the other French teachers.

Then another opportunity opened up. For the past year I had served as chairman of the board of the Vietnamese-American Association (VAA). Dan Herget, the director of that bi-national center, offered me a job as director of cultural activities. The American who had held that position had been reassigned to Washington. I had already helped inaugurate many of the VAA's events, participated in their programs, and helped formulate policy and make financial and administrative decisions. I knew the people and liked the work.

But I was not sure that I could take on the heavy load of managing all of the VAA's cultural activities. Dan encouraged me, promised to help, and was confident I'd do a superb job. While I was considering the offer, Dan paid me a visit. He told me that the board had just met and had unanimously endorsed me for the position. I said I'd try it for two months.

FIVE

WOMEN AND WAR

On February 1, 1972, I went to work at the VAA, a semi-private entity partly funded by the U.S. Information Agency and governed by a board composed of six Vietnamese and five Americans.

The VAA ran three sections: the Abraham Lincoln library, with over 10,000 books; the English as a Second Language school and its three branches, with over 15,000 students; and a cultural center where we promoted exchanges to improve understanding between the U.S. and Vietnam. Proceeds from the English courses and the cultural events completely financed the center in Saigon. We also had centers in Cholon, or Chinatown; in Dalat, north of Saigon; and in Can Tho, in the Mekong Delta. When I began to work at the VAA, I tried to resign as chairman of the board, but the board wouldn't accept my resignation. Therefore, I wore two hats.

Under Dan Herget's excellent guidance (I called him Papa Herget), we organized concerts, art exhibitions, seminars, lectures, operas, conferences, and films. My responsibilities also included publishing *Viet-My*, a semi-annual publication containing articles by Americans and Vietnamese. I worked a regular eight-hour day, then spent many evenings presiding over lectures and conferences.

I also headed a group of thirty-two part-time teachers who instructed over six hundred fifty students in photography, voice, painting, embroidery, guitar, doll-making, Ikebana Japanese flower arranging, ballet, and silk flower-making. Our classes were popular, with long waiting lists, so I hired more teachers to accommodate the growing demand.

In 1973, my second year at the VAA, we enrolled 18,800 students, organized 1,200 cultural events, and attracted audiences totaling 390,000. I more than tripled the number of events organized by my American predecessor. A host of Vietnamese and American friends attended most of my programs. I brought my mother, my mother-in-law, and my children to most of the events. I was happy with my work.

Our classes and concerts generated profits. I was allowed to donate these funds to the Thanh Mau orphanage, which housed hundreds of abandoned or orphaned children. We also adopted the Army's 18th Logistics Battalion, which had courageously defended Saigon in 1972. Volunteers from the VAA visited this unit and their families every three months, bringing small gifts. I often brought a small artistic group headed by Kim Oanh, professor at the Vietnamese School of Arts and Music. She and her students entertained the soldiers, who were living under constant tension.

Accepting a full-time job with important responsibilities wasn't the only change in my life after Bong was murdered. I now had to leave the big government house on Phan Thanh Gian street which had been assigned to Bong by virtue of his position. With my children and Bong's mother and sisters—who had all been living with us—I moved into my mother's townhouse.

I had lived in the large house on Phan Thanh Gian street since I'd married eight years before. The house, a typical French Colonial, had marble floors, tall ceilings, and big Roman columns, both in the front and on the inside, separating the living room from the dining room. The front lawn, large enough for a sit-down dinner for a hundred guests, was protected by a tall fence covered with bright bougainvillea flowers. The rear yard had bird and rabbit cages. There was also a kitchen and three small dwellings for domestic staff. Standing outside for the last time, I bade farewell to eight years of peace and happiness, all ended in one fateful moment.

Leaving the house was painful for the children as well. The yard was big enough to accommodate lots of pets: Blackie, a German shepherd; Kitty, a Siamese cat, and her four kittens; two rabbits; and five chickens. When Blackie was a puppy, Le Quoc used to carry him on the back seat of his little blue tricycle. The dog was his constant companion. Blackie had grown up and, suddenly, become a huge, handsome guard dog. The children had fed the rabbits each day and collected eggs from the chickens for our breakfast.

Le Quoc asked whether he would be able to bring all the animals with us when we moved to grandma's house. There was no way we could do it, I replied. Our new home was small—without a yard big enough for their pets. I explained that we'd had to pack up and store many of our prized possessions, including Bong's books. I tried to explain all this to the children, but it was hard for them to understand all of the difficult and confusing changes in their lives.

Thu Anh wondered whether we would still have big gatherings at her birthday or yearly festivities for all of our friends. I told her our new house was too small. We barely had enough room for our family.

Le Viet worried about getting lost and having no one to find him now that his father was dead. The year before, when he was six, he had gone to a Boy Scout outing for the weekend. He was scheduled to be back on Sunday at five. But his bus returned to Saigon and dropped him off half an hour early. Le Viet grew impatient waiting for us to pick him up, and decided to find his own way home, which he thought would be easy.

He saw a few familiar-looking villas, and crossed the street by himself. He kept walking but could not find our house. Scared and exhausted, he stopped at a street corner and started to cry. One of the policemen who guarded the house of Mr. Nguyen Luu Vien, the deputy prime minister, saw him and asked what was wrong. Learning he was Bong's son, the guard immediately alerted Mrs. Vien, who took Le Viet into her house, cleaned him up, gave him ice cream and cookies, and calmed him down. She tried to call us but we had already gone out looking for him.

Bong and I drove to the botanical garden. No one knew where Le Viet was. We circled the neighborhood in vain, then finally went home to call the police and hospitals. I was in a panic. I thought Le Viet had been kidnapped. It was not unusual for children of prominent Vietnamese families to be taken and held for ransom. The kidnappers would demand a political rather than a financial exchange, we speculated.

While Bong was frantically calling everyone, our guard ran inside to say that Le Viet was safe. We ran out and saw our little boy being helped out of a huge black limousine by the deputy prime minister's bodyguard. He ran to us and said that he had had a good time, and wanted to share his cookies with his sister and brother. He did not know how relieved we were to see him. Le Viet, or Victor, as he is called now, still remembers that impressive incident.

It was not easy moving in with my mother. She had become frail and emotional. She was sometimes bitter about her social decline. After her years of stardom in Cambodia, she'd become a nobody back in Vietnam. Not only had she returned to a new and hostile environment, but she also had to raise her many children on her own. My father, who remained handicapped until he died, was no more than a silent observer.

So my mother, a bold avant-garde woman in her younger years, spent her middle age doing hard physical work and worrying about her family's survival. Even more taxing, her children were often engaged in ideological and philosophical battles. Faced with all this upheaval, she felt exhausted and lonely.

To cope, my mother spent her time meditating, helping the cook prepare meals, and going to doctors to be treated for various ailments—headaches, rheumatism, indigestion. The doctors loaded her down with medicine and vitamins, even though no serious illness was ever diagnosed.

By the time I moved in with her, things had improved in at least one respect: my mother was fortunate enough to have profited from my father's island, and from the government's land reform program. To counter the Northern Communists, the Ministry of Agriculture bought farmland to distribute to peasants. My mother participated in this program, and received more than enough money to live comfortably. She gave part of her proceeds to some of her children, including me. I used the money to buy and remodel her house so we'd have enough room for us all to live together.

With my mother, my children, Bong's mother and two daughters, I was now in charge of a large, extended family. I had to become head of the household, bread-winner, and decision-maker—no longer just the wife of Nguyen Van Bong. My new position was not that different from thousands of other women in Vietnam widowed by war. The Vietnamese widows had to replace their dead husbands in the family and in society. They had to take men's jobs, even carrying heavy loads on their shoulders at marketplaces and ports, or driving military trucks. Women started to enlist in the army and air force. With husbands either missing or dead, a new type of working woman had sprung up.

To survive in a macho society, women had to work twice as hard as men, for lower wages, then return home to attend to household chores. Many of them were up from five in the morning, and did not stop until late at night. Others chose another path, working for foreigners for more money and less effort.

My mother's place was in Tan Dinh, a district of Saigon. I stayed in the front section of her two-story house with my children and in-laws, and my mother occupied the back part, which had a separate entrance. When I looked around the table at dinner, I counted three adults, all widowed, and five children, all without a father. Our two maids were also widows. Their husbands, drafted into the army, had died in the war. This is what the war had brought us. We celebrated the Vietnamese Lunar New Year of 1972 holding back our tears and pasting sad smiles on our faces to cheer up the children.

Bong had not left me any retirement annuity or social security benefits. To qualify for a government pension, Bong needed to have worked ten years. He had completed almost nine. He had no life insurance, since that was not common. Bong had borrowed money from relatives and friends to print a thousand books that he had planned to sell to his students. They lay stacked to the ceiling in our house. I had inherited Bong's debts.

I had also inherited certain expectations of how I should act. Being Bong's widow, I was in the public eye, under constant scrutiny. After more than a year working at the VAA, I was feeling invigorated. My energy and smile returned. I was invited to receptions and dinner parties by ambassadors and government officials. Some Vietnamese started calling me the "Merry Widow." They thought I should be like other widows—

dress in dark colors, avoid make-up and jewelry, and shun parties. I was supposed to wear my misery on my face at all times. That was the tradition. By taking an important job, I'd violated another tradition. In Confucian societies, a widow was not supposed to shine outside the home.

In 1974, in an article in *Vietnam Magazine*, I was described in this way: "She is a familiar figure in the slum sections of Saigon, this small and comely woman with a face always beaming with *joie de vivre*." The reporter meant to compliment me, but others saw it as more evidence of defying custom. I was branded an unconventional, nonconformist woman.

One day, Chi Hoa, who worked in our administrative section at the VAA, came to tell me that rumors were being spread about me. She said that every day, when she saw me pass by her office, dressed in my black *ao dai*, thin as a willow, lonely as an orphan, she almost cried. This was why she had to tell me that some people were saying bad things about me. Some of the VAA's instructors in the cultural section, unhappy that I had hired more teachers and afraid of losing their jobs, were going to hold a demonstration against me. She said that I should act quickly.

I did. I called a meeting of all the teachers in my section, and explained my plans. I said I wanted to do a survey to find out how many students were taking the various courses they were interested in. I said I was going to restructure the classes to hold them in the evenings and on weekends, too. If they were available to teach, they would teach more classes. I would open more courses and hire more teachers, as well. I had no intention of firing any of them.

I said that instead of relying on my own judgment, I had also invited a few well-known professors from the School of Fine Arts to help me select the best painters to exhibit in our renovated exhibition hall. I would rely more on their qualifications, and decisions would be based on certain criteria. There would be a few changes as we went along, I informed them.

The atmosphere was charged at first. People raised their voices. It was hard to accept changes. I was a young and inexperienced manager, while they had taught at the VAA for years. A heated discussion went on for over two hours. At the end, most of us came out smiling. We had cleared the air. Chi Hoa had helped me avoid a crisis. Had she not come to talk to me, I would have run into an unforeseen demonstration.

One evening, I invited Dr. Than to a painting exhibit at the VAA exhibition hall at 6:30 P.M. by an artist he liked. At 7:30 I had to run to the auditorium to introduce a speaker. I waited until the speaker finished so I could thank him before I went home. Around eight, as Dr. Than was leaving, he saw me eating a sandwich in a corner, outside the auditorium, and waved good-bye to me.

The next day, his wife, Dr. Bach, called and invited the children and me for lunch the following Sunday. She said they would like us come every weekend to have lunch and swim in their pool. She said I worked too much and did not even have a proper dinner sometimes. After that, whether Than and Bach took their vacation in the mountains at Dalat or the beach at Cap St. Jacques, they brought us along, as part of their family.

In Vietnam, the traditional mourning period lasts two years. During this period the widow stays loyal to her dead husband's memory. To commemorate the first two anniversaries of her husband's death, the widow is expected to invite his relatives to a ceremony. I dutifully followed these customs. Once the mourning period is over, a widow is free to marry and begin a new life. So, after November 1973, I considered myself in a position to marry again.

A few months later, the children and I spent the week of Tet, the Vietnamese New Year, at Vung Tau, or, in French, Cap St. Jacques, with Dr. Than and Dr. Bach. Since Bong's death, they had included us in their family celebrations and vacations. I relied on both Than and Bach for emotional support. Counseling centers were unheard of. Even if they had existed, I would not have set foot in one for fear of being regarded as a "crazy" woman.

Dr. De, who had proposed marriage to me at the same time as Bong, was now living in that area. We all met for lunch. De, now a wealthy general practitioner and an army captain, had gone into politics. Since his province had only one seat in the House of Representatives, he was its only deputy. I had told Bong about De, and we considered him a friend. De had visited us a few times when he came to Saigon for congressional sessions.

It is a Vietnamese tradition to visit and exchange wishes and gifts on the first three days of the Lunar New Year. So Dr. De came to our villa on the morning of the very first day of Tet to pay us a visit. He wished the children well in their school work, and told them to obey their mother. Then, holding Thu Anh's hands, he said, "Ask your mother if she would marry *Tonton* (Uncle) De. He will love you as a father from now on and will take good care of all of you for the rest of his life. Your mother will become the star and the queen of this province." I was sitting next to De. I turned to Thu Anh and said, "Tell *Tonton* De that your mother appreciates very much his kind proposal, but she would prefer to remain a widow and not change her status." My feelings for Bong were still too strong for me to consider remarriage.

I later learned that he'd married a friend of his from medical school, a dentist. They were to have two beautiful children.

A year after Bong's death, one of Bong's friends, Anh Quan, a business-man, came to visit. He had a copy of Bong's book, *Political Parties and Public Law*, and ask me to inscribe it. He said that people were clamoring for Bong's book, "like shrimp jumping up and down in a pond."

I told Quan that I had a thousand of these books piled up in the back of the house, which I hadn't been able to sell. A few days later, Quan called to tell me that a print shop had illegally printed Bong's book and was selling it. Quan helped me get a court injunction against the print shop to make it stop.

Then Dr. Lanh, one of Bong's former students and now a professor of law, came to visit. He said he was going to teach Constitutional Law at the University of Can Tho in the Delta. He took a stack of books and sold them to his students. Over the years, he helped me repay Bong's debts by selling many of these books. Those that were left were given to relatives and friends who wanted a memento of Bong.

The American military build-up in Vietnam brought optimism to the country, but it also caused radical changes in the capital and in the countryside. It promised a period of political stability and economic development, but it also caused a host of psychological and social side-effects. By 1966, 300,000 U.S. and allied troops from the Asian and Pacific nations—Thailand, the Philippines, South Korea, Australia, and New Zealand—were living side by side with fifteen million South Vietnamese. Huge military centers were set up to train Vietnamese soldiers.

Military supplies and equipment jammed the ports and streets. Aircraft roared overhead, from transport planes to jet fighters. Military barracks mushroomed overnight. Small shanty towns sprang up and construction boomed. Vietnamese businesses servicing the foreign forces flourished. The giant PXs (post exchanges) inundated the society with consumer goods, and black markets expanded. Prostitution proliferated. The dollar was king.

The imported American war machine changed the face and shape of Vietnam. The Vietnam war became an American war. The U.S. commander in chief, General William Westmoreland, introduced his "search and destroy" strategy. American bombing, whether by naval and artillery gunfire or B-52s, inflicted terrible casualties on the Viet Cong, but also hit populated areas and killed innocent villagers.

There was a period when I was regularly shaken in my bed by the ear-splitting, hair-raising roar of aircraft taking off from Tan Son Nhat airport, a few miles from our house. The thunderous reverberations sent chills up my spine and brought fever to my temples. Sometimes, I could not go back to sleep, and I imagined that the incredible noise must have sent not just the Viet Cong but even elephants and tigers into hiding. The bombing was responsible for much of the uprooting of the rural population, and that was blamed on the Americans.

Bombing strikes on the industrial areas of Hanoi and Haiphong were also condemned by world leaders. Antiwar movements, both in the U.S. and Europe, caused thousands of marches and demonstrations on college campuses and in the streets. The international protests against the Americanization of the war, which began in the late 60s, escalated in the early 70s.

In America, parents were asking why their sons were fighting and dying in a country ten thousand miles away. In Europe and elsewhere, people were shocked to see the strongest and richest country on earth bombing the poor, tiny nation of North Vietnam, whose only objective, it was said, was to unify their country. In reality, Vietnam was the playing field for a war game between the superpowers, with the Vietnamese in both North and South their proxies. For the Communists, victory meant the proliferation of their ideology in the region. To the U.S., victory meant containment of Communism so that other nations in Asia would not fall to the Communists, one after another, like dominos.

In Saigon, the older generation of Vietnamese adopted a silent but hostile stance against the war and against the Americans. These older, educated Vietnamese saw in the vast American presence an onslaught on Vietnamese culture and values. Having anything to do with Americans brought shame to a family.

A few of Bong's relatives felt that I had shamed them by going to work with the Americans, promoting their debased culture. Two of Bong's aunts who offered us a home in Bong's hometown, Go Cong, withdrew their offers. Other people thought that I had damaged Bong's good reputation by cooperating with the Americans, who had lowered the status of Vietnamese women. Even my sister Madame Tao was not happy. There were rumors that I worked for the CIA and had received millions of dollars, which I hid in Swiss banks.

Because the Vietnamese held the Americans responsible for degrading Vietnamese women, it was especially galling to many Vietnamese when an American senator, William Fulbright, returned home from Vietnam in 1974 and declared Saigon a "whorehouse." This insult shocked the Vietnamese.

At first sight, he may have been right. Bar girls, prostitutes, and street children roamed the streets day and night. It was a nonstop bacchanal. Youngsters and teenagers from the countryside, uprooted by war, fled to the urban areas to make a living. Girls who worked in the rice fields saw their livelihood destroyed as their rice fields became battle grounds. These girls had to choose between earning a pitiful wage as domestics and feeling ill-treated, or getting easy money providing pleasure to lonely foreign soldiers.

I was amazed to see nightclubs and pubs spring up on both the main streets and dark alleys of downtown Saigon and in any town where there were American troops. The bar girls—faces painted, bodies skimpily clad—were eager to sell their favors. Prostitutes were everywhere, snaring prey like bees dumped in honey. A new, nouveau-riche class of prostitutes popped up like firecrackers in the night. The "Dollar Queens" drastically changed the image of the Vietnamese woman.

The first introduction to a bar girl was to buy her a drink. Although the GI paid for whiskey, the bar girl would be sipping tea, since she needed to talk and flirt all day with different clients. Prostitutes extorted money and various privileges from the Americans who frequented their bars. The girls would ask the soldiers to shop for them at the tax-free PXs. They would then sell these goods on the black market for a huge profit. Many of the bar girls and prostitutes were country girls who had come to the city to earn money to support their families. They were the other victims of the war.

One day I went to the plush Hotel Caravelle to visit my niece, My, the eldest daughter of my brother Anh Ba. She had just come back with her family from the U.S. to visit Vietnam. When I called her from the reception area, she invited me to her suite because she had not finished dressing her children. I was anxious to see a suite in this ultra-modern, five-star hotel, then the talk of the town.

I took the elevator. On the way up, the young man who accompanied me asked me to give him some money. I said that I did not have any luggage, and that I was just visiting someone. He persisted, saying if I shared my income with him, he would not report me to the management or to the police. Highly irritated when I realized what he was up to I said I'd report *him* to the police instead. He complained that all the other girls who went to their clients' rooms had given him a big tip. Why was I different?

I went straight to the hotel's general manager, Anh Tha, an acquaintance. Anh Tha called the elevator boy into his office and lectured him harshly. Both men apologized to me profusely. To make up for that embarrassment, Tha invited me to a private dinner for twenty prominent members of the government and business community. He wanted to show me that his hotel was not a brothel.

Women of all classes were cashing in on the war. Some of my friends, or my friends' mothers, contracted with Americans to cater food, sell goods, rent their houses, buy *do phe thay*, metal scraps, and military rubbish from American bases to be resold at exorbitant prices for recycling. Some even opened massage parlors. Making money, particularly green dollars, was in fashion. Some people became instant millionaires.

Women were not the only civilian casualties. I was appalled to see hordes of children running around selling cigarettes and drugs, and harassing Americans in the streets. They picked pockets or stole watches and other valuables from any naïve foreigner they could find. Orphaned by the war and abandoned, they slept on street corners, begged, robbed, and cheated. They were regarded as if lepers.

Fortunately, there were private organizations that helped these children as well as some heroic individuals, such as Dick Hughes, an American. A conscientious objector, Dick, at age twenty-four, refused to be drafted and instead borrowed money and paid his own way to Saigon. He landed in the capital in April 1968 as a freelance journalist for the Boston University newspaper. Dick went to Vietnam because he wanted to do social work to offset the carnage. He called his Vietnam period a "temporary leave" from his acting career, the "first love of my life." For his pains, Dick was considered to be CIA by most Vietnamese.

Two weeks after arriving in Vietnam, Dick started working with the street boys of Saigon. He called them *Bui Doi*, the "dust of life." Most were homeless, some were pick-pockets. He encouraged each boy to move into a shelter, and then to a more structured "family" home. He founded and funded a project called the Shoeshine Boys—named for the corner shoeshine businesses that were staffed by his boys. Dick gave shelter, work, education, and life to hundreds of war orphans.

In 1973, I called Dick to ask if I could be of help. I went to visit two of his five hostel-type homes, and met some of the one hundred fifty or so boys, from six to fourteen, who looked upon Dick as their godfather.

Dick also funded a home for former teenage prostitutes. A British nurse, Liz Thomas, lived there and cared for them. I offered scholarships to VAA classes to Dick's boys and girls. Dick was wary. He feared that too close an association with an American-funded organization would be misinterpreted as a link to the CIA. He did, however, send some of his girls to VAA English and vocational classes.

Dick spent eight years in Vietnam, raising nearly half a million dollars from 18,000 generous donors. He gave hope to hundreds of desperate, homeless kids. He recounted his experiences in a *New York Times* article in 1976, just after leaving Vietnam. He said, "I owe the people of Vietnam so much. They have reordered my life by teaching me simplicity, brotherhood, how to touch, and [given me] a reason for carrying on."

Despite Dick's selfless work and his attempts to separate himself from American governmental organizations, there were still rumors that he was a CIA spy. Few Vietnamese believed an American could be so bighearted, without ulterior motives. In fact, in January 1976, an article in Saigon's *Tin Sang* newspaper denounced a young CIA agent who exploited street children, sending them out to shine shoes and spy. They had mistaken Dick for another American who had worked for the World Vision streetboy house at Khu Dan Sinh. That may be why, despite Dick's care to dissociate himself from American officialdom—especially the CIA—two of Dick's Vietnamese executive staff were jailed for years as alleged CIA collaborators after the Communists took over in 1975. Later Dick mounted a campaign to get the Communist government to allow them to leave the country and come to the United States. One of them, Doan Thanh Liem, an attorney, settled in California.

Now fifty-three, Dick lives in New York with Sherry Hall, a public school teacher, and their daughter, Tara. A Clint Eastwood look-alike, he has gone back to his first love, acting. But for me Dick Hughes' best role will always be the part he played in Vietnam: Santa Claus to the "dust of life."

In Vietnam, the oldest son has the responsibility for continuing the family's lineage and legacy. After Bong's death, relatives and friends constantly admonished Le Viet to be worthy of his father. Some even went as far as charging Le Viet with finding Bong's assassins and punishing them. This was an overwhelming burden for a small boy.

Le Viet did not know how to achieve what friends and relatives demanded of him. He had nightmares—ran in circles between his bedroom and mine. I took him to his pediatrician, who said that he needed time to recover from the shock of his father's death.

As the nightmares continued, the doctor finally told me it would be better if Le Viet could get away from home. The opportunity came in the summer of 1972, when I received a fellowship to attend a six-week workshop at the University of Chicago on population and family planning, with forty-five other participants from different countries. I took Le Viet to the U.S. with me.

We first spent a week in California, seeing all the rides and shows at Disneyland. This fantasyland was a great contrast with Le Viet's life in Vietnam, and a vast relief. Before returning to Vietnam, I stopped in Washington, D.C., to visit my number six brother Trung, who'd moved there after teaching Vietnamese in Texas.

Trung offered to foster Le Viet, and keep him in Washington. He had the great support of his friends, Phuong and Hanh, a married couple who, with no children of their own, were anxious to care for my son. I gladly accepted my brother's offer.

On my way home, I stopped in South Korea, Taiwan and Thailand to visit family planning centers there and to see other projects for women.

Back in Saigon, I became an advocate for family planning. My motivation was personal. After delivering twins, I was afraid that I would quickly end up with ten children like my mother and my eldest sister, Chi Hai. My eldest brother had nine children. I went to see my gynecologist about birth control. To my horror, he told me I could do nothing because of a law forbidding the use of any birth control methods. He counseled me on "the rhythm method." I carefully applied this method, and charted my temperature to determine when I was ovulating. Despite my diligence, three months after the twin's first birthday, I became pregnant again. Although I was not thrilled to be pregnant so soon, I was very happy to carry a child, and announced the news to Bong and my family. Everyone was enchanted that I was so fertile, a sign of good fortune and prosperity.

In the late 1950s, Madame Nhu, the sister-in-law of President Diem, herself a member of Parliament, had persuaded or rather forced the National Assembly to enact a "family law" that declared the use of contraceptives a crime. Repeat offenders could be imprisoned for five years. In pushing for the enactment of this law, Madame Nhu had revived a French law that had been implemented throughout France and the French colonies of the 1940s. After World War II, the French government outlawed the use of contraceptives so that families would produce more children to make up for the soldiers killed in the war. That law had been applied to all French colonies—including those in Asia and Africa—where women routinely had between six and a dozen children. France had long ago repealed the law, but some colonies—including Vietnam—were still enforcing it.

Back home, I met with the minister of Health, Dr. Cat. He felt that the law banning contraception should be repealed but warned that changing the law and attitudes would take time. Some family planning education was available at "Mother and Child" centers set up by the Ministry of Health. But the use of the words "contraceptive" or "family planning" had been forbidden. He recommended organizing a nonprofit organization to spearhead the campaign to repeal the prohibition on contraception.

I considered whether I should take on this battle. My life had already taken difficult and unexpected twists. I'd gone from being an innocent girl to a sophisticated wife, an unexpected widow, and finally a professional woman. I already had a full plate, providing for my children and my extended family and managing a full-time job. My life had settled into a comfortable routine. Did I want to stir the pot and take on the challenge of changing the lives of other women? I knew it would be a tough fight and that I would expose myself to personal attacks.

One evening, I came home, prayed in front of the altar, and asked for guidance from the invisible spirits who I believed protected and blessed me. After consulting with my spirits, I decided to take on this new challenge for the silent majority of Vietnamese women.

With a handful of doctors, I established a non-profit organization. We also had the support of a member of the cabinet. Using a euphemism, we called ourselves "The Protection of Family Happiness Association." We wrote a proposal to the International Planned Parenthood Federation (IPPF), headquartered in England. The IPPF gave us some seed money to start an educational project, gathering family planning information. With not enough money to rent a big office, I used a room in my own house to open the center. We hired a part-time doctor and a staff of nurses and social workers to run the program in the evenings.

On weekends and evenings, I would go with the social workers to slum areas to educate families on family planning. We distributed leaflets, and explained to women they should take control of their bodies, while respecting traditional values. We showed these women different methods of contraception, and told them to come to our office to see our doctors if they needed more information. Our work was officially illegal. But we wanted to give women choices, and change prevailing attitudes.

In 1972, we wrote another proposal and got more funding from the Ford Foundation. USAID (the U.S. Agency for International Development) gave us contraceptives to distribute for free. A few months later, we moved into a bigger office, and hired more social workers we called motivators, who were sent to slum areas to spread the word. These motivators educated people about how to space their children and reduce the size of their families. Gaining acceptance of contraception required more than convincing wives. We needed to convince husbands and mothers-in-law, who took care of their grandchildren and had considerable influence.

Soon, the word spread. One day, I saw a caricature of myself on the front page of a paper. I was portrayed as the pioneer of family planning and a bad example for women. The religious groups, Buddhists and Catholics alike, were against family planning. They and others made many arguments. In a war-torn country, we needed more children. Confucian tradition said more children also meant more prosperity. Children were the future of the country, and the future of the family. Children provided social security for their aged parents. Using contraceptives or performing abortions was against the will of God. Family planning was an instrument of the Americans.

Some of Bong's former law students helped me develop an economic argument for family planning. The median wage of a menial laborer or soldier with four children was the equivalent of twenty to twenty-five U.S. dollars a month. I showed that, on this salary, the wage earner couldn't adequately feed both himself and his wife, much less provide for a family of six.

I asked my audience if it made sense to produce children when families couldn't afford to care for them. Wouldn't it be better to have fewer children and provide for them decently?

I did not ask people to perform illegal abortions, or stop the reproduction process. I asked that women be given some respite and some dignity instead of being "womb factories." My simple arguments made sense to the average family and generated headlines.

My own mother was among my most fervent supporters. She told me that if she'd known those methods, she would not have had ten children. My number eight sister, Thu Cuc, was among the first to come and bring her friends to the center for the "daily pills." Relatives, friends, acquaintances, and strangers rushed to us. We succeeded beyond our expectations.

Little by little, women began flocking to our Family Happiness Center. They wanted the magic pills. The more criticism we absorbed, the more successful we became. Women's groups and universities invited me to talk to them about family planning. Even the labor unions organized a population conference and invited me and other international experts to participate. Our organization grew to six centers in the provinces. I was invited by the International Planned Parenthood Federation to attend population and family planning conferences in Hong Kong, Thailand, Singapore, Indonesia, Malaysia, and the Philippines.

In February 1973, after the signing of the Paris Peace Agreement, I was one of three women profiled in a *New York Times* article, "The Women of Vietnam: Some Grew Strong in the Face of War."

In the article, I said, "We must build a new nation with a new economy. Life is going to be hard, and old attitudes must change." I went on to say that women had always run the home and managed the money in their family. Now they were running the businesses. "We don't need women's liberation. We are already emancipated."

In 1973, the minister of Health, Dr. Cat, asked me to represent Vietnam at a three-day conference on "The Status of Women and Family Planning" organized by the United Nations in Indonesia. At the conference, other representatives said that the women of Vietnam, whom the media tended to describe as corrupt, prostitutes, or drug addicts, were lowering the status of the women in Asia. They cited astounding statistics: half a million orphans, many of them abandoned by their prostitute mothers or their G.I. fathers. A large majority of the delegates approved a motion to discuss the dreadful problems of Vietnamese women.

I asked to speak. I pointed out that the plight of Vietnamese women wasn't any different from those in any other country at war. I recalled Europe during the two world wars, and explained how prostitution and orphaned children were also commonplace in China, Korea, the Philippines, and other Asian countries under Japanese occupation.

I explained that prostitutes represented only a small minority of women in Vietnam. Widowed women now headed families. Wives of disabled husbands had taken men's jobs in businesses, the government, and the military. Had they heard of the woman, seven months pregnant, who had had a miscarriage unloading hundred-pound rice bags on the docks of Saigon? Vietnamese women were replacing men and running the country, invisible and uncomplaining.

I also told them about my own life—a widow living in a house with four other widows—all working hard to make ends meet. I urged the delegates to adopt a resolution praising, not censuring, Vietnamese women. First a few, then the majority of the delegates raised their hands in support of my resolution. After the session, women congratulated me. An Indonesian journalist interviewed me, and an article with my picture appeared on the front page of the local paper. I proudly showed it to the minister of Health when I returned to Saigon. My government had not wasted its travel money.

One evening, Ambassador Bunker invited me to a small dinner at his residence. After dinner, over coffee, he asked me whether I'd considered going into politics. He believed that as a politician I could fight for women's rights.

I replied that I didn't have the will or determination to enter politics. Ambassador Bunker argued that Vietnam needed honest and respected politicians. "Everyone knows you and Bong," he said. "You could do a lot of good for Vietnam." I knew that while I could take on social issues, politics was not my calling. "I do not think I'm cut out to be a politician," I told the ambassador. While I rejected a political career, however, I continued to speak out for Vietnamese women.

In 1974, the "Year of the Woman," *Newsweek* printed a long article entitled, "Tasting Power: the New Asian Woman." It featured pictures of India's Indira Gandhi; Sri Lanka's Prime Minister Bandaranaike; China's Chiang Ching, wife of Mao Tse Tung; and the Philippines' Imelda Marcos.

The article told how the role of women was changing in Asia. "Asia— for years a bastion of male supremacy—is finally setting store by its women." Talking about these changes, I was quoted: "It's challenging to be an active Asian woman today. The men can't keep us down much longer."

In the fall of 1974, I finally tasted the fruits of my labor. I was invited to work with the Health Committee of the Vietnamese National Assembly to draft legislation repealing the anticontraception law. Working with medical groups, women's organizations and labor unions, we hammered out the precise wording for a measure to repeal the law. Our law passed that year. I had the satisfaction of knowing that what I believed in and fought for had finally come to pass.

In the space of three years, my life had changed dramatically. I'd gone from being the wife of a beloved politician to becoming my own person. I had gone on to change the lives of millions of women in Vietnam.

SIX

Escape from Vietnam and Passage Through Three Refugee Camps

When the end came for South Vietnam, in April of 1975, I was director of cultural activities at the Vietnamese-American Association. The VAA was booming, with twenty-five thousand Vietnamese learning English, and a full round of concerts, plays, art exhibits, lectures, conferences, and other cultural presentations. My program had grown tremendously during my three years there, and now I was working hard, putting on events days, nights, and weekends.

At the same time, things were deteriorating badly for South Vietnam. The play had entered its last act. President Thieu, with his inept cabinet and failing army, was making a desperate effort to hold off the iron-fisted Communist Le Duc Tho, whose ever-stronger forces were closing in on Saigon. In the United States, President Gerald Ford, who in my memory seems always to have had a golf club in hand, was facing a hostile Congress.

The Watergate scandal, which had led to President Richard Nixon's resignation in August 1974, confounded the whole world, especially Vietnam. In its wake, Congress cut U.S. economic aid to Vietnam by half, and military aid to a third of the previous year's. Neither my Vietnamese friends nor I understood how such a small incident could cause such devastating consequences.

Looking back, it seems that President Thieu was influenced by an analysis prepared by Major General John Murray, the second-to-last American commander in Vietnam. In 1972, when Murray was U.S. chief of logistics, he reasoned that, once our military assistance slid below

186

certain levels, the South Vietnamese government would be hard-pressed even to hold on to Saigon and the Mekong Delta, to the capital's south. This opened the possibility that, one day, the government might have to decide to abandon the northern part of the country to try to save what was left.

With aid cut back badly, the situation on the battlefield did worsen. I read in the morning newspaper on March 11 that the North had attacked the central provincial capital of Ban Me Thuot, one hundred fifty miles northeast of Saigon. It had already taken over Phuoc Long province, only seventy five miles away. Both attacks were blatant violations of the 1973 Paris Peace Accords. I watched President Thieu on television denounce the Communists for resupplying their army with new Soviet weapons while sending a force amounting to two hundred fifty thousand troops down the Ho Chi Minh Trail into the South.

In mid-March, Thieu decided to act on General Murray's logic, strongly supported by Australian advisor General Ted Serong, and to redeploy and consolidate his forces. He ordered his generals to withdraw from the central highland towns of Ban Me Thuot, Pleiku, Kontum, and Hue. My family and I heard on the BBC and the Voice of America the shocking and fearsome news that our South Vietnamese troops were fleeing the highlands with their families in military convoys, flooding the roads. Terrified, the people fled, too. Pandemonium broke out. Stories spread of people walking on top of children and soldiers shooting at civilians who panicked and got in their way.

The disastrous retreat from the highlands eventually involved half a million people. The BBC was predicting that the Communists would reach the outskirts of Saigon within two to three weeks. Embassies were closing in quick succession. I was invited to a series of farewell dinners as foreign diplomats said their hasty farewells. "Nonessential" staff from the U.S. embassy were also departing.

Only now did it hit me that Saigon was close to falling, and that my family and I were in grave danger. I had always thought that our American allies would never abandon us.

However, the most urgent task at the moment was to feed the refugees who had walked to Saigon from the central parts of Vietnam, their feet blistered and bleeding. They were without food or shelter. At the end of March, incongruous as it seems, I organized a fashion show at the VAA to raise funds. I asked my dressmaker, the famous Mr. Thiet Lap, for help. He and his wife called on their twenty-five clients and assorted beauty queens to participate. We made enough money to buy basic foods for the refugees, and went out by convoy to visit them. We saw hundreds of people with young children on the ground in the forest, fifteen miles from Saigon, huddled together in the pouring rain.

President Thieu tried to prevent panic by announcing that any Vietnamese trying to flee the country would be arrested. Meanwhile, the VAA's new acting director told the staff to make lists of our families for the American embassy in case there was an evacuation. To avoid showing signs of fear or panic, he said, our Cultural Center should remain open to the public. There was nothing to worry about. We just needed to bring canned food and blankets and be ready to sleep in our offices in case things changed.

In mid-April, I went to see Nancy Bennett, a dear friend and the Chinese-born wife of the political counselor at the American embassy. I asked whether she could help get my children out of Vietnam, at least temporarily. Nancy was the first person to call me "Jackie," shortening my French name. Therefore I was called Jackie Bong, and it has stuck with me ever since.

Nancy said that there was about to be an evacuation of Vietnamese orphans called "Operation Babylift." She could easily get my children out through that project: my children had no father, she said, so they could be considered orphans. They could leave at any time.

I was happy to hear that there was a way out. But then Nancy said that the orphans would be adopted once they arrived in the United States. My three children would live with their new parents. Did that mean that I would lose them? There was no way I could do such an abdominable thing. Thank God I felt that way: On April 4 the massive C-5 plane that was implementing Operation Babylift crashed after takeoff, killing many of the children and others on board. It was one more disaster on top of all the others that were occurring.

I still needed a solution for my children. The first task was to get them passports so they could leave the country legally. I went to see the minister of the Interior, who told me that, by order of the president, he could not possibly do anything. He could issue the passports only if they were authorized by someone higher up.

I then called on Nguyen Van Hao, deputy prime minister for economic affairs, and asked him to write a note to the minister of the Interior on the children's behalf. At this late stage, I knew that the situation was irreversible, and the Communists were about to encircle Saigon.

Hao, in his late thirties, smart and ambitious, resisted at first. He said that, although he respected my late husband, Bong, and was grateful to him, he thought that a well-known person like me should not be fleeing the country. He said that he, his wife, and his children were staying. I told him that I was not afraid to die, that I was not fleeing, but that my children deserved to live in a free country because their father had given his life for Vietnam.

A few days later, on April 20, Hao called me at my office and said that he would write a letter to the minister of the Interior to allow my children, and them alone, to go. I went to Air France to buy them tickets to Paris. I intended for them to stay with my sister number nine, Thu Thuy.

After a week of encountering red tape from one end of the Ministry to the other, I finally got approval for the children's passports. Once I had the appointment to pick them up, I was elated, believing that my children would be safe at last.

I went to the designated office. A old *planton,* or messenger, sitting outside the office, asked me to sit in the hallway. After waiting for forty-five minutes, I asked to see the director. I was told that he was very busy. After an hour, more and more impatient, I got up and started to knock at the door. The old man stopped me, and told me to return the next day because the director had other urgent matters to deal with. As I was leaving, he followed me out and said in a low voice, "You know, when you come back tomorrow, would you mind bringing a gift for us?"

"What kind of gift are you talking about?"

"Well," said the man, "the normal fee for an exit visa."

"What is the amount required?"

"I suppose a couple of hundred thousand dong would do."

"You mean that I won't get the passports and visas if I don't give you the money? That's four to five times an entire year's salary for your big boss, the minister himself."

"Please understand that we government employees are paid very little, and, besides, we have to share the gift with a lot of other underpaid people in the section. We can negotiate and come up with the right amount, if you like."

I did not know whether to empathize with him or give him a punch. He saw that I was upset at such open extortion. I immediately turned around and, after a quick knock, went straight into the director's office. I sat down on a chair and looked at him, redfaced. I introduced myself, and he greeted me, *"Kinh thua Ba Vien Truong,"* addressing me with respect as the wife of the director of the National Institute of Administration, Bong's old title, which I had now inherited. The official told me he had been Bong's student at the NIA, a fact I could have guessed because most government directors, chiefs of cabinet, or higher-ups were NIA graduates.

"I came to get my children's passports, and I wonder whether they are ready. Here is the appointment paper, with the passport numbers."

"Oh yes," said the official, "They came to me this morning. In fact, they are in the in box here in front of me. I have been expecting you to come for them."

"What else do I need to do?"

"Well, you need to pay a fee of fifty dong for each one. After you give me the receipts for the three of them, I will stamp an exit visa on each passport."

"Is there anything else I have to do?"

"No. That is all. The cashier is at the end of the hall on your left."

I went outside to pay and passed the old man without saying a word. He did not blink an eye. I handed his boss the receipt, and finally had the three precious passports in my hand. I felt so relieved—the lives of my children depended on these three little booklets. As I thanked the director, I wondered whether I should tell him what his subordinate had demanded from me. But I did not know whether they were co-conspirators or whether the official was totally unaware of what was going on outside his office door.

I was weighing the pros and cons when it occurred to me that this was not the right moment for whistle-blowing. Would it help me or them if I spoke up? Instead of correcting the situation, I might get myself in trouble. With so many urgent things to do, I had to run. My children's lives were the most important thing now. I couldn't waste time trying to change practices that were so deeply rooted in the system that they qualified as a tradition. So I bade farewell to the people who were paid with my tax money to serve me, leaving fast and refusing to give them anything from my pocket on the way out.

The children now needed entry visas to the place where they were going, and it was not easy to get visas for France unless the president of Vietnam himself approved. It was too late for such a request.

So that evening, I asked the Belgian ambassador, who had invited me to a farewell dinner, whether there was any way for the children to go to Brussels. My sister could go there and drive them back to Paris. The ambassador agreed, and even arranged for his deputy, who was going home the following night, to accompany the children. The deputy would call my sister when they arrived in Brussels.

The flight was scheduled for 11:30 P.M. on April 22. A curfew was in effect from six P.M. to six A.M. Bill Johnson, a friend from the U.S. embassy, said he would have an embassy car take us to the airport. His wife, Pat, had left a few days before and had invited me over for a quick farewell dinner with them. Bill invited the children and me to dinner at his house on the night of the children's departure. The embassy van would pick us up there at ten P.M.

During dinner, we watched President Thieu give his bitter, scornful, tearful resignation speech. Thieu blamed the Americans for deserting Vietnam.

I put the children to bed and stayed next to them. I was sad, but happy that they would be safe soon. God only knew when I would see them again, I thought.

At a quarter to ten, the phone rang, and Bill spoke to the caller. Then, very calmly, Bill told the children and me to stay still and not move. He went to the garage and returned to the living room with an M-16 rifle, which he loaded with bullets. He said that the embassy security officer had told him the Communists were closing in on Saigon. There was no way we could go to the airport.

Bill's house was on Tu Xuong street, across from the residence of Vice-President Tran Van Huong, and he thought they might attack that area first. Smoking his pipe and wearing a fatigue jacket, Bill continued loading bullets into his rifle. Each bullet equaled ten of my heartbeats. As my heart pounded, I put my right index finger on the vein of my left wrist to try to calm myself. The more I pressed, the more the vein stood out—it was as if Elvis Presley were dancing rock-and-roll inside my wrist.

We stayed up the whole night, waiting for the attack. It would be my first on-the-scene war experience. We would be in the middle of the battlefield. I had to be brave and face death with my children. We were armed only with our prayers. I told them to pray for their father and ask him to come to our rescue. We waited, yawning and half-asleep, for the massacre to come.

The universe seemed to be making fun of us. April Fool's Day seemed to be lasting all month. I did not know any more whether to laugh or cry. Deceit and reality seemed to run together, confusing people. Calamities piled on top of one another.

In the dark of the night, I lay still, trying to make sense of what had been happening. It was like a game of roulette inside a roller-coaster, or a documentary in fast forward. I remembered that April 1 had started with the loss of Danang. On April 3, Prime Minister Tran Thien Khiem resigned, bringing down the whole cabinet. And President Ford, playing golf in Palm Springs, criticized President Thieu for his hasty withdrawal from the central highlands. On April 9, the Communists reached Xuan Loc, thirty-six miles east of Saigon, and destroyed that city.

Earlier, President Ford, in his State of the Union speech, failed to ask Congress for military support for South Vietnam, as promised by President Nixon. We South Vietnamese heard the news with much apprehension, but we held on to a last ray of hope, telling ourselves that it was near to impossible that the Americans would let us down. We reasoned that, with so much at stake and with so many of America's allies involved in Vietnam as well, the United States could not back out without sacrificing its leadership and its reputation in the world.

On April 18, the U.S. House of Representatives Committee on International Relations authorized President Ford to use U.S. military forces to evacuate Americans from Vietnam. We knew then that that was the end.

And tonight, April 22, it was Thieu's turn to give up power. I learned later that Thieu, Prime Minister Khiem, and their aides had left for Taiwan that very night. Their wives, children, and other family members were already gone. I wondered how Thieu could have had the gall to leave Vietnam in violation of his own decree, while abandoning the rest of the nation to its misfortune. While the top Vietnamese leaders and their American counterparts washed their hands of us, what would become of the millions of people left behind, the victims of their global game? The Communists were on top of us, ready to smash whomever they could lay their hands on.

At that moment, Bill's comfortable refuge felt like an inferno to me. I did not know whether I was facing death or about to escape to freedom. I was in between—curled up on a chair with my head on the bed where my children were sleeping—full of agony and tension. It all came to an end when Bill awakened me at seven A.M., and I saw that nothing had happened during the night. Bill said he would take us home.

I was having breakfast at our house when a dozen aunts, uncles, cousins, and friends poured in. The situation was alarming, they cried. Their friends were running around to different embassies for help, but to no avail. Could I ask the U.S. embassy to evacuate their families? They had no other recourse, they told me. Was there any other way out? I could only tell them even I did not know what to do. I called the VAA director and told him that I would be late for work.

At nine A.M., one of my two assistants, Tuyet, phoned and said that Nancy Bennett's driver had been waiting for me at the VAA since 8:15. I said to tell him to go home, and that I would drive to the Bennetts' residence. When I arrived, I saw Nancy packing her belongings. She said that she had a way to get the children and me out of the country. She told me to sit down, be strong, and not be shocked by what she was going to tell me.

All Americans and their dependents, she said, were allowed to be evacuated to the United States. An American pilot, Pat Barnett, who worked in Singapore and was married to a Vietnamese, had come to Saigon to try to rescue his in-laws. He wanted to rent a plane to bring them out, and had about $10,000 to do it. Jim Eckes, head of Continental Airlines, told Barnett he would arrange a way for him to get his in-laws out free of charge if he would say that my children and I were part of his family and take us out, too. Pat was delighted with the easy proposal, and agreed.

Nancy said this was now the best way for us to get to the United States, but I had to agree to pose as Pat's wife, and my children had to pose as his children. Pat was from El Paso, Texas. I knew the place. I had visited my brother, Trung, there in 1972, when he was teaching Vietnamese at the military base. But I still didn't understand. "Do I have to marry him officially? When can I divorce him so he can go back to his wife and children?"

Nancy laughed, and said it was just a formality. Pat would sign us all up as his dependents at the processing center at the airport. We would not need to show any documentation.

I had to make a quick decision, because we had to leave in one hour. I thanked Nancy and said we would go. We were each allowed one piece of hand luggage.

In fact, I was not ready to leave. I raced home and told my maid to pack some clothes. I was confused by the rush of events. I would be leaving everything and everyone so suddenly, with no time to say good-bye to my family or to my staff at the VAA. I asked my sister, Thu Cuc, who had happened by for a visit, to go with me to the bank to withdraw my money. At least that way I would be spending my last moments with someone in my family.

I told my bodyguard to follow us on his motorcycle. After Bong's assassination in 1971, the government had provided me two full-time bodyguards for life. I was also given an M-16 rifle, which I put under my bed. I never touched it and could not have handled it anyway. The police had also given me a little handgun. I kept it hidden in my safe and had forgotten all about it.

When my sister and I arrived at the bank, hundreds of people were there trying to get their money out. It was like a crowded marketplace. The bank teller gave me a number and said it would be at least half an hour to forty-five minutes before I was called. Even then, she said, there was no way to exchange the dong, our currency, into U.S. dollars. So I gave my sister my number and asked her to withdraw the money in the afternoon and use it to take care of my mother-in-law, stepsisters, and maids. She said she would.

Back at home, I opened the small safe in my bedroom and gave all the money I had left in an envelope to my mother-in-law. My own mother had enough money to care for herself. I also found the small handgun in the back of the safe. I gave that and the M-16 rifle to my bodyguard and told him to return them to the police. I also told him to keep the motorcycle I had bought him to follow me around every day, and handed him some money. I also found a precious U.S. twenty-dollar bill, left over from my last trip overseas, that I kept for myself.

I called my boss at the VAA and told him that I was going to the United States. Then, in tears, I talked to Tuyet, my assistant, and wished her and my other staff well. She could keep all my paintings, ornaments, and personal belongings from my office.

I then said my farewells to my mother, my mother-in-law, and my other relatives. My brother number six, Trung, had just arrived at my house. I asked him whether he wanted to go to the United States, from which he had returned a short time earlier. He said no. The Northern Communists, he said, were also Vietnamese, and would not retaliate against the South Vietnamese. "Are you sure of that?" I asked.

"Yes," he said. "I will have the chance to do business and work under the new regime. The new rulers will need all the resources they can get to rebuild the country."

These were my brother's last words to me. Later I learned that he had been put into prison. Subjected to extreme mistreatment there, he died, with no one in our family present to bury him.

Nancy Bennett's driver came to my house and drove me to the airport at eleven on the morning of April 23, 1975. I could not believe that it was the last time I would see Saigon's pretty houses, its familiar streets, its squalid outskirts. Pink magenta frangipanis perfumed the air of our neighborhood, and bougainvillea overflowed gardens and spilled over fences. I asked the driver to pass by the Mac Dinh Chi cemetery. At its gate, I looked through the car window at the tombs—miniature marble mansions and pantheons built by French and upper-class Vietnamese families to extend their high status in this world into the next.

I caught a glimpse of Bong's monument, the part extending upward with his epitaph written in marble. I closed my eyes to speak to him. I promised him I would try someday to repay the many people who had paid him homage at his funeral and helped me through the ordeal. If I could not show them my gratitude in person, I would compensate by doing something for others. Then I asked him to protect and bless the children and me as we set out on our journey to an unknown destination and a different life.

Passing the Cong Ly bridge, I looked back at the squatters' wooden shacks, perched on stilts along the filthy banks. I wondered whether I would ever smell the river's foul air again. Continuing down Cach Mang street, I fixed my gaze on the gray roof of the house where I had spent part of my childhood, and where my father had died. I stared at the row of coconut trees in the front, the cherished mango trees, the huge scented guavas, the apple custards, the emerald banana bunches, the tall sweet sugar cane. My mother had planted all of them with care and love. They shook in the breeze, sadly waving good-bye to me. I opened the palm of my hand, placed it under my chin, and blew a last kiss with my hand to return their grace.

I touched my chest and felt my heart aching. The pain spread out and descended, cutting into my stomach. In a flash, I prayed for my parents, brothers and sisters, aunts, uncles, and all their children. I prayed that the Viet Cong would spare them and spare my friends, and that there would be no bloodbath, as there had been in the 1950s. I had seen pictures of people buried alive up to the neck, then decapitated with machetes in Central Vietnam. I had seen documentaries of Vietnamese Communist cadres spraying innocent people with bullets and throwing them into mass graves.

Suddenly, the driver veered into a villa's drive. Two guards opened an iron gate. Inside, a big black sedan with an American flag on one side and a Vietnamese flag on the other stood parked in front of the house. Nancy's driver opened the door of my car to let us out. Another driver and a security guard from the other car opened the doors of the black sedan and let us in. The villa had served as a safe house over the previous two weeks for embassy Foreign Service officers who were evacuating Vietnamese from Saigon. I did not understand what was going on.

Jim Eckes, head of Continental Airlines, was in the front seat. He introduced me to my "husband," Pat Barnett, a man in his late thirties, around one hundred fifty pounds, with brown hair and eyes. He was in the back seat, wearing a white shirt and brown pants, waiting for us. We shook hands and headed for the airport. The children sat between us.

Jim told me that the American ambassador, Graham Martin, had lent us his car for the drive to the airport. He wanted to make sure the children and I would be safe. The day before, the Vietnamese police had arrested the minister of Economy and his family at the same airport for trying to leave Vietnam. The police were acting on President Thieu's decree to jail any Vietnamese caught fleeing the country. I was being shipped out clandestinely with the help of the Americans. It reminded me of the stories of Jews being helped to flee Europe during World War II.

To break the ice cold atmosphere, and needing to say something, I told Pat about being in El Paso, his hometown, in 1972. I had visited my brother, Trung, who was working there, and he had driven me to a hill on the outskirts. We could see the border with Mexico.

Five minutes later, we were at Tan Son Nhut airport, not the regular international departing area, but the American section. The American security officer in the front seat told us to say nothing if we were stopped. He had papers ready. But the Vietnamese police, seeing the ambassador's car with its flag and tinted windows, simply waved us in. I breathed a deep sigh of relief.

I saw groups of people crowded into the yard of a large complex. Jim told us to wait inside the bowling alley, which was air conditioned. It was late morning, and nearing a hundred degrees outside. Pat said he had to go back to town to pick up his Vietnamese in-laws. He would be back within an hour at the latest.

I looked around. Hundreds of Vietnamese were sitting or lying on the floor, or in the bowling lanes. Some were sleeping, some snoring. I found a small empty space, and told the children to sit there. Exhausted, I was ready for a good sleep, too, but the heavy smell of hundreds of people packed inside the bowling alley overwhelmed me. I decided instead to walk around and see what was going on.

There were no familiar faces, only people hunched low on the ground, speaking quietly and looking worried.

I sat there holding my children. Thu Anh and Le Viet were ten, and Le Quoc eight. They were excited about going on such a long trip, and did not understand what was happening around them. I tried to explain, but they couldn't really grasp the situation. Thu Anh asked whether we would go to Paris, and I realized that, in my haste, I had forgotten to tell them that our plan to go to France had changed, and we would be going to the United States, but that I did not know where exactly we would end up. The most urgent task was to get out of Saigon first, I told them.

Would they be going to French schools, as they had in Vietnam? Would they see their classmates again? Would their grandmothers join them soon? When were we leaving? When were they going to eat lunch? These were some of the questions I had no answer for. I could only ask them to be patient.

An hour passed, and Pat did not come back. Two hours passed. I could not believe that my brand-new husband would abandon us. I did not know what to do. With the children on either side of me, we went out to search for him.

We looked at one American face after another and tried to find my fake husband. I asked the children whether they remembered what Pat looked like. I had met him so quickly that I could not recall his features. The children pointed to a man with a beard, and I said it was certainly not him. They pointed to a fat, sturdy man, and I shook my head. After fifteen minutes of this, I started to panic. Where could he be? How could he leave without us? What were we going to do?

Then I saw a familiar car and a familiar face. It was Nancy, and we hugged her as if she were made of gold. Nancy took us to the Defense Attaché Officers' Club and treated us to a good American lunch—by that time we were very hungry. Miraculously, the kitchen was still operating. General Homer Smith, the defense attaché and the highest-ranking American military man in Vietnam, joined our table, but did not eat. General Smith explained to me that we would go to Clark Field air base in the Philippines on a C-130, a cargo plane, then on to the United States in a bigger plane. We would have to stay in the processing center in the Philippines, spend time in a camp in the United States, and be sponsored out by an American. Only then could we start living normally in our new country.

Nancy said that former Ambassador, Ellsworth Bunker, had sent messages asking that the children and I be well taken care of. She promised that she would see me again in Washington, D.C.

After lunch, Nancy went home. More relaxed, I sat on the floor outside the bowling alley and waited for Pat. I leaned my head against the wall and took a nap in the ninety-seven degree sun. The children were lying on the ground around me. It was better than being inside the suffocating bowling alley that smelled of sweat and fear. Outside, people talked in faint voices and walked around nonchalantly. They were more lively than those inside, but I could also see their dispirited eyes and their stunned faces, devoid of khi, "kinetic energy."

I was perspiring in my light blue short-sleeved shirt and dark blue pants, baking in the blistering noon weather. I suddenly became afflicted with paranoia. I heard percussions of drumbeats reverberating inside my head and my chest. I closed my eyes to try to center my thoughts. Instead I felt a thousand repugnant ants creeping slowly from my toes to my knees, and from my fingers to my elbows. They were gradually sucking my blood cells and paralyzing me. I felt anesthetized and lost myself in a deep sleep, sitting up against the wall.

Someone tapped me on the shoulder. I started and saw, first unfocused and then clearly, a Caucasian man talking to me. I recognized him and felt reassured. Pat had finally returned, and he apologized for being so late. One of his brothers-in-law had gone to visit a friend without telling anyone in the family, and the parents would not leave without him. He eventually came back, and now they were all here. Pat introduced me to his seven in-laws. From then on, we total strangers would stick together like a family.

Pat told us to wait, and went to register our names at the crowded processing center—me as his wife, my children as his, and his in-laws as mine. I chatted with my instant relatives, trying to get to know them. Two hours later, Pat came back and said we would be out on a flight that night. Until then, we were confined to the restricted area of the compound.

In the evening, in the cool courtyard, I saw some of my friends. Mrs. Trieu, the head of Claire-Joie, one of the best kindergartens in town, a branch of Regina Mundi (Les Oiseaux), was there with her two girls. To follow the progress of my children, I had taught there during the two years they attended that preschool. Her husband, a politician and businessman, had stayed behind with their two boys. Present too were Professor Lam Thanh Liem, deputy minister of education, his wife, and their three children. He was going back to his office afterward; he was only there to see his family off. Dr. Bao, head of the faculty of liberal arts, former minister of education, and my French literature professor, introduced me to his cousin, Dr. Bui, who had returned a few months earlier from Paris to teach French literature. I was happy finally to see a few friends.

Then, suddenly, Dr. Bui exclaimed that he was missing a Samsonite briefcase he had left unattended on the ground next to his suitcase. It contained $2,000, all his savings. He needed it to survive in the United

States until he could find a job. He said he did not want to have to beg for money there.

We looked for the briefcase for an hour, and it was obvious that someone had stolen it. Stricken, Dr. Bui decided to go back to Saigon; he would not go to the United States with nothing to live on. Dr. Bao said he would not leave without his cousin; he did not have any money, either. So they went back to town with Dr. Liem. Later, I heard that all three had been put in reeducation camps.

That night, we lined up to leave. The C-130s were swooping in every fifteen minutes to take the refugees away. They flew to the Philippines, unloaded their passengers in Manila, and returned immediately to Saigon for more—a nonstop ferry service. It was spectacular to see these giant crickets, with their bright eyes, flying up and down in the dark.

At two A.M. on April 24, armed American soldiers helped us to board the plane by the gaping rear door. Pat went ahead, got two empty seats for me and the children, and told us to sit down. It was first come, first served. There was only one row of seats, which followed the shell of the plane and formed a large, cigar-shaped oval. We faced the empty space in the center, which started to fill up with latecomers, who had to sit on the floor. Pat sat there, too. The roar of the plane was deafening.

I felt a sense of revival. Finally, I thought, we were on our way out of Saigon. At the same time, we had not made it to freedom yet. Something could still go wrong at the eleventh hour.

A tall American in his late thirties, with a big bag in his hand, and a Vietnamese woman were among the last people to board. The American looked around, came over to me, pulled my seat belt, and gestured to me and my children to vacate our seats, while motioning to his companion to come and take our places. I shook my head and held the children down with my hand, refusing to let go of our seats. Angry that I was disobeying his orders, he dropped his big bag on my feet. I felt as if a hundred pounds of iron had smashed my toes. The pain was so acute that tears ran down my face.

I was tied to the seat, unable to move. The plane was about to take off. The man pulled his companion over to him, sat on the floor, and looked at me with disgust. "Hey, girl, do you know what you're going to do in my country? You'll be washing laundry." As if I had not heard or understood what he meant, he rubbed his hands together to show me the way people washed their clothes. I looked away and closed my eyes. His bag still weighed heavily on my feet.

So I left my country with a heavy heart and crushed feet. I felt humiliated and ashamed. I was not a criminal. Why did I have to flee my ancestors' tombs like a coward or a fugitive? What evil had they or I done to deserve that kind of treatment? Where could we turn to find peace? My mind went black. I wanted to forget everything, run away from everything—jump headlong into a new environment.

We arrived in the Philippines around 3:30 on the dark morning of April 24. We went to the processing center at Clark Field to register our names with people working at small tables. We were kept waiting there until 6 A.M., when someone finally took us to a large dormitory with clean beds. Families would stay together. All of us dropped our bags next to our beds and fell into a deep sleep, without even changing our clothes.

In the afternoon, we got up and went to a big cafeteria for dinner. I was overjoyed to see some of my friends who had arrived earlier. We were free to wander around a small area of the base, more relaxed and better fed. Not knowing what to do next, Pat went to the processing center for more information. He was told to wait for new orders.

After a couple of days, I met former Colonel Dang and his wife. They used to manage the Grand Hotel, the biggest in Vung Tau, a white-sand beach resort one hundred twenty miles southeast of Saigon. Colonel Dang was listening to the BBC and the VOA with his small, short-wave radio. We were all curious to know what was going on in Vietnam.

Colonel Dang told us that on April 28 North Vietnamese artillery fire had destroyed helicopters, C-130s, and other airplanes at Bien Hoa, thirty miles from Saigon, and had captured the air base. North Vietnamese commandos had attacked the Newport bridge, a few miles from the center of Saigon. The Saigon-Bien Hoa highway was closed, and a USAID warehouse on the other side of the river was burned down.

The capital, we learned from the radio, was in a state of chaos.

Thousands of people, soldiers and civilians, jammed the streets, running for their lives. Army officers were shedding their uniforms for civilian clothes. The North Vietnamese were approaching the Saigon suburbs. At the Defense Attaché Office, from which I had departed the night before, six thousand terrified Vietnamese were slowly being airlifted out.

Ambassador Martin and his CIA station chief, Tom Polgar, had been convinced that the North would negotiate a political settlement and a cease-fire with the South, I learned later. They had delayed evacuation of many high-risk Vietnamese for as long as possible, until there was no other hope. At this stage, it was too late for many.

In an act of desperation on our side, on April 28, General Duong Van Minh was installed as president. He called for an immediate cease-fire, and offered to form a government of reconciliation. Ten minutes later, Communist planes attacked the capital and the airport. General Smith was ordered to dismantle his DAO complex. Back in Washington, Henry Kissinger would ask the Soviets again whether they could get Hanoi to agree to a cease-fire.

On April 29, the Saigon government imposed a twenty-four-hour curfew. Some two hundred of my VAA colleagues, USAID personnel, and other U.S. mission staff had assembled at the U.S. Information Service compound on Le Qui Don street. Chi Hoa, my friendly colleague at the VAA, later told me that she and her family were among them, huddled there, ready to be airlifted out. American companies such as Esso, Shell, IBM, and others had their people waiting at other safe havens to be evacuated. It was too late. Many of them were left behind. At the embassy, thousands of fearful Vietnamese, squatting inside and outside the compound, were waiting, as well.

Thirty miles from the capital, the North Vietnamese leaders—General Van Tien Dung, Le Duc Tho, Pham Hung, and Tran Van Tra—were looking at their battle maps. I visualized them clapping their hands, fortissimo, as the North scored each successive conquest. I imagined them putting red dots on the places they had captured, destroyed, and left in flames.

I saw them pointing their fingers at the ultimate prize, Saigon. General

Dung would move in full force, handing out his death warrants. The Communists were demanding total withdrawal of the United States, and declaring that the Saigon government must be swept away.

On April 29, after Ambassador Martin had gone to Tan Son Nhut airport himself and seen that it was no longer usable for fixed-wing aircraft following a night of Communist shelling, President Ford ordered him to go to the last phase of the evacuation. The fall of Saigon was a living event on that last, frantic day.

At the DAO "Dodge City" processing center at Tan Son Nhut airport, Marine Corps helicopters flew in with over eight hundred ground security forces to protect the helicopters that were taking evacuees from the DAO. By nightfall, they had evacuated nearly all three thousand people remaining.

Meanwhile, two huge, sandbagged barges had been pulled down the Saigon River and were sitting at the nearby docks at Khanh Hoi. Each could accommodate several thousand people, but poor communication within the embassy meant that many fewer actually made it. Many of the Vietnamese for whom the barges had been set up were left in the safe havens. For Chi Hoa, stuck at the USIS compound, the result was ten years in prison for her husband, an army officer. My own fate would have been worse if I had stayed.

Some of the key American evacuating officers at the embassy, like Ken Moorefield, had not been told of the barges, which finally left half-empty. They could have accommodated some of the thousands of high-risk Vietnamese who had worked loyally for the U.S. government and American companies and were left behind.

That afternoon Marine Corps helicopters started arriving at the embassy to evacuate people from the roof. Both the roof and the parking lot were turned into landing zones. By then, a number of Vietnamese had been let into the Embassy compound to be evacuated.

As time passed and the Vietnamese allowed onto the embassy grounds became more and more desperate to leave, the compound became a junkyard. The swimming pool was filled up with handguns, which people had to discard to board the choppers. They also used the pool as a urinal.

Ashes from documents and U.S. currency the Marines had been burning on the roof settled everywhere.

The helicopter evacuation went on all afternoon and into the night. From the air, frightening beasts, with flaring eyes and sharp, enormous blades, swooped down every ten minutes. They swallowed groups of fifty to seventy humans, flew away, and vomited them out like ferocious dragons onto the American ships offshore. Outside the embassy gate, more than a thousand Vietnamese, some yelling and others crying, were trying to fight their way inside. A few were recognized by embassy officers and pulled in. Marines, armed to the teeth and newly reinforced, kept out the rest.

In the early afternoon, Ambassador Martin instructed a sergeant to escort his wife, Dorothy, and their dog, Nit Noy, to an Air America helicopter that would take them out to the Seventh Fleet. Mrs. Martin departed, but left Nit Noy behind at the Ambassador's office.

At nine, Ambassador Martin told Eva Kim, his secretary, that it was time for her to leave. George McArthur, the *Los Angeles Times* correspondent who later became Eva's husband, offered to bring Nit Noy along. They joined Lacy Wright and others, snaked up the stairwell to the roof, and boarded a chopper.

Lacy remembers looking down and seeing, to the west, the huge fire that was consuming the U.S. base at Long Binh. He was exhausted from the previous ten days of evacuating the Vietnamese relatives of Americans. He and fellow embassy officers like Joe McBride, Art Kobler, and Charlie Currier, used a series of safe houses to assemble people and drive them clandestinely to the airport for flights out of the country. Now he fell asleep next to George McArthur—a lapse that George recorded in his next dispatch to the *L.A. Times* and of which he reminded us twenty years later in a letter. Alan Carter, director of U.S. Information Service, dejectedly boarded the same flight. He had desperately tried to save his staff, but the buses never came. Innocently, Nit Noy looked on.

Back at the embassy, Ambassador Martin, who was getting pneumonia, looked desperately tired. Around 10:00 P.M., we learned later, he cabled Brent Scowcroft, head of the National Security Council, in the

White House situation room and Admiral Gayler in Honolulu that he needed another thirty Chinook helicopters, immediately, to get everyone out. An hour later, the reply came: the Chinooks were on their way.

At 11:30, a rumor circulated that, at midnight, the embassy would be shelled and the helicopters shot down. All Americans except the Marines at the gates were ordered into the building. No shelling occurred. Wolf Lehmann, deputy to the ambassador, CIA chief Tom Polgar, Ken Moore-field, and other officers were still working inside the embassy.

Down in the compound, the Vietnamese were starting to panic; they calmed down only when the Americans said they would get them all out. Ominously, the Marines then withdrew from the part of the compound where the Vietnamese were waiting, and sealed it off. From that point on, the choppers landed only on the roof.

After midnight, the head count inside the embassy compound was reported at seven hundred thirty, but it was actually one thousand one hundred, including a handful of non-official Americans. At two o'clock that morning in Saigon—two in the afternoon in Washington—Kissinger was telling reporters that the evacuation was going very smoothly. He would talk to them again at four that afternoon.

We read later that, around three A.M., Ambassador Martin got a message from President Ford himself. It said that nineteen helicopter sorties were authorized for seven hundred thirty evacuees, and that the President expected Martin to be on the last one, no later than 3:45 A.M. Martin sent back a last message to Scowcroft: he would close the mission at 4:40 A.M. local time, April 30, 1975. At 4:40 A.M., Martin, CIA Station Chief Polgar, Colonel Jake Jacobson, and press spokesman John Hogan boarded the *Lady Ace 09* and flew out with a group of Marines who had finished their work at the DAO.

But there were still more flights. At about 5:30 A.M., another chopper brought the last American officials out. That still left eleven Marines, all of whom retreated to the roof and locked the door. Now the Vietnamese below saw they were being abandoned. Panicked, they entered the embassy, climbed the stairs, pushed away the barricades, and desperately made their way to the roof, hoping for a last chance at escape. But the Marines pushed them back with tear gas grenades.

Among those outside the Embassy was my friend, Phuoy Tran, a U.S. Agency for International Development employee, her husband, and her four young children. They were left behind, petrified. Later, the family escaped as boat people.

At eight A.M., a Chinook-46, escorted by six Nimble Cobra gunships, approached. To protect themselves, the Marines were still holding the Vietnamese at bay with tear gas. The Chinook sucked the last Marines into its belly, and spirited them away into the iridescence of the early morning.

Neil Davis, an Australian correspondent for NBC, was filming the scene from the street. In Chelmsford, England, my seventh sister, Thu Ha, and her husband, Alan Bell, were watching. Alan, a quiet, phlegmatic Englishman, threw up, and Thu Ha had burst into tears. For days afterward, she had stomach cramps and was unable to eat.

Now refugees in the Philippines, we were following developments every hour, our ears glued to the radio, eager for every detail.

In Vietnam, a new day was dawning. It was April 30, 1975. North Vietnamese soldiers and Soviet tanks streamed into Saigon. Big Minh, the man who had become the president of South Vietnam in its death throes, asked over the radio that the soldiers of the Republic end hostilities and lay down their arms. Shortly afterward, the North Vietnamese were inside the presidental palace, and Minh was told to announce total surrender over the radio.

At Clark Air Force Base in Manila, we sat on the floor after dinner, listening to a rerun of the surrender. Some exclaimed, *"Troi Dat!"* (Heaven and Earth). Others shook their heads, still others sobbed. Some were holding their knees to their heads. Some were praying for their loved ones in Vietnam. Some remained silent.

As for me, I lay on the ground and looked up into the infinite, starlit sky. I thought of the innumerable galaxies, there for tens of millions of years. Under that expanse of hundreds of billions of stars, I gazed sadly at the vast Milky Way. The nearest star, Sirius, blinked intensely. Lady Venus stared at me, frozen in place.

Animals charged through the sky: the Great Bear and Serpentis, Aries the ram, Scorpius, Taurus the bull, Cancer the crab, Gemini the twins. Standing still in their planets were Mars, Mercury, Jupiter, Saturn, Neptune. Finally, I saw Diana, queen of the night, fixing me with her crescent eye. Orion, the hunter warrior, unleashed his sword and split me in two. Like a meteor, I descended into a black hole, suspended in the middle of the stratosphere.

I woke up in the middle of the night at the airport in Guam. The long flight had been tiring. After a week in the Philippines, a hundred of us were asked to stay next to a hangar. Exhausted, most of us lay on the floor and slept soundly. Minutes earlier, I remembered seeing Pat Barnett, immobile on the ground, covering his head with an empty box of toilet tissues. Not far from him was a portable toilet. Uncompromising, Pat snored away.

It was still dark when we were told to go to our quarters. We walked past rows of big tents, and saw Marines cutting trees while others set up more tents to house us. We entered a tent that had twenty cots arranged in two rows.

Late that morning, I woke up and saw that many more tents surrounded ours. The Marines must have worked all night long. A block away, in the rear, four ready-made portable toilets welcomed us. Four blocks down, long lines of refugees waited impatiently for the four showers. The wooden doors revealed people from the knees down while they washed.

I lined up with the children. In front of us, people were shouting that each person was allowed only five minutes. Those who dared to linger longer had stones thrown at their feet. A lady emerged shouting that her clothes had been stolen. People laughed as she covered herself with a hand towel.

I returned to my tent and saw a little girl, about six years old, lying in a cot by herself, tiny and pale. I went over to say hello and put my hand over her forehead to feel whether she had any fever. I talked to her and saw that her name was written on a plastic bracelet, like patients wear in hospitals. A small plastic bag with all her papers hung around her neck. She was traveling by herself, and been put in our tent because we happened to have an empty cot.

She did not say anything and did not want to do anything. She looked scared and traumatized. Her long straight black hair was on one side of her face. The papers on her neck said that she was on her way to join her older sister, who was married to an American and lived in Hawaii. I told my children to play with her to cheer her up. I took her under my wing and treated her like another daughter. It seemed that my instant family kept growing. In times of stress, total strangers feel closer. We supported each other and did things together.

We ate in a huge mess hall that served American food all day and late into the evening. People arrived at all hours. I saw sandwich bread, butter, potatoes, ham, cheese, eggs, and steaks left half-eaten on plates.

My instant relatives and the other refugees were tired and dejected. All they wanted was a bowl of hot rice and *nuoc mam*, the pungent fish sauce that no Vietnamese can do without. None was available. But we were being fed for free so we didn't want to complain.

After two days of going to bed half-hungry, some of the refugees urged me to say something to the chef. They thought we could mobilize refugees to help him cook the rice and other Vietnamese dishes.

Steeling myself, I told this to the chef. He said he was not allowed to let anybody in to help him do his job, but he would give us more rice, and serve us more Asian food. The next day, the rice came out like porridge. We complained, and the next day it was half-cooked and hard to eat. One old lady said she nearly cracked a tooth. But after a few days of trying, the chef learned, and the rice was cooked to near perfection. Feeding thousands of refugees four meals a day was not easy.

On my second day in the camp, I walked around with the children and saw a Red Cross center where American volunteers were distributing toiletries, basic medicine, used clothing, and shoes. They were also giving out paper and envelopes so people could send mail to the United States. Postage was free of charge. They needed interpreters, and I volunteered. As I was handed my own basic necessities, I smiled: I had been performing the same service for refugees in the forest near Saigon only a couple of weeks before. Now we had changed places, and I was on the receiving end.

It was funny to see Vietnamese wearing American clothing one or two sizes too large, but it was much better than nothing. We all had to try to adjust to our new environment. We had to be patient until we were self-sufficient. But how were we going to cope? No one knew what we were going to do next. *"Troi sanh voi, sanh co"* (God creates elephants, and grass to feed them).

After three days, the little girl, whom I called Mimi, caught a fever and began throwing up. I went to the processing center to tell an American officer, who arranged for a van to take her, and me as interpreter and escort, to see a doctor at the Health Unit ten minutes away. I was carrying Mimi in my arms. She was so light; she seemed to weigh only twenty-five pounds. I registered her with the nurse, and asked whether I could see the doctor, as well. I had been sick since I arrived, and did not feel well.

While we were waiting to see the doctor, I took Mimi to the bathroom. It was so clean and orderly. After I used the dirt-free toilet, I had no more irregularity, no more stomachache, no more headache. When the doctor finally asked me what my problem was, I told him that I had found the right medicine: a clean toilet. The filthy portable toilets, used by hundreds of people, did not suit me well. Two days later, Mimi felt better, and was the first person to leave us. I gave her a kiss on the forehead and never saw or heard of her again.

The tents kept mushrooming. More and more refugees arrived, and all of us kept waiting. I wrote to friends at the State Department, but it was not easy to get an answer. There was no incoming mail yet, and no phones were available to us—unless we went to a certain place and had enough quarters to call long distance. There were long lines day and night at the phone booth. I knew people in the United States, but I had few addresses or telephone numbers.

After a few days, Pat said that he had accompanied us to safety; now it was time for him to go back to his wife and children in Singapore. We would wait until someone or some organization sponsored us into the United States. So my "husband" left. I thanked him, and told him to send my best regards to his wife and children. After a few days, his in-laws were sponsored and were able to go to the U.S.

Twelve days passed, and I had not heard from anyone, so I went to the processing center to see how we could get out of the camp. I was told that no one could go anywhere unless sponsored out by an American.

What was I going to do with three young children? How was I going to live? What kind of work was I going to get? I had been so preoccupied with events in Vietnam that I had not given myself a chance to think about my new life in the new world.

It rained the next day. I was stepping carefully along a path of stones and boards, trying to avoid the mud, when I saw Julio Andrews, the former director of the Asia Foundation. His organization had given me a fellowship to attend the "Population and Family Planning" workshop at the University of Chicago. He was looking for his staff, and wondered whether I had seen any of them. I had not, I answered. I asked him whether he would sponsor me out of the camp. Without any hesitation, he said, of course, he would.

We went together to the processing center where there was a man, a Marine I suppose, sitting at a desk. He said we had to fill out some papers, and give them to another man sitting at another desk behind him. He also explained that we had to satisfy certain criteria; an American could only petition for a refugee as a member of his family or of his household.

I did not belong to an American family. My fake American husband had left me to go back to his real wife. There was one option left—to be sponsored out as a member of a household. The man explained that a household member could be a servant or a chauffeur who worked for an American family. I did not belong in those categories either, but I could think of no other way out. After reflecting a while, half-serious, half-joking, I asked whether Julio would mind sponsoring me out as his servant.

Julio flushed, "Oh, Mrs. Bong, I would not dare!" he exclaimed. But what else could I do? I did not want to be stuck in the camp forever. The man at the desk said that we did not need to show any papers, just fill out the form, and the children and I would then be able to fly out on the next available plane to the American mainland. More relaxed, we looked at each other, acquiescing, and filled out the forms. Two days later, the children and I boarded a plane for California, with over a hundred other refugees.

Finally, California, the beautiful West Coast, with its temperate climate and vast green spaces. I would love to find a job and live here, I thought. At the huge Camp Pendleton, we were assigned to tin barracks, where the military used to live. This time, the children and I occupied two sets of bunk beds and were reunited with some dear friends in the same barrack: Dr. Than and his wife, Dr. Bach; Professor Khoa, whose wife was Dr. Bach's older sister; and their children. Khoa had headed the book publication section at the VAA, and had taught me Oriental philosophy at the University of Saigon.

At the far end of the barrack were Khuong Huu Dieu, an M.I.T. graduate and a former director of the Vietnam Industrial Development Bank, and his pretty wife, Marie. I felt more secure among people I knew. But, in mid-May, the weather was still cold by our standards; it dropped from seventy degrees during the day to fifty at night. We had no warm clothes to wear, and were given military jackets to keep warm.

My children also found some friends from their school to play with. They ran around, and had a good time. For them it was like a scout camp or a nonstop picnic. By late afternoon, most children looked like bronze penguins, draped from neck to feet in their enormous military jackets. From the top of a far hill, one saw what looked like small clusters of Indians next to their tents. Farther away, long queues of penguins lined up in front of the mess hall, shivering. We all thought we were at the North Pole.

The general in charge of Camp Pendleton asked for volunteers to handle the information center. The camp was divided into five sections, with a few thousand refugees in each. We formed a committee: Than, Dieu, and I, as well as other Vietnamese, some civilians and some army officers. We worked in shifts of two or more hours to welcome the refugees flowing in.

Soon the number of arrivals swelled. The mess hall could not accommodate all of us. Some of the newly arrived had to walk for ten to fifteen minutes to the mess hall and line up for more than an hour outside in the cold, then spend another hour inside getting their meal. As soon as they finished breakfast, many started lining up for lunch. After lunch, they lined up for dinner. After dinner, there was supper if you were still hungry. There was nothing else to do but line up for meals. Besides, it was the only place to gather and talk to your friends.

You could hear outbursts of joy here and there in the lines, as people recognized their relatives or friends. You also saw tears when people learned that, at the last minute, someone had not made it. People jumped the line to run to their loved ones, and stayed there to talk and walk along with them. Refugees who had been in line for a long time told the "jumpers" to go back to their places. There were shouts and sometimes fistfights. This became a common occurrence; people were distraught.

Our committee proposed that another mess hall be set up near the section where the tents were located so people would not have to walk so far or line up so long to get their meals. A huge tent was erected as the second mess hall. We were also better fed, with more rice, soya sauce, and chow mein, noodles cooked with chopped meat and sauce— American style. Than often said that, after eating so much chow mein, we risked turning into chow mein ourselves. We were not yet rewarded, however, with the familiar *nuoc mam*. The old people, in particular, missed it a great deal.

Another woman and I were assigned to make announcements. Our voices were heard over the loudspeakers all day and sometimes at night, if there was an emergency. The camp had become a massive fair. People roamed around looking for their lost husbands, wives, or other relatives who had become separated from them fleeing the country. A father with a crying baby and a child of five asked me late one evening to try to find his wife and his other children.

People lost their baggage, their money, their papers. Some had come with suitcases filled with Vietnamese currency and asked me where they could change it into U.S. dollars. Some wanted to sell their gold pieces, or jewelry. Some came and simply cried, traumatized by the radical uprooting. Americans came looking for their relatives to take them out of the camp.

American sponsors asked me to read the same written announcements again and again. They had reversed the order of the Vietnamese names in such a way that they were not recognizable. After half a day, not having gotten any response, sponsors would come back to me to ask for an explanation. I told them that, although we were on U.S. soil, they were still dealing with Vietnamese within a Vietnamese community. I explained that the family name went first, then the middle name, and, last, the first name, not the other way around.

After a week in the camp, the general in charge came to us and said that General Nguyen Cao Ky had just arrived. The camp commander wanted to give the former prime minister and vice-president of the former South Vietnam a tour of the camp by a jeep. He asked whether our committee would assemble and welcome Ky at our reception center the next day. We convened a meeting that night to discuss the matter.

Not everyone wanted to welcome Ky. They recalled his radio address in Saigon, just days before, an eloquent appeal to stay and fight the Northern Communists. He would set the example and defend the South until the war was won, he declared. Why did he then flee and leave his troops to their fate? Some pointed out that Ky was no longer our prime minister, and asked why he should get the red carpet treatment while others did not. They thought he should be treated like any other refugee. The majority voted not to line up to give him a formal reception. Whoever wanted to go could do so.

The next morning, I went to work as usual and made the regular announcements. I was alone in the reception center when I looked out and saw a jeep parked in front with the American general and General Ky standing next to it. Dr. Vinh, a former member of Parliament, was showing Ky into the center. As they entered, Vinh recognized me and introduced me. Ky said that he had fond memories of Bong, and that when he was prime minister, he had invited Bong to become a state minister in the Prime Minister's Office. I replied that Bong had declined because he preferred to remain a professor, a career that was untainted and respectable. Ky looked around and said good-bye.

Ky, with his pencil mustache, had become chief of the Air Force at thirty-two. His star rose higher when he married another star, Mai, a former stewardess. Flashy and flamboyant, they used to parade around in identical black flying uniforms with mauve scarves trailing behind them, wearing dark sunglasses. Ky became prime minister and then vice-president of the republic. Ky had been born in North Vietnam. Back in Saigon in the late 1960s, my family was eating dinner one evening and watching the news. My mother-in-law, from Camau, the remote southern tip of the country, asked me who "the American" was who had been shouting something on the television for the past ten minutes. What was he saying? I laughed and told her that it was our prime minister, Nguyen Cao Ky. He was Vietnamese, not American, speaking with a northern accent. He was saying he wanted to fly to the North to bomb the Communists, and to have public executions *"phap truong cat"* of people who were corrupt.

After the war, Ky and his wife settled in California. They opened a liquor store, then closed it and filed for bankruptcy. A few years after that, the Vietnamese newspapers said that he and his wife had divorced. Ky then went to live in Bangkok, where he advocated doing business with Communist Vietnam. Again, he made headlines in the Vietnamese newspapers.

Seeing Ky made me think of his former chief of police, Colonel Nguyen Ngoc Loan. I would later encounter them together at a dinner in Virginia in 1984. The photo of Loan shooting a Viet Cong at point-blank range during the 1968 Tet attacks in Saigon had made him infamous. The picture made the covers of *Time* and *Newsweek,* and shocked people around the world. The photographer had caught Loan, his arm outstretched, firing into the temple of a young Viet Cong whose hands were tied behind him, grimacing in death. It became the most famous photo of the Vietnam war, and must have turned millions against South Vietnam and been a great boon to the Communists, not only in the United States but around the world. When Lacy and I visited the National Museum in East Berlin in 1977, a huge oil painting depicted the photo, which by then had become a symbol. After the war, the man who had achieved such unwanted notoriety ran a fast food restaurant with his family outside Washington.

Meanwhile, at Camp Pendleton, it was early morning, but still dark. We were all sleeping. Six or seven men ran into our barrack shouting, "Where is Khuong Huu Dieu? Come out here." Dieu was standing next to the bunk where he and his wife slept. He had just come back from his morning shower. He made himself known.

The men jumped him and began beating him about the face and body. Dieu's cousin and teenage son jumped out of their beds and came to his rescue. Dieu ran out shouting as two American military police arrived. They just watched, saying nothing. Seeing the MPs, the intruders left with threatening words: "This is to give you a lesson so you show people more respect." We did not understand what was going on. In the afternoon, the refugees in our barrack were moved by bus to a faraway section of the camp, about ten minutes distant.

It was rumored later that some former army officers had been complaining that they were not being treated well. They had to eat in the lower mess hall, in a cold tent in the bad area, where they and Nguyen Cao Ky were staying, instead of the warm mess hall in "upper class" tin city, where we were staying. And Dieu had been the prime mover behind the creation of two mess halls.

I had written to some of my American friends, but I had heard from no one. The latest news was that refugees could be sponsored by voluntary organizations if they had no family in the United States. After six weeks of being moved from one camp to another, I had become wary, particularly after witnessing the incident involving Dieu. I kept quiet, confining myself to walking around the camp with my children and friends as my daily exercise.

One day, Tuyet, a former member of the staff of Dr. Than's Dong Phuong Bank, was telling some refugees their future with a deck of cards. Curious, I asked her when she thought I would get out of the camp. She told me to draw a few cards, and she set them down in rows. She showed me the queen of hearts, and said that it was me. Next to the queen was a jack of hearts. She said he would be my future husband, and he would be young. She added that I would get out of the camp soon.

I laughed, asking, "Who, first of all, would be crazy enough to marry a widow? Worse, a refugee with nothing but three small children? And a young man? You're kidding me." She said that it was not she who had said it. The cards I drew showed it. That was it, she retorted. Whether I believed it or not was up to me.

A few days later, I was called to the processing center. A Vietnamese man working at the desk recognized me and said that I was being sponsored by Sanford McDonnell, chairman of the McDonnell-Douglas aircraft company. I would go to St. Louis, Missouri, as soon as the next plane was available, within the next day or two. Then the man remembered something and went to a stack of letters in a box on the wall. Lots of friends had written to me as Mrs. Nguyen Van Bong, using my late husband's name, while I was registered in my maiden name, Thu Van. I had moved four times in the past seven weeks, and, having registered in a different name, it had not been easy to locate me.

Reading the mail, I learned that a number of my friends had offered to sponsor me out. But I was very happy with the first choice. I had first met Sandy McDonnell when he visited Bong and me in Saigon in 1966. He had called us at the suggestion of Dr. Hugh Chaplin, whom I had met in London in 1961.

In 1967, when I went to Harvard to attend a summer seminar on marketing, Sandy had invited me to fly to St. Louis to meet his charming wife, Priscilla, his two children, and his parents. I also met Uncle Mac, the founder of the McDonnell aircraft company. Sandy gave me a tour of the McDonnell plant in a two-seater car. The plant had sixty-two thousand workers then and was located right at the St. Louis airport, Lambert field. I was very impressed indeed, and overwhelmed that there could be companies so gigantic in the United States. When the company later merged with Douglas aircraft, it got even larger with the addition of the California branch.

And so I bade good-bye to Camp Pendleton, and to my fellow refugees.

SEVEN

RESETTLEMENT, DEPRESSION, AND RECOVERY

My children and I went to St. Louis to stay with the McDonnells. Their two children had gone away to college, so we were given their bedrooms. To cheer us up, Pris, I learned later, gave up her tennis sessions and various civic activities—the St. Louis Symphony, the St. Louis Art Museum, and the Opera Theatre of St. Louis—and took us nearly every day to her friends' houses so we could swim, have lunch, and meet other people. The McDonnells took us to church on Sunday, and a week after we arrived, took me to the opera.

Sandy and Pris, then in their early fifties, were soft-spoken, good-humored, and extremely kind. They were both tall, Sandy at least six foot three and Pris not much shorter. They both towered over me. They were also patient. For weeks, they had been asking the State Department about my whereabouts in the refugee camps. Like the Chaplins, who lived not far from them and had known me as a student, they knew me by my maiden name, Thu Van. That was why they had been the first people able to trace me to the California camp.

Strangely enough, after a week in St. Louis, instead of feeling more secure and relaxed in our comfortable environment, the children and I started to get sick. Victor had nightmares, Alex had headaches, Annie could not eat well, and I could not sleep at night. The trauma of the past few months of refugee life was weighing heavily on us. Pris took us to a doctor, who prescribed only vitamins and told us to rest and relax.

We were not the only ones who felt disoriented. One day, Pris asked me to telephone a Vietnamese man who had just resettled in St. Louis. He told me that, in a desperate moment during the shelling in Saigon, he had jumped onto a barge and now found himself sponsored by a church here. He did not know anyone, and had not spoken Vietnamese for a month. He had left his wife and children, and did not know whether they were alive or dead. The church had found him a cleaning job in a hospital.

He was so happy to be able to speak Vietnamese, and he begged me to talk to him as long as I could. He was very homesick and said that some nights he roamed around the house or paced his bedroom for hours, and he was becoming crazy. I did not have any way to visit him, and he had no way to visit me; we lived too far apart. So we just talked on the phone. Not long after that, I learned that he had moved, and had not left a phone number. I never heard from him again.

The next week, the children and I felt better. Part of the reason was Sandy: no matter how busy he was, Sandy made sure that every evening after he came home from work he spent at least half an hour talking to us. That must have been a real effort on his part, because at the time Sandy was CEO and chairman of the entire McDonnell-Douglas Corporation. He had spent his whole career there, after graduating from Princeton University in 1945 with a BA in economics, getting a BS in mechanical engineering from the University of Colorado in 1948, and then joining his uncle's corporation, the McDonnell Aircraft Company. While still working, he finished his studies in 1954, with an MS in applied mechanics from Washington University in St. Louis.

Sandy and Pris surrounded us every night with a family atmosphere. We felt relaxed and secure with them. After a month, Sandy suggested that the children take American names. He proposed a few, and the children chose to be called Victor, Annie, and Alex. After six weeks, the McDonnells went on a trip, and we moved in with our second sponsoring family, the Chaplins.

Kate, whom I had met as we both lined up at the French Lycée in London in 1961, had gone to Harvard and married a bright young man she met there. Victor and I had attended her wedding in 1972 after I had finished the population workshop at the University of Chicago that summer. The fairy tale-like ceremony was held at her grandparents' home, in the suburbs of New York. It was the first time I had attended such an unconventional wedding, held in a home. The clergyman held forth at the back of a manicured garden, and Kate recited a small poem she had written. Later, Kate and her husband went to work for The American School in Switzerland.

David Chaplin, whose babysitter I had been in London, was studying medicine, and experimenting with some of his inventions. Monique and John, the Chaplins' late bloomers, were much younger, my children's age. It was good to see them all playing with each other. It was also great for Alice, whose mother was French, to practice that language with me. She was also a former French teacher. Hugh was teaching at Washington University in St. Louis and doing research. He explained his latest discoveries to me, little of which I could understand.

It was around this time that I heard from Barbara Clary, who had been a secretary from 1966 to 1969 at the U.S. Agency for International Development (USAID) in Saigon. She worked then in the office of Bob Clary, a USAID public administration officer and her future husband. Both had worked closely with Bong and with the National Institute of Administration.

Unlike some Americans, Barbara liked socializing with Vietnamese, and she and I developed strong ties. We had many things in common. She came from a large family (nine children), enjoyed a prestigious education at an exclusive girls' school, and loved cultural and social activities. She remembered that when she left Saigon, we had said our farewells at a lovely restaurant where Bong and I hosted a dinner in her honor with fifteen of her friends. We had *bo bay mon*, Vietnam's famous seven-course beef dish, and we ate and danced all evening. It was 1969, and Barbara was leaving for Dacca, Bangladesh, where she and Bob would be married.

Now, six years later, Barbara wrote to me, offering to let the children and me live in a house that she and Bob had bought recently in Old Town Alexandria, outside of Washington, D.C. She said she would give me her old Mustang to drive, and would help me find a job. She mentioned that Ambassador Ellsworth Bunker and many of my old friends from the embassy in Saigon would like to sponsor me too. I told her that I would like very much to be among friends, but I did not want to leave the McDonnells and the Chaplins. They had taken good care of the children and me, and their friends had showered us with clothes, toys, and other gifts.

When the McDonnell's returned from their trip, we went back to their house to stay. One night, Barbara called and talked to them. Sandy and Pris flew to Washington, and had lunch with the Clarys. They came back the same evening, and told me that, if I wanted to, I could move to Washington. They had looked at the house in Alexandria, seen the car, and had a long talk with the Clarys. They thought that I would be better off moving there. I had their blessing to go.

It was early September 1975. The McDonnells sent me and the children off in a private, six-seater plane that landed at Washington National Airport. The Clarys took us to what they called their "little townhouse." It was small and attractive, with two tiny bedrooms and a bath on the second floor, a living room downstairs, and a table for four in the kitchen. It was just perfect for the children and me. Years later, Barbara would write of the house, "Right away, God gave us a good use for it."

The Clarys were public servants of the kind the U.S. government is fortunate to have. When we took over the house in Alexandria, Bob was operations officer in USAID's Office of Foreign Disaster Assistance, where he worked from 1972 until his retirement in 1980. Barbara worked in administration in USAID's Division of Policy Development. When Bob retired, Barbara kept on working, taking executive assistant positions at American embassies in Egypt, Malawi, and South Africa. Bob played golf and did volunteer work. She retired in 1993, and they settled in Peoria, Illinois, where they set about redecorating their new home.

Friends of the Clarys' and mine came to help furnish and decorate my house while I helped paint the bathrooms and kitchen. I also cleaned the overgrown backyard. People brought enough furniture to fill the house from top to bottom. They even gave me chopsticks and *nuoc mam*, my beloved Vietnamese fish sauce. When the house was ready, the Clarys gave a housewarming party and invited our mutual friends to see the children and me again. Twenty-one years later, Barbara wrote, "I hope you never regretted leaving the McDonnells. We loved having you with us and having you share our lives with us, even today."

After I arrived in Washington, Ambassador Bunker invited me to visit him at the State Department. He asked whether I had bought any insurance for the car Barbara had given me. I had not. He wrote a check for me to buy insurance and gas; with it, I opened my first checking account.

I needed to get a driver's license. Barbara was very patient; she sat next to me while I learned the streets and street signs. When she told me to drive on to the Beltway, I panicked. Everything was so enormous in the United States: the people, the buildings, the supermarkets, the cars, the highways. Seeing four lanes on each side and cars speeding by on all sides made me dizzy. After a few minutes, I held my knees up, sweating, then came to a complete stop on the shoulder of the highway. I was shaking.

My mother had taught me how to drive when I was a teenager. In Vietnam, I had to get a special permit because I had passed my driving test under the legal minimum age. I had been driving for more than fifteen years—in France, England, and elsewhere in Europe. But I suddenly became so incompetent, so inadequate, so gauche that I could do nothing right. As a refugee starting from scratch in a new country, I felt uprooted and had lost my confidence. I chickened out every time I had to do something.

After another week of training, Barbara encouraged me to go to the Division of Motor Vehicles, the DMV, to get my driver's license. I passed the written test. When it came to the practice part, I was asked to drive with an officer sitting next to me. She told me to go two blocks. I did. She said, "Go right." I kept going right straight ahead. She said again, "Go right," so again I went right ahead of me. Then she told me to go back to the DMV. I parked and was so proud that I was about to get my license. It was not so bad, I thought.

Then the DMV lady came out and handed me a paper that told me to come back for another test. Had I failed? What did I do wrong? She said that I had not gone right as she had asked. Barbara was upset and told the lady that she should not have used slang when talking to a foreigner. She should have said, "turn right," not "go right." Two days later I went back, and this time I did "go right" and made it.

Ambassador Bunker and his wife, Ambassador Carol Laise, sometimes invited the children and me to their house for lunch on weekends. They also gave me a lacquer coffee table from Thanh Le, the best known lacquer store in Vietnam, and several Vietnamese watercolor paintings for me to keep as souvenirs of my country. Mrs. Bunker also offered me a job: to be company for her mother, who was in a senior citizens' home in Alexandria, not far from my house. Three evenings a week, I would go to Mrs. Laise, read and talk to her, and have dinner with her. It was my first paying job in America. Mrs. Bunker would visit her on weekends.

Mrs. Laise introduced me to some of her friends at the home. At dinnertime, dressed up as though they were going to an elegant restaurant, the ladies and the men, in their seventies, descended from their rooms to the big dining room. One or two of them always played the piano and sang, to the delight of their peers, and me. Inspired by the music, some of them danced, too.

Certain evenings, people from outside were invited to talk on a topic they had selected. Other times, the residents played cards, read books, or watched TV. There were also trips, both short and long. Doctors and nurses were available around the clock. I was amazed at how well senior citizens' homes were organized in the United States. They were not the depressing places I had imagined.

In Vietnam, the eldest son in the family took care of the parents in their later years; this was our social security system. The parents came to live with their son and his family, and they, in turn, acted as babysitters for their grandchildren and guarded the house. Those who, for some reason, were not lucky enough to live with the eldest son or daughter, had to go live with relatives. If they were really unfortunate, they turned up at the home of friends, but rarely were left to the streets. Senior citizens' homes did not really exist in Asia, so having as many children as you could brought security as well as prosperity.

In the home where Mrs. Laise lived, I had become the pet. The senior citizens competed at inviting Mrs. Laise and me to sit at their tables. Seeing me, they would reminisce and tell us of their trips to the exotic Far East.

In the meantime, the McDonnells, the Chaplins, and other friends had set up a fund in my name to help me and the children with our basic expenses for the first six months, or until I found a job. The Clarys helped me to look for work. We asked friends, sent out resumes, scoured bulletin boards, and looked at ads in the *Washington Post*. I went to a few interviews, and was usually told that I was either overqualified or underqualified. I did not know how to type and had no previous experience working in the United States.

I needed a chance to get a start so I could acquire some work experience. If employers only looked for experienced staff, how would I ever get a job? It was a chicken-and-egg puzzle for me, looking for a job in the land of plenty. I heard that the two secretaries who had worked for me at the VAA had already found secretarial jobs. I was trailing behind.

The Clarys thought I should learn to type. I took a typing course and flunked the exam by only typing twenty five words a minute. I retook it, and flunked again, with thirty five words per minute (even today I have made no further progress in typing). I must be very dumb, I told myself, not suited for anything. What would I do in my new life? I felt embarrassed at being so unfit.

The man who dropped his heavy suitcase on my poor feet as we departed Saigon on the C-130 might have been right. After many job interviews, the only thing left for me to do was laundry. I had none of the skills or experience that the U.S. job market required.

I could not cook, either. I had never gone inside a kitchen to make anything serious. In Vietnam, we had always had cooks. One day, Alex's English teacher asked to see me. She wondered whether Alex had been telling her stories. She could not believe that an Asian mother, and a refugee, did not know how to cook. Alex had told her that he often ate sandwiches because his mother burned nearly everything she touched, even the rice.

Embarrassed, I confessed that I burned a lot of the Vietnamese meals I tried to prepare. I said it was partly the fault of the electric oven, which I did not know how to control: it was either not hot enough at the beginning, or too hot afterwards. She sent me some Oriental recipes, but I felt so incompetent and helpless. The prospect of opening a Vietnamese restaurant was now gone, too.

My identity was printed on two small pieces of paper: my social security card and an I-94 form from the Immigration and Naturalization Service. The I-94 listed my status as a "parollee." I got out the dictionary and found to my great consternation and anxiety that I was a "person who has been released from prison on parole." I looked up the word "parole" and read: "the release of a prisoner whose sentence has not yet expired, on condition of future good behavior; the sentence is not set aside and the individual remains under the supervision of a parole board."

My heart nearly jumped out of my chest. My god! Was I a criminal under supervision? I thought that, having been freed from the Communists, I had found freedom in a democratic country. I did not know that I was under strict scrutiny. I could not sleep that night. My life was shaken from top to bottom. Chairman of the board and director of a prestigious center one day, then a refugee, later a domestic in Guam, and now a prisoner under close examination. I had worn many hats on my head in the space of three months. The Vietnamese saying, "len voi xuong cho" was right: "riding on top of an elephant, then trailing on the ground like a dog."

The next day, I asked the Clarys about my status. They tried to calm me down, saying that the immigration office used the word "parole" to legalize the refugees' presence in the United States, and I should not worry about it. I would become a permanent resident in two years, then a citizen in five. But that meant that, for two years, I had to wear that shameful sign on my forehead. I felt like disappearing into a tunnel.

Another American couple had expressed their desire to sponsor me out of the refugee camp. Jim Keyes was with the embassy in Vietnam; his wife, Gerry, was a judge in Washington. They lived in the plush Watergate apartments and invited the children and me to stay with them a few times on weekends. Other friends were Wilson Hart, a USAID officer in Saigon, and his blonde wife, Frances, who was always perfectly coiffed. Wilson had also worked with Bong. They maintained strong relations with me and gave me a lot of encouragement during my adjustment and transition into my new life. They boosted my morale whenever I became depressed.

It was during that unemployed period that I started to develop fatigue and depression. I was affected by the traumatic moves from Saigon to the three camps, and from St. Louis to Washington, within a span of four months. Settled now in Alexandria, I spent my days cleaning, washing, cooking, and shopping. I finally received mail from Ho Chi Minh City, Saigon's new name. My number six brother, Trung, had been sent to a reeducation camp, and had not been heard of since. My Communist sister, Nam Ly, and her family were staying at my mother's house. My mother wrote that everything was rationed, and she had to sell things from her house to survive. My mother-in-law had gone back to Camau, at the southern tip of Vietnam, to live with the family of her eldest daughter. My own house had been confiscated by the Communists and used as one of their offices in the district. Everyone was having a hard time adjusting to the new regime.

After doing my chores around the house, I would read and reread my mother's letters, and spend hours crying. They were thousands of miles away, and I could not do anything for them. I was helpless and desperate, and I missed my family, my friends, and my country. I could not write to any of my relatives using an American address. My family might be arrested if the Communist police knew of that connection.

I started to have nightmares. Sometimes I saw myself bound and gagged by the Viet Cong. Wearing painted African masks, they surrounded me and pushed me into a bonfire. Other times, I was caught in a big bomb explosion. I also saw myself running in the jungle like a fugitive, hunted by a helicopter while American troops set off firecrackers above my head and laughed at my fear. As though I had been contaminated by secondary smoke or inhaling lethal chemicals, I developed a postwar syndrome. I was supersensitive, gifted with a sixth sense that picked up all the wrong signals.

At night, I dreamed of my brother, Trung, and thousands of my friends wailing behind barbed wire and prison bars or chained in small, solitary metal boxes. I also dreamed of my mother and other relatives selling their household items on the street, begging, or lining up under the sun to buy a kilo of rationed rice.

Ambassador Samuel Berger, former deputy to Ambassador Bunker, and his wife, Betty Lee, advised me to volunteer at the Indochinese Reception Center in Washington, an information and referral office. Volunteers gave out information to refugees from Vietnam, Laos, and Cambodia, and they tried to match up refugees with different jobs available in the area.

I had been volunteering there for two weeks when an American lady called and asked whether I knew of any Vietnamese who spoke English and would like to work for a vocational school. I said I would like to try that job but, unfortunately, I could not type properly. She said she did not need a typist, but someone who could interview refugee applicants, and place them in the right courses—keypunch, secretarial, accounting, or TV and radio repair. The position was at the Lacaze-Gardner School in Washington.

The lady interviewed me and offered me the job. The salary was about eight hundred dollars a month with benefits, adequate for an inexperienced parolee, and I gladly started work the following day. I learned how to fill out the forms to get the refugees federal grants to study at the school. For any course that cost more than the basic grant, the student would have to pay the balance in five years at a low interest rate of five percent, but only after the school had found him or her a job. It sounded very good to me. I would be able to help my fellow refugees. I wished I had known that such a program existed; I could have prepared myself better to look for a job.

I started advertising in the Vietnamese churches, shops, and local papers. Word spread, and the Vietnamese filled up one, two, then three classes. They studied in the upstairs classrooms with the other students, mostly Hispanics and blacks. A group of former students from Bong's National Institute of Administration registered to study business accounting. Most Vietnamese women and young girls studied keypunch. A Vietnamese engineer was hired to teach radio and TV courses in both languages.

After a month, I felt at ease working at the school. I was glad to be helping my compatriots, who would become self-sufficient after they graduated—within six months or a year at the latest.

One day, a secretary in a primary school in Alexandria called me looking for the father of a girl who had been injured at school. The girl was named Anh Thi, and the father's name was Van Nguyen. The girl had been hit by a ball and was bleeding; she needed a parent to sign a document to allow the school to take her to the hospital. It was an emergency.

I ran upstairs to the classrooms where the Vietnamese were studying. None of them had a daughter by that name. So I called the school and asked whether they had gotten the right location and name, I could not find anyone whose father and daughter had the names they had given me. Ten minutes later, the school called me back and said that it was the girl's mother, not the father who was at the Lacaze-Gardner School. I asked the caller to spell the mother's name. It was me.

I rushed out of the building and drove as fast as I could. If I had been stopped by the police I would have become a real prisoner, but I did not care. When I reached the school, my poor daughter, Annie, was still lying on the ground in the courtyard, her nose bleeding. The nurse and I rushed her to the hospital. It was nothing serious, thank God, but it scared me to death. I later changed all our names legally to Jackie Bong, Annie Bong, Victor Bong, and Alex Bong. It would be easier to identify us that way.

When it comes to study, or to work, Vietnamese are very serious and industrious. Most, then all, the students graduated and got jobs. I still see some of them. Mr. Thang Tran has been working for the past twenty years as a CPA for the courthouse in Arlington, Virginia. Mr. Emerson Le opened his own accounting firm in the area, and has been doing accounting and taxes for various businesses ever since. Ms. Nguyet Anh, who worked as a keypunch operator after graduation, now publishes her own Vietnamese newspaper. These are but a few of the success stories.

It was around the end of September 1975, after I moved from St. Louis to Washington, D.C., that Joe and Nancy Bennett invited me to dinner at their temporary quarters, Michele Towers, across from the State Department. I was to call Joe from the phone booth in front of the drugstore next door, and he would open the security door and let me in. As I finished my call, I saw Lacy Wright, a young foreign service officer who lived in the next building, going into the drugstore. I had met Lacy a few times in Saigon when he attended lectures I had organized at the VAA. He worked as a political officer at the U.S. embassy in Saigon, then in Can Tho, the second-largest city in Vietnam. We shook hands and exchanged phone numbers. I apologized and said I had to run to the Bennetts' for dinner.

Lacy called me a month later and invited me to dinner. He had completed an economics training course at the Foreign Service Institute, and was about to go to Milan, Italy, he explained. We went to a French restaurant in Georgetown and had a good time exchanging stories about Vietnam. To return his gesture, I invited him to our house for dinner. Still unable to cook well, I watched as he tried to swallow the hard meat that I had overdone. The following weekend, he invited the children and me to go to the zoo. Alex, my youngest, was so happy to ride on Lacy's shoulders and watch the animals. We really had a good time eating hamburgers and ice cream and sitting on benches talking.

We felt attached to each other and wanted to see more of each other. Lacy initiated us to bowling, and we went together to children's movies. Each time he came over, Lacy would spend some time teaching the children English. He had become a dear friend who really cared about me and the children. He brought warmth to our cold house that winter.

He was a fine man, the kind of man I had dreamed of. His eyes were strikingly tender and kind.

Lacy was in Washington only temporarily before being assigned to another country, so he had not bought a car, but was using a motorcycle he had brought back from London, his second post after Saigon. So we went around in my old Mustang, with one or the other of us driving. We became more and more in love with each other.

Two weeks before Lacy went to Milan, he invited me to dinner and said, "If I asked to marry you, would you accept?" He was afraid that a direct question would elicit a direct negative answer.

"I love you very much, but you should have more time to think carefully," I said.

"Why?" Lacy asked.

"I have had so many problems in my own life, and three young children would be a big burden, especially for a man who has never been married before."

Lacy said calmly, "I have thought about that."

"You call me in a few days after you have thought it through," I replied. Very early the next morning, Lacy called and confirmed again his desire to marry me.

I told him that I would like to ask the children's opinion before giving him an answer. That night, at dinnertime, I asked whether the children would like to have Lacy as a father. They all jumped with joy. I said that it meant that we would move to Italy in the summer, and live there for the next two years. The two boys did not see any problem and applauded with delight, but Annie did not want to move again. We had just moved from Saigon to St. Louis, then to Washington, D.C. She did not want to lose more friends than she already had, and did not want to change to another school. She had started to feel comfortable with the school she was in, and was attached to a friend who sat next to her. But she agreed that I should marry Lacy.

I told Lacy about the children's reactions, and said I would be happy to marry him. But Lacy had to endure another test: I had to consult an astrologer before I could give him a final answer. At the Lacaze-Gardner

School, I had come to know Nguyet Anh, whose father, Colonel Y, was a well-known astrologer in Vietnam. After President Diem's coup, Colonel Y, who used to work for the police, had been imprisoned.

Colonel Y had spent his time in jail reading and studying astrology. He had predicted the date of his release from prison, and it happened the month he said it would. He had also foretold the future for some of his inmate friends, and they spread the word to others about his ability. Once his reputation was established, he spent most of his time telling people's futures.

Nguyet Anh's eldest sister, An, had learned astrology from her father and knew how to read horoscopes, as well. So I asked An to interpret my future, with the help of her father. I gave her the hour, day, and year of my birth, and that of Lacy. Not mentioning marriage, I asked whether we would prosper if we joined in a business venture.

An came back to me after three days with charts of the zodiac drawn on a piece of paper and interpreted the two horoscopes. I wrote down what she said about Lacy's past, his parents, his family, his career, and his immediate future and mine. She concluded, "If you wanted to do business with that man, there would be no problem, but if you wanted to marry him, it would be much better. Both of you would prosper in the area of diplomacy and foreign relations. The more you traveled, the better it would be. He would do well, and you would be the bright star that would shine on him. Say yes if he proposes to you."

How did she know? Neither she nor her father had ever seen me with Lacy. We were in different circles, with different friends. I did not tell them that Lacy was an American, either, yet An said that he came from a different race, that he was not Vietnamese. No Vietnamese knew I was dating Lacy or had seen us going out together.

When I read to Lacy what she had said about his past and his family, Lacy had no explanation. How could it be? An's family had just resettled in Springfield, Virginia, while Lacy's family had lived for decades in Springfield, Illinois. And yet, she knew that Lacy's mother had died, and that his father had remarried and had a second set of children. She even predicted that Lacy would travel soon, and work somewhere in Europe.

She added, "Your star showed a new passage into a new family life. It was his destiny to carry you and your children on his wings. If he is willing to do it, why should you worry?" After thinking for a few days about my future, I gave Lacy a firm yes.

Lacy took me to Springfield, Illinois, the home of Abraham Lincoln, to introduce me to his family. I told Lacy that I wanted to visit his mother's tomb. It was a very cold winter, and a thick, white blanket of snow covered the cemetery.

Lacy drove me to his mother's burial area, but the snow was falling so hard we could not find the grave. After fifteen minutes, Lacy started to give up. He headed toward the car, saying we would visit again the following year. Lacy was pulling on my hand, but I said I wanted his mother to bless our union, and that I wanted to pray in front of her tomb. I would not leave the cemetery until I found his mother.

I was determined. I crept back up and looked around for another five minutes. "Please lead me to you, Mother. Let me meet you at least once before we get married. You should agree to your son's marriage to me," I repeated to myself. Something directed me to go farther to the right. I looked up and saw her name, Florence Wright. "Lacy, I found your mother; she was right here." Lacy ran up, and, holding hands, we asked her to unite us and bless us.

Lacy's father gave a big party and invited his relatives and friends to come and meet me. Lacy's three small half-brothers and two small nieces followed me wherever I went. They were in awe of my Oriental face and asked me why my eyes were so small and slanted. Could I see as well as everybody else? Why did my eyes close as if I were sleeping when I laughed? Would I grow taller than five feet? They were competing to hold my hands, and nearly broke my fingers. When I sat, they held onto my knees and legs, and stared at me as if I had come from another planet.

Lacy was the eldest of five brothers and three half-brothers. When all eight met, I heard nothing but laughing and jokes all day long. They all had a good sense of humor, particularly Lacy's fourth brother, Dennis, a medical student. For me, Dennis was a replica of Steve Martin. He and his wife, Cindy, a nurse, now live in Joliet, Illinois, with their two girls.

Bo, the second brother, whose real name is George, was teaching chemistry at the University of Massachusetts. He showed me an article he had written but it was like Greek to me; I could not understand the formulas and signs. Lacy could not decipher them either. George and his wife, Donna, a former nurse turned artist, had three children. Michael, Lacy's third brother and the father of lovely identical twin girls, was a computer analyst for the state of Illinois. John, the youngest, was working at the Park Service in Springfield. He was still living with his father and Clara, his stepmother. The three younger half-brothers were Tom, Brian, and Paul. At five, Paul looked very much like a picture of Lacy when he was that age in the family album. Both had the same handsome, smiling face.

Lacy's father took me to visit one of his old friends, Virgil, now an invalid and confined to his armchair. He introduced me as his son's fiancée. Virgil paid me no attention, but talked instead to Lacy senior. Finally, he turned to me and asked, "And you, my dear, are you a Springfield girl?" I said no, that I was from Vietnam. At that, he again lost interest, and continued reminiscing with Lacy senior.

Back in Washington, Lacy wanted us to announce our engagement: he did not want to lose me to anyone else. A hundred of our friends attended our engagement reception at the Foreign Service Club, just down the street from Michele Towers, where we had met. This was before Lacy left for Milan to work as number two officer at the Consulate General.

Ambassador Bunker invited us to dinner the day after our engagement party. He asked me whether he could give me away at my wedding, and play the role of my father. I was very honored and touched by his gesture. Like an orphan, I had no father or mother to witness my marriage in the United States.

We were planning to hold our wedding in the summer at Holy Trinity Church, in Georgetown, for which Lacy would return from Milan. Right after the ceremony, we would have a buffet-reception in the Hall of Nations auditorium at Georgetown University, a block from the church. Lacy had already decided to adopt the children.

In January, Lacy left for his new post, and I stayed on working until the summer, when the children would finish school. But piles of red tape awaited us.

An Immigration and Naturalization (INS) officer told me that if I got married abroad, I could get my permanent residency as soon as I returned to the United States. I would hand over all my documents to an INS officer at the airport, and have my status changed quickly. If I didn't do that, the process would take a long time. And because I was accompanying my husband abroad to serve his government, I could expedite the process and become a citizen within a year instead of the usual three.

So, to speed up my citizenship process, Lacy applied for us to get married in Milan in April. Tom Fina, the consul general, and his charming wife Eleanor, gave a big wedding reception for us at their apartment. After spending a two-week honeymoon with Lacy touring towns in the north of Italy, I had to go back to the Washington, D.C. area to my work and my children. Lacy would return in June for our real wedding, the one we had planned from the start at Holy Trinity Church in Georgetown.

Lacy had studied to be a Catholic priest—first in Springfield, Illinois, then in Chicago, and finally in Rome. There he studied theology at the Gregorian University from 1962 to 1964. He knew Latin because the Gregorian still taught most of its classes in that language, and he also spoke Italian. His aunt, Kitty, his mother's older sister, told me that he had been a "brilliant" student in Springfield (a fond aunt's exaggeration, according to Lacy). He studied with Catholic nuns and priests and was an altar boy on Sundays. Then, after high school, he entered the seminary. He stayed for more than six years, but decided to quit in 1965, a year before he would have been ordained.

After Rome, Lacy taught high school in Chicago for a year (Latin, world history, English), then went to study international relations at the University of Chicago. He met people there who would become his lifelong friends. One was Malcolm Dean, who became an editorial writer for the *Guardian* in London. Another was Antonio Martino, who became a well-known economics professor in Rome and, later, Italian foreign minister. In 1966 Lacy took the Foreign Service exam and passed it. Like most of the other foreign service officers in his class, he was assigned to Vietnam. In 1973, after a short tour in London, he went back to Vietnam a second time.

Lacy met me the first time in 1974 in Saigon when he came to the Vietnamese American Association to attend a lecture I organized. We met a couple of more times at the VAA, but we only shook hands and said a few sentences. I did not know Lacy well in Saigon.

Although I did not want to believe it, Tuyet, who read my fortune in Camp Pendleton, was right. She said that I would marry a handsome young man. Lacy was five months older than I was. He had the most pleasant and positive disposition. A head taller than I, slim and elegant, he was smart and well dressed. I felt very lucky and proud to have him as a husband and a partner. He was also a loved and respected father and friend to my children.

To prepare for the wedding, I went first to a Vietnamese priest in Virginia and asked whether he would officiate. The answer was that the children and I had to convert to Catholicism. I wanted to remain a Buddhist, so I went to another Vietnamese priest, in Washington. The requirement was the same, and my reply was the same. A friend told me that Holy Trinity Church in Georgetown was more lenient and would not force me to change my religion. It was true, so I made arrangements to hold our wedding there.

Lacy came back in mid-June to get married a second time in a church ceremony. We went to meet the priest who would marry us, and he wanted Lacy and me to come to a few sessions of marriage counseling. We did it dutifully. The priest said he wanted Lacy to raise the children as Catholics, but Lacy said that it was up to the children to decide whether they believed in the church; he could not promise to do so.

Lacy and the priest were arguing, and I was afraid that the priest would throw us out of his office. We had already sent out two hundred invitations. Would our wedding ceremony be ruined by a religious dispute? I could not imagine what other obstacles we would have to overcome to finalize our union. Fortunately, the priest was less dogmatic than he might have been, and we went on as planned.

The night before the wedding, Ambassador Bunker hosted the rehearsal dinner for everyone involved, including Lacy's family. Lacy had asked a priest from his class in Chicago, Father Bob McLaughlin, to perform the ceremony. The best man was Al Wilkins, another former classmate. On my side, I invited Sandy McDonnell, Gerry Keyes, and Barbara Clary to be in the wedding. The Chaplins were on a trip and could not attend.

Annie was the flower girl. She, Victor, and Alex led the procession. Annie told me afterward that her knees became two pieces of rubber as she walked down the aisle. Ambassador Bunker, in his early eighties, erect and distinguished, acted as my father and gave me away to Lacy. It was a moving and marvelous event—no turbulence this time around. I only wished that someone from my family could have attended. Lacy's Dad and his family were all there.

With the wedding over, the fairy tale phase had ended, and it was back to the real world. My next task was to get passports and visas for the children and me to go to Italy. My documents, which I had left as instructed with the INS at Dulles Airport had gone astray within the INS bureaucracy. No one could find them anywhere. I had gone to the INS office in downtown Washington many times, but each time, the answer was, "we will call you when it is ready."

Finally Lacy and I both went. Lacy asked to see an officer, to whom I told my story. The INS man explained that they were deluged with mail, and a lot had not even been opened. As a last resort, he asked if I wanted to go look in the mailroom with him. There, boxes and mounds of letters were strewn everywhere. He got down on his hands and knees and started sifting through manila envelopes. Miraculously, he found mine. The children and I could now travel to Italy with Lacy the following week—finally.

The shock of Bong's death and the trauma of fleeing Vietnam had been ticking inside me like a time bomb. I had been going on for so long trying to survive, to work, and to live like a normal person, I did not have the opportunity, nor did I take the time to share my worries and my fears with anyone. So I had no way to express my bereavement, my sufferings, my anxieties, or my deepest feelings. And now, I did not want to bother Lacy with these problems. I should have been bringing him happiness, not pain.

I felt guilty at living well, eating well, and dressing well in Milan while my family in Vietnam was in such a desperate situation. I felt that my hands were tied, my mouth taped shut, my brain clouded by morbid thoughts of a Communist hell.

One night, after getting up from a Valentine's Day dinner at a friend's house in Milan, I blacked out and fell over backward onto the marble floor. The next morning, I saw Lacy and the children looking at me with frightened eyes. Lacy explained that I had had what the doctors diagnosed as an epileptic seizure. I had fallen and hit my head against the corner of a door, and had gotten five stitches. After a week, a group of Italian doctors, after checking me from head to toe, released me from the hospital. They could not find anything abnormal in my body or brain. I concluded that it was me who was abnormal. The *yin* and *yang* inside me were unbalanced. I slipped further and further into my depressive state.

Lacy did not understand how I could be such a sweet and wonderful person one minute, and turn sullen and moody the next. I sometimes got upset or cried for no reason. I often blamed myself for the sudden switch inside me, and became more and more frustrated with myself. I was worn out and burned out.

People who had known Bong often spoke of him as a "living Buddha"—always wise, calm, balanced, and gentle to me and everyone else. But why should Lacy have to carry this cross on his shoulders like Christ? Who had "chosen" him to bear this burden? He could do it only if he were strengthened by an unlimited love for me and the children. There was no other way, I thought, for him to be able to put up with all the trouble I was causing him. At times, I asked Lacy to leave me to my misfortune. I wanted to release him from the burden I had become, but he would not give up on me.

Little by little I felt better, but the children had to make the change from one country to another in a short period of time. Their radical shifts made it hard for them to adjust, too.

After a year of depression in Milan, feeling helpless and hopeless, I started to drown in questions I could not answer. The more I tried, the less I could understand or accept. Why did Bong have to sacrifice his life? Why did my brothers have to die? Why did I have to suffer Bong's loss and the loss of my country? Why did Lacy and the children have to bear the cross of my depression? Why had my country been selected to be punished constantly by wars and calamities? Why did people kill each other? The more questions I asked, the more absurd the answers became. At night, I dreamed of being burned like a torch in the middle of a bonfire.

Like Don Quixote, the hero of the fifteenth-century satirical novel by Cervantes, I shielded myself inside a suit of armor and waved my sword in the wind, trying in vain to fight evil and rescue the oppressed. At once chivalrous and unrealistic, I thought that it was my responsibility to struggle against impossible odds. I did it so incessantly that I found myself distraught during parts of the day and self-destructive in my sleep at night.

In the time that remained, I was doing my regular duties as a wife, mother, foreign service officer's spouse, and citizen in good standing. Seeing me every day, no one would have suspected that my life was partitioned into such different layers of struggle, both imagined and real. At times, I withdrew completely into myself. Sometimes I sat on a chair and gazed straight ahead for hours, into a vacuum. That protected and pacified me but also divorced me emotionally and physically from the world outside.

My reentry to the United States was another hard experience because we started from scratch again. After two years in Milan, we went back to the Washington, D.C. area, and stayed there for the next seven years. Lacy, the children, and I needed to recover from our turbulent Vietnam experiences. The children needed to be rooted in the United States for a while. From 1975 to 1976, they had lived in three countries, trying to learn three different languages—English, Italian, and French—while keeping up their Vietnamese with me at home. They needed to find their own identity.

We settled in Falls Church, Virginia, near Seven Corners, a block away from Lake Barcroft. The children walked to a public school, J.E.B. Stuart, four blocks from our house. Victor and Annie were fourteen, and Alex, twelve. They needed to be "mainstreamed" and live like American kids. They also needed to learn to be strong and independent. I asked them to share in the household chores—cleaning, washing dishes, doing the laundry, and vacuuming.

Lacy and I also encouraged them to deliver the morning newspaper in our neighborhood. This, we told them, was not only to earn their own money, but to raise their self-esteem and self-confidence, as well. They, on the other hand, saw it as hard labor, especially during the winter. The big, thick Sunday *Washington Post* was delivered in front of our garage while it was still dark. At 5:30 A.M., I woke them up and helped them slide the ads and magazines into the bulky papers and put them in plastic bags.

Assembling the papers took all of us forty-five minutes to an hour before the children were able to set out in the heavy snow, with bags nearly as big and heavy as themselves on their shoulders. When I saw the three of them, their thin frames struggling and falling in the snow, my heart sank, and I blamed myself for forcing them into such hardship. My fingers wiped tears off my cheeks, and I wanted to call out to tell them to come back. They should have been sleeping in their warm beds. What was I doing to my children?

But they were now at an age when American kids were doing the same thing. Lacy had delivered papers when he was their age, too. As a teenager, their father, Bong, had done more onerous odd jobs to earn money to go to school. Work was not a shame, work was a virtue. In whatever job they did, they had to try their best. They had to earn respect by working with their own hands. It was for them, for their future, I explained to them.

After three months of delivering papers, the children were praised by their boss, who raised their commission for doing such a fine job. They also got congratulations from their customers, who were kind enough to tip them. But Annie could not forgive me for making her do such hard work. She said that the heavy weight of the newspapers shrank her body, and kept her from growing taller than five feet. She forgot that she had inherited the stature of her mother and her grandmother. Why, I asked her, did Victor, who worked harder and carried heavier papers, grow more than a head taller than she? And little Alex, too, had grown taller than Annie. But she was not convinced by my explanation.

Our neighbors liked Victor, and some asked him to mow their lawns on weekends. He earned good money, and became known around the neighborhood. Alex learned calligraphy on his own, and decorated the programs for school plays and concerts. He also wrote poems and composed musical pieces. His grades improved from Bs in the beginning to practically straight As. At graduation, he organized an international show that involved classmates of some twenty nationalities and in which he performed some of his own compositions.

Annie became more beautiful, more sociable, and more rebellious. As a teenager, she was at the age when kids went out with their friends. Victor and Alex were not much interested in partying, but Annie was often invited to parties and movies, with both Vietnamese and Americans. I followed some of my American friends' example and imposed a curfew of ten o'clock for Annie. She would come back an hour late, and complain that her friends stayed later at parties. So I extended the curfew to eleven, then midnight, and finally there was no more curfew. Maybe I was too hard on her with my backward rules and regulations. She did not understand why she was not free to do whatever she wanted, like American kids, including smoking and drinking.

My poor children must have felt disoriented trying to adjust amidst so much culture shock. I had to find my own identity, as well. I seemed to be constantly switching from past to present, or from the future to the past. I was neither Vietnamese nor American nor French nor international. I was like a bowl of bouillabaisse, all kinds of seafood mixed together. I was confused. Sometimes I found myself mixing up two or three languages at the same time, not completely at home in any of them. I had forgotten some of my French and Vietnamese, having not spoken either for a few years. But I had not mastered English, either. What was I actually? I was at a crossroads. I had to choose a direction to go.

Nineteen seventy-eight was the year that hundreds of thousands of "boat people" started to arrive in the United States. This new wave of refugees had bribed their way out of Vietnam, setting forth across dangerous seas in fragile boats. Most came from the fishing villages and the countryside, or from Cholon, Saigon's Chinatown. Many were teenagers or single adults, and many had health problems after having lived under the Communists in a country that was now more and more impoverished.

These refugees were totally different in composition from the first flow in 1975. The boat people had had to stay for months (and later for years) in refugee camps in places like Thailand, the Philippines, Malaysia, or Indonesia before being accepted into the United States. Most were less educated and less sophisticated than the early wave of refugees, and they were less equipped to cope with the Western style of living. They had suffered from fear, imprisonment, and lack of basic care. They had more physical and mental health problems than the Indochinese who had come in 1975. Looking for a way to help, I volunteered to interpret for them in their dealings with Americans.

Then, in 1979, the Department of Health and Human Services (HHS), aware of the refugees' urgent needs, funded a six-week intensive training course by an American psychologist, Dr. Karen Shanor, and a Vietnamese psychiatrist, Dr. Tran Minh Tung, for seven mental health paraprofessionals. I was one of them. When the course was over, I was sent to intern at the Northern Virginia Family Service, a counseling agency in Falls Church, Virginia.

It was not by chance that so many of the refugees came to this area. When Saigon fell, and a hundred thirty thousand Vietnamese fled the country and came to the United States, the State Department made a deliberate effort to place them in as many states as possible to spread the public-assistance burden widely. Even today, I imagine, there are Vietnamese in every state in the union. But America is not a police state, and people can live where they wish, so many of the Vietnamese did not stay where they were resettled, especially those who were sent to cold parts of the country. The largest number migrated to California, where the warm climate reminded them of Vietnam. The second-largest number congregated in Texas. A lot of them gravitated to the Washington, D.C. area, where many had friends in the military, State Department, or other parts of the government who were willing to help them start their new lives.

The second wave of refugees tended to go where they could be with other Vietnamese, and many came to the Washington area. A large number of them moved to the suburbs of Fairfax and Arlington counties in Virginia, districts where housing, services, and jobs were more available than in the capital itself.

My responsibility was to counsel these new refugees, and help resettle about a hundred of them over a period of six months.

I met some of them at the airport when they arrived, found housing for them, and acted as their interpreter as we went around to doctors, health departments, hospitals, schools, and social service agencies.

The main responsibility for getting the refugees resettled was in the hands of the voluntary agencies, mostly nationwide refugee resettlement organizations that were often religion-based. The government assumed responsibility for getting the refugees started, but contracted with the voluntary agencies to do the work. I worked with such agencies as Church World Service, the International Rescue Committee, Catholic Charities, Buddhist Social Services, the Czechoslovak Service, and the Hebrew Immigrant Aid Society, or HIAS. Some agencies had staff in the Washington area. Those that did not referred refugee cases to people like me.

Jobs were a big problem. I helped refugees do the paperwork at the Social Security office and other agencies so they could find work. Sometimes that meant getting vocational training so they could qualify for a job. The boat people had all kinds of health problems, too, mostly skin diseases and stomach trouble. A couple of tuberculosis cases were also detected.

I provided orientation and counseling for the refugees, and created a support group that met weekly at the Knox Presbyterian Church in Arlington, on Route 50 just outside Washington. The minister there let me use a room for our meetings and supplied the refugees with basic kinds of food. Other churches in the neighborhood gave used clothing, shoes, and household items.

Housing was very difficult. There were not enough apartments big enough to house people with four to six children. Such families were willing to live almost anywhere, but American regulations sometimes forbade it. Some boat people were evicted for a kind of overcrowding they could not understand. The rules said that two children of different sexes could not stay in one bedroom, or that eight people of whatever sex could not stay in a three-bedroom apartment, for instance. That put many large refugee families in a quandary, because they could not afford a place large enough to comply with the regulations.

Near the church was a complex of nearly a hundred low-rent town-houses—the perfect place for me to try to resettle the boat people, some of whom were already living there. Usually, my husband and I had to guarantee the rent. If for some reason a refugee family did not pay, we were liable. But almost all the refugees did keep up with their payments and were happy to be there. As the complex was near the Knox Church, the boat people called it Knox Village and mispronounced it as *noc*, which means "roof" in Vietnamese. After six months, over a hundred refugees lived in "Noc Village," and some Americans started calling it the boat people ghetto.

I became a familiar sight in the housing complex. On Sundays, I often enlisted the help of American friends, who came in vans to bring the refugees brooms, laundry baskets, bowls, chopsticks, towels, and other necessities. The refugees kidded me by calling me Ba Lang, Ba Xa, "Madame Village Chief," as I made my rounds.

Sometimes it was the boat people themselves who did the best job of helping one another. At one point I rented a house in Knox Village for a new family named Chin. The house was only two doors away from the house of another group of refugees, five young, single men who had gotten a reputation for being troublemakers. The term used then was "cowboys." The police told me that these boys were on welfare, did not go to work, and bothered Americans and other Vietnamese alike.

I went to see these young men and introduced the Chin family to them. Mr. Chin came from a fishing village in Vietnam, and he had a wife and four small children, all of them sick. I singled out the most softspoken of the five "cowboys," and asked him to call me if there was any emergency in Mr. Chin's family. A few days later, I asked the boys to take Mr. Chin across the street with them to the supermarket the next time they went so he could learn how to shop.

After three weeks, the "cowboys" announced to me they wanted to take over as the official sponsors of the Chin family so I could devote more time to other newly arrived boat people. They had risen to the occasion and were proud to have been given some responsibility.

The story has a sequel. In 1980, when my mother came to live with us in Falls Church, I took her to a Vietnamese restaurant one Sunday. A young man came to our table and asked permission to be seated. He took my mother's hand, kissed it, and wept like a baby. He said he badly missed his mother, whom he had not seen for years. It was then that he reminded me that he had been one of the five wild "cowboys" in "Noc Village." He was now working as a sanitation engineer in a hotel, which meant that he cleaned the floors. He had a second job, in a restaurant, where he was "general manager of bowls and plates," washing dishes. He told us that his roommates had moved to other states, and they were also working. After he left and I asked for the bill, the waiter said the young man had already paid it.

It is hard for outsiders to appreciate how new and different life in America was for the boat people. At one of the support group meetings at the church, three families told me that they had written to their families in Vietnam but had not heard anything back for months. They asked me to check with the post office to see whether their mail had been lost. I asked them how they had mailed their letters. They said they did exactly what I had told them to do: they had put the stamps on the right corner of the envelopes, and dropped them in the mailbox on the corner a block from the rental office. I went to look, and found that they had confused the mailbox with a trash can, which was neatly covered and nicely painted. They had carefully dropped their letters into the garbage. They could not believe that a trash can could be that neat and clean.

Another example: One evening, I got an urgent call to go to the house of Chi Tu, who would be delivering a baby at any minute. When I got to Knox Village, I saw three fire trucks with a dozen firemen, hoses in hand, running between the narrow rows of townhouses. Two firemen emerged with Chi Tu to carry her to the hospital.

I found Anh Tu, her husband, and asked what was happening. Had there been a fire or some other accident in their house? "No," he explained. When I had not arrived after fifteen minutes, he called the 911 number I had instructed him to use in case of crisis. It turned out that, although he did not know how to speak English, he was able to utter enough strange and alarming sounds to cause the fire department to send all three of its firetrucks to his rescue. Two police cars had arrived as well, but no ambulance, which is what was needed.

Sometime in 1979, Nuccio and Lili Abbondanza, friends from Milan, and two other Italian couples came to visit us. At dinner, we talked about "Noc Village," and they wanted to see it, especially since they had heard so much about the boat people, even in Italy.

We went the following day. The refugee who moved them most was a Chinese-born man in his mid-sixties. He had watched his wife and two of his children drown at sea when a storm began and a big wave swept away half of his family. Then, as they approached Thailand, they were assaulted by Thai pirates, who raped his teenage daughter and robbed everyone on board.

Now, the man lived with his two remaining boys, in their early twenties, and the girl. He was suffering from high blood pressure, while the girl was being treated for venereal disease and depression. I used to take them to the hospital regularly. During the conversation, in which I acted as interpreter, the father looked often at a table that served as an altar. On it lay a small, yellowish photo of his wife next to a bowl of rice, a cup of tea, two oranges, and some burned incense sticks. The girl looked at the floor, and did not say a word. She had not wanted to talk to anyone since they settled in their new place. It was a sobering day for my friends, and one of those times when there is nothing a person can say or do to lighten the tragedy that has befallen other human beings.

Other refugee stories were much happier. Next to Knox Village was a small shopping center with about a dozen shops. One Vietnamese family opened a small Asian grocery store there, and, after several years, other Vietnamese opened a restaurant, a tailor shop, a jewelry store, a travel agency, and a laundromat. So when I came back to the area in the summer of 1996, I was not surprised to see that most of the stores in that shopping center had signs in both English and Vietnamese.

Curious to see how things were going, I ducked inside a gift shop called "My Linh." The owner of the shop, a sturdy lady, recognized me and shouted my name. Happy to see me, she lifted me up in the air with her two strong hands. "Chi Bong, you are just as light and as frail as you used to be. I've thought about you a lot and always hoped to see you again some day. Do you remember me? Then she said that she and her husband, Anh Sau, and their four children had come to the United States as boat people in 1979. "You saved my family, especially my baby."

I told her honestly that I did not remember her, and asked her what had happened.

"Well, we had been sponsored by a relative who lived far from here. We were such a big family that he rented two separate apartments for us, but we could not stay like that forever. It was too expensive. We did not have enough money for our food, either. To make matters worse, I did not have enough milk to nurse my baby."

I agreed that that period was a hard time for a lot of refugees.

"But you came along and saved us. You and your husband helped us to rent a house in Knox Village, and that allowed us to be reunited under one roof. You brought milk for my baby and food and clothing and beds for my family. I still keep the two little chairs you gave me for the children. And I remember how your husband helped to carry those heavy beds and mattresses to our empty house. Now I want you to come and meet the 'baby' we were just talking about. We've bought a house near here, and she is there right now."

She then told me that her oldest daughter had gotten married, and had a jewelry shop. She showed me a photo of her two grandchildren that was sitting behind the counter. Another daughter, who was eight when I met the family, was also married, and she owned still another shop. Her husband helped her there. The other children were in college, doing fine. "It's amazing," I said, "how successful the children of the boat people have become." I said I was proud of them.

Chi Sau then took me to her house, not far from her shop. She asked whether I recognized the big girl of sixteen she called out to say hello to me. "This was your little baby," she said. Now a beautiful young lady, the daughter was doing well in her last year of high school, and was readying herself to go to college.

Chi Sau said that she and her husband had done all kinds of odd jobs when they first arrived in America. With tears in her eyes, she told me how hard it had been, not knowing English or having any real skills, to raise so many young children. Now, they owned a gift shop and a jewelry store. She oversaw the shop and worked as a dressmaker, while her husband repaired and sold jewelry.

Chi Sau kept asking me what she could do to show her gratitude to me. I said that I was going to Brasilia in a few days and was preparing my house to put in on the market for sale. She recommended a professional Vietnamese builder who could fix my kitchen and repaint the house. (In fact, I hired him, and he did a very nice job.) I said I had some furniture I wanted to give away to refugees, and other things, including books, I needed a place to store.

The next day, Chi Sau sent her brother with a van to come and pick up everything. She stored my books and a few other things at her house. I was very touched and could not help but think that our roles had been reversed. Returning to the United States after ten years abroad, it was I who was a stranger, as Chi Sau had been before. It was her turn to help me, and my turn to adjust to a new environment.

But back to 1979. After helping to resettle boat people during my six-month internship with the Family Services counseling agency, I was hired by the Fairfax Department of Social Services as a refugee case worker. My work became less hectic and more orderly. I collaborated with colleagues from Laos and Cambodia who did the same work for the refugees of their different countries. Afghan refugees started to pour in, too. The United Nations High Commissioner for Refugees (UNHCR) and the U.S. administration had their hands full.

The plight of the refugees seemed to reach its most acute point in the early 1980s. In 1980 a group of Indochinese refugees sponsored by churches in Alexandria asked for help. There were no refugee agencies there to provide services for them.

About that time, I went to a party where I met a retired naval captain who had served in Vietnam. He and his wife asked me whether they could do anything to help the boat people. I said that the most pressing problem was housing; big families could not find houses to rent, and I knew of many who had been evicted from their apartments. The couple said that they had just bought a house in Alexandria, and would let me rent it at half price. They would not set any restrictions as long as I managed it and kept it in order. It was a golden opportunity to take care of refugee families with emergency housing needs.

I asked some of my American friends—Ambassador Bunker, Ambassador Sam Berger, and others—whether they could do anything to help rent a house to serve as a temporary shelter for refugees who otherwise would fall between the cracks. Within days, they called together a group of their friends and formed a committee. Everyone chipped in a few hundred dollars, and it was decided that we would form a nonprofit organization so we could function within U.S. laws when handling money.

William Colby, who had just stepped down as director of the CIA, was introduced to me for the first time. Bill was a lawyer, and he helped us incorporate our organization as a nonprofit entity. We called ourselves the Indochinese Refugees Social Services (IRSS), Inc. It sounded like "IRS," but with an S added at the end. The difference was that we did not pay tax to the IRS, and whoever donated anything to us could deduct it from his or her taxes.

A twelve-person board of directors was established, composed of Vietnamese, Laotians, Cambodians, and Americans. We rented the naval captain's home and called our shelter the "Welcome House." I left the Fairfax Department of Social Services, where I had a secure job, and went as a volunteer to be coordinator of the IRSS. I moved a couple into the Welcome House, and asked them to help clean and paint the place. We spent a week on our knees scraping the floors, painting, and climbing ladders to clean the gutters. I had had some experience with all this in my first house in Alexandria, the one given to me so kindly by the Clarys.

I went to the neighbors, who were mostly blacks and Hispanics, and asked if they would object to refugees living near them. They said there was no problem, and that they would help, too. I went to two churches in the neighborhood and enlisted their support. The ministers raised funds and provided clothing and food for the refugees.

Typically, refugees would stay at the Welcome House for a few weeks until I found permanent housing and employment for them. In the meantime, I tried to show them how to live in the West.

They needed to learn not to squat on top of the toilet seat with their shoes on. They were not to take baths by scooping up the water with a plastic cup and pouring it over themselves while standing outside the bathtub. They should not roll up their sheets and mattresses every morning. They had to learn how to use the electric stove. They did not need to wash their clothes by hand, but could put them in the washer and dryer instead. It was not easy at first to remember all these details.

I used to take the refugees to the supermarket the first two times, and then they bought their groceries on their own. What thrilled them most was to see such a huge market under one roof, a vast place where you could buy whatever you wanted without having to bargain with anyone. During one of these trips to the supermarket, Vinh, a boy of ten who had come by himself from a fishing village, reminded me that I had promised to buy him a belt, and told me he had seen one. The pants the church had given him were too large at the waist. I told him that we should wait and go to the shop around the corner, but he insisted—he had found just the one he wanted. He led me to it and pointed. He wanted the red, not the green. We were in the pet section, and it was a dog's leash.

I explained to him and the others that, in the United States, dogs and cats were loved and cared for. They had their own special food, brushes, serving bowls, medicine, doctors, and even leashes and necklaces. "Good Lord, is it true?" they exclaimed. Vinh said sadly, "I wish my three brothers and sisters back home could become pets in some rich American family."

After two weeks of "Americanization" drills, I told Chi Mui, a twenty-five-year-old woman from the countryside, to go and buy a few things at the Giant supermarket. She came back with two brown bags of groceries, but said she couldn't find milk anywhere. She said she asked a man for *sua*, the Vietnamese word for milk. "That strange man," she said, "insisted that I buy a bag of *sugar*. I shook my head and put it back. But he said that it was really what I wanted, and he took it himself, bought it, and gave it to me." We all enjoyed the caramel I showed her how to make for dessert.

Once I drove a refugee family to the health center, and stopped by a drive-in bank to get some money. Sitting in my car, I wrote a check, put it in a box, pushed a button and sent it to the teller behind a glass window, ten yards away. A few minutes later, the teller sent the box back to me, asked me to count the money, and said thank you and good-bye through the microphone. I counted my money, thanked him, and drove away.

The whole process was such a spectacle that the couple and their three young children looked at each other and at me in bewilderment. The father said, "How did he do it? He said a few magic words, and the tube flew back to you filled with money. It was so wonderful. Do you think he would do the same trick for me?"

After two weeks at the Welcome House, Chi Mui started having nightmares, and cried at night. In her dreams, people were strangling her. She finally confessed to me that she had been raped many times by pirates in Thailand. I took her to the doctor so she could be treated for venereal disease. The following weekend, so she could have a change, I let her stay at my house. She told me the next morning that my house did not have ghosts like the Welcome House. She could sleep straight through without nightmares. I explained to her that she felt more secure being away from the other refugees.

That Sunday, I asked Phung Sherper, a friend and neighbor, to take Chi Mui to the Buddhist temple. When Chi Mui returned, she told me that Phung had told her that my late husband Bong was an actor in Vietnam. Now she understood why I painted my face so beautifully, and she asked me to show her how to use cosmetics. Bewildered, I called Phung for an explanation. She said that she had asked Chi Mui whether any of the refugees I had been helping knew who I was. Mui said that they all called me Sister Bong, that was all they knew.

Phung said she explained to Chi Mui that Bong had been well-known in Vietnam. She said he had had a high position, and mentioned that senators (*nghi si*) had been elected from Bong's political party. Chi Mui instead heard *nghe si*, which means "actor." She concluded that both Bong and I were actors in Vietnam. Phung and I had a good laugh.

I tried to find employment for the men. With no knowledge of English, it was not easy for them to work. What was available were cleaning, gardening, and painting jobs, and menial work in stores and churches. The government, however, started giving incentives to certain factories to hire refugees. There were a string of them along Route 1 in Alexandria, and I began to go to them, talk to the managers, and leave my name. A metal factory called me, and I placed one, then two, then five refugees there. The factory manager was satisfied with the refugees' industriousness. Word spread.

In the same industrial complex, a poultry plant needed people to cut the chickens into pieces with a special knife and separate the flesh from the bones to sell to supermarkets. The workers had to be covered from head to toe, like astronauts. I sent them five, then ten, then twenty-five Vietnamese, Cambodians, Laotians, and Hmong (Laotian mountain people). They had to work standing in meat-locker conditions every day for eight hours. I asked the manager to let them listen to their own music, which they brought on cassette tapes. After a month, I negotiated with him for benefits for them. The refugees did such an excellent job that another poultry plant, in a neighboring county in Maryland, called and asked me for Indochinese workers.

Those refugees who still had no job were sent to learn English and a skill at Job Corps, a training center for unemployed adolescents and adults. Old people and homebound mothers with young children received welfare benefits, as did the other jobless until they found work.

I also went to the Alexandria office of the Virginia State Employment Service and asked the director to help the refugees. He called me back one day to tell me about jobs available at a newly opened Hyatt hotel in Crystal City, near National Airport. He said Indochinese could apply, and asked if I would interpret. The hotel needed about a hundred people, and interviewed applicants in a big hall for a whole week. Hundreds of people lined up to apply for the jobs. I helped the refugees fill out their application forms and be interviewed. The hotel selected quite a few of them, which pleased me a great deal.

One Sunday, an American lady called me at my home, hysterical. I had sent her a refugee to do yard work that morning. She said she asked him to mow the grass, but instead he took the hoe and dug chunks of grass out of her lawn. He even dug up some of her flower beds, too. "What can you do?" she asked me. I apologized and said I should have given him more training. "And what," she said bitterly, "should I do now?"

"You can fire him right away," I sighed. When cultural differences and the inability to communicate produce a situation that has gotten out of hand, sometimes there is nothing to do but retreat.

The problems with the thousands of boat people were so acute that the government developed more federal and state projects to cope with the flow. The Department of Health and Human Services provided grants to private organizations to help out with education, employment, and medical and other services. Some of our IRSS board members, like Myrna Pike and Shirley Feary, helped me to write proposals for the HHS. Other board members—Mrs. Creighton Abrams, Mrs. John McCain, Mrs. Hillman Dickinson, Mrs. Barbara Colby, Ambassador Charles Whitehouse, and Robert and Catherine Lincoln—supported my work by bringing the refugees furniture and other household items.

One Saturday morning, Mrs. Abrams, who was IRSS treasurer, drove me to a bank to sign some documents. She used to make sure that every check was in order and that our tax forms were filed on time so our tax-exempt status would not be jeopardized. Suddenly I saw something and asked her to stop. In front of a house, there were two good mattresses about to be discarded. I said that a family I was going to move to an apartment needed mattresses urgently. We talked to the owners of the house, who said the mattresses were there to be picked up and taken away as trash, so Mrs. Abrams and I put them on the back of her car and delivered them to the family. I often called on the Salvation Army, too, to get things the refugees needed.

Mona Ruoff, another member of our board, wrote a fable on the Legend of the Dragon, with drawings by her daughter, to help raise funds for the IRSS. A hardy group of Indochinese and other Asians helped by coming to our numerous meetings and contributing ideas, food, clothing, and funds to the Welcome House. To celebrate the first year of our existence, General John Vessey, later chairman of the Joint Chiefs of Staff, honored my board and me at his residence with a big reception. Finally, my Asian board members were a huge help. Proum Im from Cambodia, Mrs. Boumsoum Sanamikone and Somchanh Vinaya from Laos, Father Pham Quang Thuy from Vietnam, Helen Heyes, and Dr. Victor Yu from the Chinese community came to my monthly meetings to offer ideas, bring food and clothing, and raise funds for the Welcome House and our many projects.

In 1981, after that first year of hard work, the IRSS was awarded three grants. We received two in Alexandria for social services and vocational training, and one in Fairfax County for bilingual tutoring and basic English. I thus became a paid executive director for the three projects, each of which had a coordinator in charge.

In Alexandria, we rented three rooms on the second floor of a small office building, and we were in business. We hired a coordinator to supervise the staff of Vietnamese, Cambodian, Laotian, and Afghan workers. Someone generously gave us an old station wagon to drive refugee families to health clinics and other places. Not far from our office, we found another apartment complex where we began moving refugees when they left the Welcome House, making it another "refugee ghetto."

Our vocational section trained refugees in professional cleaning, gardening, and house painting, the jobs that people requested the most. Ly Tri, a former USAID interpreter in Vietnam, headed the training section. He showed the refugees the right tools to use and the proper way to conduct themselves in American residences. We supplied what people demanded. The more highly qualified refugees I sent to do more professional vocational training with other centers. Some Afghan refugees wanted to be taxi drivers. We showed them how to get their driver's licenses, where to rent cabs, and how to read city maps.

Two Afghans in particular worked with me closely to help resettle their own refugees. They had been well-educated professional people in their own country. I told them that, like all of us mortals, they would have to go through purgatory before they reached heaven. One distinguished Afghan man in his late fifties—I do not remember his name—who had been head of a big company, became a taxi driver. For his wife, a beautiful lady with manicured fingernails, I found a job cleaning houses, after she had been trained at our center. Having never worked in her life, with little English and no skills, she did not know what else to do. After three months of cleaning houses seven days a week, she was so exhausted that she became sick. She showed me her dirty fingers and blistered hands. Her husband came to me red-eyed and talked about her poor health, but he never complained about their work. They refused to be on welfare. He said that when things got better, he and his compatriots would go back to join the *mujahedeen* to fight against the Russian aggressors who had invaded their country.

Six months later, one of the man's Afghan friends told me that he had died the night before of a heart attack. After dinner, he had felt a strong pain in his chest, and was rushed to the hospital. He died quietly, not uttering a word. There was no way to console his poor wife. I could only tell her that her husband had finally found peace in heaven.

For the third project, in Fairfax County, the Whittier Intermediate School kindly gave us free office space. We hired Vietnamese, Cambodian, and Laotian teachers to tutor the refugee children after their regular school hours, at 2:30 P.M. They were taught English, math, science, and social studies, both in English and in their own language, in six selected schools. This was only for a transitional period until they had mastered English and were moved to regular classes.

Councilman Tom Davis, now a congressman in the 11th district in Virginia, also helped. He generously allowed us free use of his office copying machines for our courses, provided we brought our own paper. He encouraged me, too, to participate in school board meetings and other public gatherings that had to do with refugees. It turned out that there was a great demand among public officials and other administrators for information on how to deal with the refugees. I was often asked to give talks to them and to health organizations and mental health centers.

Most refugee children did well in school. Their parents encouraged them to study, and study all the time. It was in their blood and souls. Most Asian children did so well, in fact, that after a few years in the United States, many had become the best students in their class, their school, and their state.

For their parents, the IRSS organized basic English-language skill training and survival English, taught day and night in the neighborhoods where there were the greatest concentrations of refugees. We borrowed rooms in churches and schools for the night classes. We also took the refugees on field trips to the store, the bank, the post office, the supermarket, and the laundromat.

My mother was one of the students. She knew absolutely no English when she came in 1980 to live with us in Falls Church. Alone at home during the day, she was alarmed when the phone rang. She said that she did not dare answer. So I tried to teach her to pick up the phone, say "hello," and then, no matter what the other person said, say "Call the office," so that the caller would phone me or Lacy at work. She learned the phrase by heart, repeated it like a parrot to anyone who called, and immediately hung up the phone. She was always afraid that the other person would continue to talk, and she would not be able to reply.

One day, she told us all at dinner how the mailman had come to the door and asked her to sign a registered letter. She smiled with satisfaction as she related that, after she signed, she said to the man, "Call the office," and he had responded, "Thank you very much." She was so proud to have talked to someone who, she thought, understood her and answered her. She asked whether he had called me at my office.

Some of the old refugees told me that English came in one ear and left immediately through the other. They tried to retain some of the words they learned, but it was not easy. It was good nonetheless that they made the effort to go to class and meet other people; it made them feel less isolated and less fearful. Being a former teacher and having learned French, my mother was eager to study English and did well.

The drastic adjustments the refugees made to their new environment brought positive and negative results. The first wave of refugees—those who came in 1975—were working and paying taxes by the early 1980s. Their children spoke English and led normal lives. When I called my friends and asked the children in Vietnamese for their parents, almost all of them answered me in English.

I did not want my own children to forget their Vietnamese, so that is what we always spoke. One evening, a boy named Greg called, speaking English, and asked for Annie, who was not at home. I insisted on speaking Vietnamese to the boy, explaining that Annie was doing her homework at a friend's and would be home in two hours. Later, I relayed the message to Annie and told her that she should remind Greg to speak Vietnamese to me next time he called; I would refuse to speak English to him. Annie said that Greg was a classmate at school and an American. I was so embarrassed. Greg probably thought that Annie's mother was a boat person from the countryside who was unable to speak proper English.

It was not only the children of the first wave of refugees who learned English quickly, but the children of the boat people, too. In a household, they were the first to answer the phone, and they acted as interpreters for their parents in anything that had to do with English in their everyday lives. For their part, the parents often complained to me that, although they were happy that their children were doing well in school, the children had become the bosses. Parents were so dependent on their children that they felt they had lost control. They were no longer the heads of the household. Children talked back to their parents and showed them little respect.

Parents felt a strong rift between themselves and their Americanized children. They did not understand that it was natural for their children to ask questions, to doubt values, and to regard conventional traditions as backward. The children confronted their parents and grandparents. They felt they were free to do whatever they wanted in their new, democratic country. Clashes occurred. Asian parents could not agree with the American concept that freedom of expression started at a very early age, at school and at home.

I tried to explain to refugee parents that it was the American tradition to educate children to be independent and free. But the change was too radical; the older people could not accept the insolence and arrogance they felt their children displayed. Freedom could not mean total rejection of traditions and values. Vietnamese parents lost faith in a system in which American children felt proud to insult their own parents in public. The Vietnamese heard stories of American children complaining bitterly, shouting angrily at their parents on talk shows, and divorcing or suing their mothers and fathers.

Vietnamese parents argued to me that it was the solidarity of the family and the clan that had kept Asians strong. If we lost that, what would be left? Were we to devote ourselves only to having fun, making money, and becoming consumer kings? Was that what happiness was?

Added to the problems with their Americanized children, Asian parents could not find the secure, respectable, high-paying jobs that they needed to be the leaders of their families that they had been in their own country. Most had to do menial work at minimum wage, and many could find no job at all. The fathers suffered the most; they felt themselves unfit, with no skills. They also felt inferior to their wives, who were often more flexible, more industrious, and earned more money than they did. The men had to help clean, cook, and babysit, activities almost unknown to them in Vietnam. They became demoralized and depressed.

The women were more independent. If they could not find a normal job, they took to catering Vietnamese food, making clothes, or babysitting to earn money. Even if they had no job and no authority over their children, the women felt that at least they were bosses in their own kitchen. The men, on the contrary, were no longer bosses anywhere.

With such radical changes taking place, the boat people had a hard time coping with conflicts, whether in the family or in society. Battering, separations, and divorces became common.

Referring to this period a few years later, one man jokingly told me, "We refugee men were ranked number seven. Do you know why? Wife was number one, children number two, cats and dogs number three, house number four, plants and trees number five, cars number six, and us men number seven. Please call me 'Brother Seven' from now on."

But it was perhaps worst of all for the grandparents, who, as old people in Asia, always ranked above the parents, at the top of the ladder. Now, they thought of themselves like the four symbolic monkeys—their hands over their eyes, ears, and mouth, and holding their legs. Not reading English, they were blind. Not understanding English, they became deaf. Not speaking English, they became dumb. And not being able to drive, they felt crippled. They had to depend so much on others that they felt useless and hopeless. They were afraid to ask for anything from their children or grandchildren, all of whom were busy working or studying. So they became lonely and desperate, without relatives or friends to talk to or confide in.

One day, I was asked to visit an old, ailing couple who lived in a senior citizens' home in Crystal City, near Alexandria. They told me that there were three other Vietnamese couples in the same building, on different floors. I met one of the couples, who happened to know my mother. I then took my mother to visit them, so that she, too, could meet some old friends. And I asked the director of the home if she had room for more Vietnamese senior citizens in her building. She did not, but she told me there was another home in Alexandria, and it was accepting applications.

I applied there for a few old couples, and also for my mother, and they all went there to live. This way, I felt, she would be able to live with friends her age, and would not feel frightened staying home alone all day, as she had with us. I remembered my first job as a companion for Mrs. Laise, and knew that my mother would be better off living with her peers.

I explained to the director that it would be better to have several Vietnamese couples on a floor instead of scattering and isolated them all over the building. They needed to be able to speak to each other in their own language, and to support one another in case of sickness or emergency. After I went to see her three times, the director finally agreed, and let two couples stay on each floor.

So, after nearly four years of living with us, my mother, then nearly eighty, moved into an ultra-modern home called The Claridge, off Duke Street in Alexandria. The apartment house had the best amenities: a big dining room, a game room, a workshop where residents could learn pottery or engage in other hobbies, a TV room, a library, a solarium with high glass doors and a roof for sunbathing. Residents also had their own barber shop and beauty salon, and a little grocery store in the basement.

My mother was put next door to a "younger" couple, only in their mid-sixties. Cau Nam Sac (which means Uncle Sac number five) and his wife, Mo Nam. They were from my mother's hometown, Go Cong, knew her well, and were like family to her. My mother loved to walk for an hour every morning and evening on the building's grounds, filled with trees and flowers. She had always been independent and now she had her own home where she could do what she wanted, and her own group of friends she felt comfortable with.

There was always a birthday or other celebration at The Claridge. I used to make up my mother's face and dress her up so she could dance the tango and waltz with Cau Nam Sac and other partners. She also loved to take free bus rides once a week to go shopping at the huge shopping malls. She played cards and reminisced with her friends about the good old times in Vietnam.

Old people's homes are not in the Vietnamese tradition. My brothers and sisters back in Vietnam must have thought that I had abandoned my poor mother, in her old age, to an isolated "cage." But it was in fact a golden cage, where everything was organized in such a way as to make the residents feel happy and at home.

Later, some of the Vietnamese established a nonprofit organization called "Vietnamese Senior Citizens," which I, too, joined as an associate member. I drove my mother's friends to its monthly meetings. Once the organization's leaders had gotten settled themselves, they saw the need for reacculturation. They held talks on Vietnamese culture, organized shows, and celebrated Tet, the Vietnamese Lunar New Year, to remind the younger people of the customs and traditions of Vietnam. They helped each other and enjoyed each other's company, and they became the most respected group among the refugees, helping to instill self-confidence and self-esteem in the others.

The adult refugees, by now permanent residents and citizens, also organized themselves. They formed mutual assistance associations, or MAAs. The MAAs helped the refugees to resettle, and were active in providing social services. They also became identified with the old political parties in Vietnam, and became a vehicle for Vietnamese to preserve their former political affiliations. The MAAs proliferated to the point where more than two hundred of them, large and small, had been set up, all across the United States. They did a lot of good work, but they also embodied the divisions and dissension that existed in the Vietnamese community, sometimes carrying on the fight against the Communists, and sometimes simply fighting among themselves.

In 1981, the board of the Asian Pacific American Women's Club (APAWC), an advocacy group of which I was a board member, nominated me for a national award in the field of social services. They had worked with me in the different "refugee ghettos," and had raised funds to help IRSS and the Welcome House. They had also gone with me to the State Department and Congress to lobby and fight for measures on behalf of

Asians in general, and the refugees in particular. They often called on me to discuss refugee issues, as did other civic groups and the media.

The award was one given by the U.S.-Asia Institute to ten outstanding Asian-Americans for the year. The general purpose was to raise the profile and status of Asian-Americans in the United States by honoring those who had made a significant contribution to U.S. society. I was the newest naturalized American citizen in the group. In addition to recognizing work in the social services, awards were given in politics, the arts, business, architecture, and others. Mrs. Anna Chennault, a prominent political advocate, and Maya Ying Lin, the young architect who designed the Vietnam Memorial, were among the awardees, as was Zubin Mehta, the Indian-American symphony conductor. Connie Chung, the TV anchor, had received a U.S.-Asia Institute award a previous year.

Not long before the award was to be given, I went to visit Ambassador Martin Herz, then in his early sixties and director of the Center for Diplomacy at Georgetown University. He gave me an article he had written about the Vietnam War.

I asked him what he thought of the national award I was about to receive.

He surprised me. "You don't really want to accept it, do you?"

"Why not?" I asked. "It's the first time that the refugees as a group will be recognized."

"But you don't want the Vietnamese to knife you in the back, do you?"

I said I understood that some of them would be jealous of me and would criticize me. But this was not for me alone. It was a recognition for all overseas Vietnamese.

Martin continued. "Do you think they will unite behind you? Most Vietnamese want to be at the top, and will fight to bring down anyone who is notable. They are always bickering among themselves. I wish I could see even three Vietnamese united like the Japanese, or two parties working together without being at each other's throat. If I were you, I would not want to receive that award."

"You know us too well," I told Martin. "But this is the first time since the war and the arrival of the boat people that the Vietnamese will be shown in a positive way, making a contribution to American society. I admit I hesitated at first. But I am not accepting the award for me. I want people to know that the refugees are not just parasites or criminals."

"If you think that way, then good luck," he said with doubt in his eyes and a cynical smile.

The award dinner took place at the Hyatt Hotel on Capitol Hill. I invited Vietnamese, Laotian, Cambodian, and Chinese social workers from different states to attend. They filled two tables. In my acceptance remarks, I said that I was honored to receive the award as a symbolic gesture on behalf of my fellow social workers, some of them present, who had worked so hard to help their compatriots. I said the honor was not only for me, but for all of us, newly resettled and proud voting citizens who had contributed to the well-being of our new country. I did not think that I had done a better job than my colleagues. We all worked very hard. I just happened to be in the right place at the right time.

I was happy to see that we refugees were recognized, and that we were not simply regarded as welfare recipients eating away the taxpayers' money. We had become taxpayers ourselves, and we were contributing to the improvement of our own community. Whether we were paid for our services or not, we had a vested interest in helping to support our own people in need. By then, the Vietnamese had concentrated mainly in California, Texas, and the Washington, D.C. area. They had set up businesses and founded small shopping centers with restaurants, grocery stores, and jewelry shops to cater to the wants and needs of their community.

On the other hand, we also had criminality among the refugees. In the 1980s Vietnamese gangs, made up mostly of young, single men, started to break the law. They went to Vietnamese stores and demanded a monthly "stipend" if the Vietnamese businessman wanted to live in peace. If the man refused to be intimidated, the gangs would throw a stone through his store window, or come back with knives or guns to extort the money. The Vietnamese newspapers reported these crimes weekly. Other gangs went around with trucks and robbed houses of their entire contents. They even shot and killed people.

My own children, meanwhile, were becoming well rooted in their adopted motherland. So well, in fact, that at one point Victor refused to eat with chopsticks or to speak Vietnamese. He wanted to be like the other Americans. Some of the "real" American children started calling the Asian students "boat people" or "refugees," and told them to "go home to Vietnam." I told the children to ignore them and not be confrontational. Instead, they should report any behavior like that to the school authorities. To understand the local educational system better, I volunteered to be on the board of the Parent-Teachers Association of J.E.B. Stuart High School, where our children went. I was elected treasurer.

I kept feeding the family both Vietnamese and American food, and kept speaking Vietnamese to the children. Little by little, they understood that they had to retain and be proud of their origin, their identity, and their culture. In his last two years of high school, Victor was eager to know more about his family roots, and about Vietnam and Asia. Annie, meanwhile, had always had a lot of Vietnamese friends, gone to Vietnamese parties, and liked to speak Vietnamese and eat Vietnamese food. She also remembered how to read and write in Vietnamese. After graduation, Victor went to Duke University and Annie to The George Washington University. Alex, the youngest, was still in high school, where he excelled. After graduation, he went to Yale, where he studied international economics.

Needless to say, we were very proud of our three "refugee" children. They, and thousands of others, proved that they could contribute to the well-being of their new country. They were not merely absorbed into the "melting pot," but to use a better metaphor, they added new flavors to the "fruit cocktail" that is the United States today, where each ingredient keeps its own identity, but, mixed with the others, produces a rich combination and greater dimension.

Meanwhile, the boat people continued to arrive, and more mutual assistance associations received federal funds to provide them services. The IRSS continued on as well: by now we had resettled nearly two hundred families in the Alexandria area. Even so, our staffing and funding had been cut. One morning, a journalist from a local paper in Virginia came to see me at my office, unannounced. He said he had heard that I was not doing a good job for the refugees, and that they had complained to the authorities. This was why my funds were cut. He said that I was cramming the refugees into ghettos, and not providing them with the services they needed.

I asked who his sources were, and exactly what he was looking for. He said he had to protect his informants, and asked me to respond to the charges. If I refused, he would write what he had been told. I had no choice. I pulled out the more than one hundred file folders of the refugees I had resettled, and asked him to select any families he would like to interview. It was better than my defending my own case. I said I would show him where the people lived and introduce him to them, but he would have to find his own interpreters. I did not want him to think we were misinterpreting or trying to influence the refugees.

The reporter selected five families from each refugee nationality, and off we went on our expedition. I introduced him to them, told them to answer truthfully, and left. Two days passed. Naturally, I was eager to hear what had gone on. Then an article appeared on the front page of the *Alexandria Gazette*. There was a photo of smiling Cambodian, Laotian, and Vietnamese refugees living under one roof at the Welcome House. They described how they had been treated and cared for, and other families living nearby told the journalist how they had fared. There were no complaints, just facts about their hardships when they first arrived and words of gratitude at the end.

I always believed there was a Supreme Being somewhere in the universe, hidden behind the dark, thick clouds, who was looking after me and protecting me. Whenever I hit an impasse and did not know what to do, the clouds seemed to clear enough to let an angel appear. That is what happened in this case.

In 1982, my sister, Thu Thuy, came to visit me from Paris. She was impressed by the excellent services provided for the refugees in the United States, particularly for the senior citizens. The French government was doing its part, as well, resettling boat people in France. Canada, Australia, and a number of other countries were also involved in resettling nearly half a million Indochinese.

Thu Thuy and I could not believe that, in the span of seven years, such a fundamental change had taken place, both for good and bad, for us Vietnamese. We had scattered to the four corners of the globe to flee an authoritarian government. A thousand years of wars with the Chinese, the French, and the Japanese, even the famine that had killed nearly two million Vietnamese in 1944 and 1945, had not seen such an outflow, such a flight of skilled labor and brainpower. Abstract concepts of liberty and democracy might be subject to interpretation, but there was no confusion when it came to individual freedom. All South Vietnamese, educated or not, preferred it over dictatorship and oppression. The boat people voted with their arms and legs, determined to swim to other horizons. And although freedom was the ultimate goal, the chance for personal development—for education, training, and the opportunity to compete—was another strong attraction for those who fled.

So we refugees, no matter how homesick, felt much better off, both mentally and economically, in our new environments. Some had escaped the reeducation camps; others, just the regimentation of life in post-war Vietnam. The decline and failure of the Communists in the Soviet Union and Eastern Europe confirmed the legitimacy of our flight from Vietnamese authoritarianism.

I had been working for the refugees for four years. It was time for me to move in another direction. I decided to go back to school, and applied for the master's in foreign service program at Georgetown University—an experience I describe later.

While Thu Thuy was visiting, she asked about a photo I kept in our living room. It was taken at the White House in 1981, and showed Nancy Reagan and me standing side by side, holding hands, with a handwritten dedication from her to me. I told my sister how I had first met Nancy in 1972 in Saigon, at a lunch held for her by Ambassador Bunker. She and Ronald Reagan, then governor of California, were visiting Vietnam. While Reagan was having lunch with President Thieu, Bunker arranged for a separate lunch at his residence so Nancy could meet the wives of various Vietnamese officials. I was by then a widow, but the ambassador invited me, as well.

In 1980, right after her husband was elected president, the First Lady published her autobiography, *Nancy*. The *Washington Post* printed excerpts, and one of them concerned her trip to Vietnam.

Mrs. Reagan recalled her deep emotion at seeing young American soldiers wounded when she visited them in the army hospital the first morning of her stay. She then described how her dismay lightened a few hours later when she saw a totally different vision: pretty, beautifully dressed Vietnamese ladies at Ambassador Bunker's residence for lunch. It was as if, she thought at the time, we were living in a totally different world, devoid of terrorism or war or worries. After lunch, she shared her thoughts with a woman from the embassy who escorted her back to the airport. The woman told her that among those merry faces was that of a young widow with three children whose husband had been assassinated by a bomb blast only a few months earlier.

The wife of the governor of California recorded her Vietnam trip in her diary, and it later appeared in her autobiography. In that book, she remembered the luncheon and concluded her description of it by asking about me, "Whatever happened to her and her three children?"

At a dinner given in Maryland by Ed Fullner, head of the Heritage Foundation, I was seated at one of the tables of eight people. It was a few months after President Ronald Reagan took office. And the hot topic of the evening, at least at our table, was how dreadful Nancy Reagan was. She had refurbished the White House, replaced the chinaware, dressed expensively, and thought only of her millionnaire Hollywood friends without giving any regard to underprivileged Americans.

It amused me to hear the harsh criticism that Americans themselves were pouring on their First Lady. I listened and said little, but when we neared the end of the main course, I finally spoke: "I do not know Mrs. Reagan well, but I think she is absolutely right. First of all, she redecorated the White House and bought the china by raising money from her rich friends, so the taxpayers did not have to contribute to any of these expenditures. I can't understand why the American press is up in arms against her."

A lady sitting in front of me was not convinced. She retorted, "Even so, can you believe the huge amount of money she's spent?"

"Don't you think that the White House should look its best when it has to receive the heads of state of other countries—presidents, prime ministers, kings, queens? As for her clothes, I am proud that Nancy dresses elegantly to represent the United States. In Asia and Europe, people criticize American women for their bad taste in clothes, all except Jackie Kennedy. I don't see any problem in her buying brand-name dresses with her husband's money."

Another person jumped in. "But isn't that out of order? Her dresses are extremely expensive while there are unemployed people who have to struggle hard to get by. She should spend her time visiting poor neighborhoods, and giving them money instead. Does she care at all for the needy?"

"Well, I only know that she cared for the injured GIs when she visited Saigon. And I know that she remembered and asked about me and my children in her book. I was just a widow in Vietnam, and later a refugee here. She could have forgotten us entirely. I was touched by her thoughtfulness."

One lady at our table, who had been critical of Nancy at first, was interested in my story, and asked me to tell her more about my encounter with Mrs. Reagan. "After our meeting in Saigon," I recalled, "the only thing I still remember are her big, deep eyes, full of kindness. I don't recall anything we said to one another. She was softspoken, and did not talk much. But I have always remembered her eyes."

My table-mate told me her name was Judy Bachrach, and that she was a reporter for the *Washington Times*. She wanted to interview me and invited me to lunch the following day in downtown Washington. I said I would be there.

I had no idea who Judy Bachrach was. For two hours, over a delicious

French meal, she grilled me with intelligent questions and I told her genuinely what I thought. It turned out that Judy Bachrach was a regular newspaper columnist known for her trenchant writing and acerbic views. When her column on me appeared a few days later, it was entitled, "Nancy, Wonder no More," a reply to the question Mrs. Reagan had asked in her book. Then her column began: "Today, Jackie Bong Wright is going to write to you." And Judy continued with a moving story about me.

So I did write to Mrs. Reagan. I told her that I had gotten out of Vietnam safely, that I was married to Lacy, that the children were doing well in school, and that my mother had come to the United States to live with us. Two weeks later, I received a phone call from the White House inviting me to have tea with the First Lady, and we set the date. Two days before we were to meet, however, the President was shot. Of course, I called and canceled our meeting. It was not until eight months later that I received another invitation to the White House—to attend an afternoon concert featuring Leontyne Price and several young singers from the Metropolitan Opera. We got instructions on how to park our car behind the White House, and were told to arrive a half hour in advance.

When we got there, Lacy and I found ourselves in the smallest car, a Toyota Tercel, among a Hollywood-like line of vehicles, mostly long, chauffeur-driven limousines. In that company, even the Mercedes-Benzes looked small. Now I understood what Judy Bachrach meant when she talked about the millionnaire jet setter friends of the Reagans.

The one-hour concert made us feel nostalgic for our time in Italy, where we had gone to the opera at La Scala as often as we could. After a show that we found enthralling, we joined the receiving line to meet President and Mrs. Reagan.

When I shook Nancy's hand, I told her that I was very touched to be able to meet her again after so many years. She squeezed my hand hard and looked straight into my eyes. Both of us were holding back tears. But we had no time to talk; we could not hold up all the people waiting behind. With the other guests, Lacy and I moved into a room where refreshments were being served. We were congratulating some of the singers, when a young woman in naval uniform tapped me on the shoulder and asked me to go with her to meet President and Mrs. Reagan.

By now all the guests had gone into the tea room, and only the security guards were left with the first couple. This time Nancy hugged me and asked about my family and me. The President stood next to me, and smiled as I spoke. He looked fit, as though he had recuperated entirely from having been wounded. Then Nancy asked a photographer to take a few pictures with me, one with her hand tightly holding mine, and the other with her arm around my back. I felt extremely honored and pleased that she had not forgotten me. She asked me to write to her again. I have not done so, but I have often thought about her and her husband, and prayed for them both.

EIGHT

REFLECTIONS ON THE VIETNAM WAR AND ITS AFTERMATH

"I forget what I hear, I remember what I see, but I understand what I do."

Confucius

Like a global gypsy, I had been hopping around to different parts of the world, still searching for myself. After more than four years of refugee work in the United States from 1978 to 1982, and as my three children entered college, I wanted to go back to school. I yearned for answers to questions that had been bothering me. I wanted to understand the relationships among countries, how different political systems functioned, and why the United States lost the war in Vietnam. With its great strength, the United States had wiped out the enemy in two world wars and had become the savior and hero of the free world. I wanted to analyze, without personal bias or emotion, how the Americans could have been defeated in Vietnam. It was unfinished business for me.

In the fall of 1982, I applied to study international relations in the School of Foreign Service at Georgetown University in Washington, and was accepted. I was more thirsty for knowledge than for a diploma. I also focused on foreign trade in Asia as a minor. Where did Japan, Korea, and Singapore get the discipline to become "tigers," economic powerhouses? And what were the chances that more Asian tigers would follow in their footsteps?

About a hundred students were accepted for the master of science in foreign service (MSFS) program each year. We were divided into groups of up to twenty-five, and we took courses that fit with our specialties. We did research papers for each course, and presented them before classes for discussion.

Although my Asian background led me to be submissive, my Western education pushed me to be assertive. In the MSFS course, I had to be aggressive, too. I had to participate actively in class, ask questions, talk, and discuss. I learned to say whatever I thought. There were no silly questions or comments, my professors said. My active participation and my papers would determine my grades at the end. The final exam would be a grueling, two-hour, oral test with four experts from different government agencies. We were warned that we would not be able to take the course again if we failed the oral test, even if we had good written grades. The decision was final.

We studied in the newly built Intercultural Center in the far rear of the imposing old Georgetown University building. When I was not attending classes, I studied in the library, where I stayed all day long. I went home at five and, after dinner, I studied until midnight. We were given tons of books and articles to read for each course. After two months, I was so far behind in my reading that Lacy had to prevent me from getting up at four or five in the morning, when it was still dark.

At forty-one, I was not as alert as the young people, who assimilated everything very quickly. They read and wrote like computers. I had to ponder, think, and learn new subjects I had never set eyes on before, such as economics and statistics. It was not easy, and I had to take some tutorial courses to keep up. Like a boat person, I had to try to sail my heavy ship, loaded with books, term papers, and anxiety attacks, across a vast ocean. But I was determined to reach my destination, no matter how hard it was, and earn my forty-eight credits.

Despite many sleepless nights, I was fortunate enough to pass all my courses. I got As and Bs in all of them except for a couple of Cs in the business courses.

I have forgotten all the readings, the papers, and the tests. What is left in my mind now is the information that captured my attention and that made sense. I learned how different parts of the government function or should function. Dr. Madeleine Albright, who taught me foreign policy, repeated to us over and over that the first question to ask in dealing with other countries was, "What are the United States' national interests? How do they mesh with our government's foreign policy?" She had served at the White House under President Carter as a liaison with the Congress, was an ambassador to the United Nations, and then became our first female secretary of state. She herself fled Czechoslovakia, her country of birth, for Belgrade, Yugoslavia, during the German occupation in 1938, and fled a second time to the United States at the age of eleven after pro-Moscow Communists staged a *coup d'état* in 1948. Her experience with the Nazis and the Communists helped her formulate the views on human rights and freedom that she taught her students. She invited me to give an informal talk on how Vietnamese women fared during the wars in our country.

Dr. Theodore Geiger, in his intersocietal relations course, gave us an overview of the history of mankind. Learning how different societies were formed and evolved gave us a better understanding of the cultures we had to deal with. Why did people react differently under different circumstances? It was because they carried with them a host of traditional, societal, religious, economic, and political ways of thinking and making decisions. It was all interrelated, we were all interdependent. So it was necessary to know all the dynamics involved before negotiating with others.

No society could live in isolation. The world was shrinking into a smaller and more cohesive entity, with ever more sophisticated communications. But if we misuse state-of-the-art technology, it could be deadly.

I also learned that policy formulation and decision making by leaders in all countries required them to take account of global politics and the superpowers. In a course called "System of International Dynamics," I was taught that, for most leaders, relations among countries resembled the action of a yo-yo. Nations were friends, became enemies, and became friends again whenever their interests altered—and sometimes even when the mood of the people changed. Too bad if they made mistakes at the top; those at the bottom of the pyramid had to suffer the consequences of their errors of judgment. How to avoid those errors was the question.

Dr. Allan Goodman, our dean, showed us how to do briefings. Whether making a presentation or testifying before Congress, we were to describe concisely the background of the issue at hand and then make a few essential points. We were supposed to look at both sides of an issue, and understand other people's views. We were to analyze the pros and cons, not be one-sided. Therefore, getting the right information was crucial when it came to understanding a person, country, or situation. Negotiating was to be tried before using force or going to war. But when you made a decision, you were to be consistent, and stick to your guns until the end.

With Professor Earl Ravenal, who had worked for the Pentagon, we studied the threat of nuclear arms and terrorism. We could see even then that the economies of the Soviet Union and its satellite countries were in shambles, and wondered how long those governments could survive. We did not predict the crumbling of the Berlin wall or Gorbachev's *perestroika*, but we did foresee that radical change would take place from within the Communist states.

I especially enjoyed the plenary sessions, where a hundred of us engaged in spirited discussion with three professors, who challenged us to explain the events that were taking place in various parts of the world. Visiting lecturers from the United Nations, Congress, the Pentagon, international organizations, and other countries came to talk to us regularly. For me, the whole experience was an eye-opener.

We were not given the answers or urged to take any particular stand on any issue. Instead we were encouraged to assess the various angles of each situation carefully, to ask questions, and to come up with appropriate answers. We sometimes wrote papers in teams of two or more to prepare us for a world in which we would have to interact and cooperate with partners in our future workplaces.

For most of my issue papers, I zeroed in on the countries of Asia, particularly Japan, China, and the members of the Association of South

East Asian Nations (ASEAN). How did Japan become the leader in Asia after World War II in international trade? Would China decentralize and become a real market economy? Would it absorb Taiwan? Hong Kong? How? Would Vietnam open up and join ASEAN? We were not going to solve the problems of the world, but we were learning that just asking the right questions was learning part of the answer. I came to realize that there was usually no one perfect solution to a problem, but a number of options from which we should try to pick the best.

We discussed the controversial double standard whereby some democracies applied different policies to different countries. This phenomenon was described in a book by Jeanne Kirkpatrick, former ambassador to the United Nations and now a professor at Georgetown. The United States punished some of her allies for not observing the human rights of their citizens, and rewarded other countries that failed just as miserably in the same area. Obvious cases of American support in the 1970s and 1980s, including President Ferdinand Marcos of the Philippines; Mohammed Reza Pahlavi, the Shah of Iran; and General Augusto Pinochet in Chile, illustrated Kirkpatrick's point.

In my second year, there was an optional, four-week course on the Vietnam war. It was mostly facts, questions, and discussion about the war and its legacy. No presentation or paper was required. I stayed mute most of the time. The words, "Vietnam war," hurt my joints, my bones, and my muscles like an incurable case of arthritis. There was not enough Tiger Balm or Ben Gay in the world to soothe me or relieve my mental agony. I could not utter those two words without feeling as if I were being strangled. And the more I tried to avoid talking about the war, the more I realized that the wounds were still deep inside me.

Afterwards, I was told that I had done well and to get ready for my graduation. It had taken two years of desperately hard work, but I had achieved what I wanted.

After the course, I was lucky enough to be selected by another professor to do in-depth research on Ho Chi Minh. The professor wanted to write a book on this surreal figure, and asked me to find anything written about Ho that I could lay my hands on. So, twice or three times a week,

I went looking, mostly at the Library of Congress, and made copies of books, magazines, and articles in Vietnamese, French, and English. My job was to read them, write up summaries, and, every two weeks, report back to the professor.

It was amazing how many hundreds of books had been written about Ho Chi Minh by foreign writers, including Bernard Fall, Jean Lacouture, Paul Mus, Gerard Tongas, and Ellen Hammer. There were also tons of articles in Vietnamese by Ho's Communist disciples. They recounted various segments of his now legendary life in Europe, the Soviet Union, China, Southeast Asia, and the jungles of Vietnam. They all praised him for his theatrical exploits and his heroism. Their propaganda made him out to be a god, as if he had never sinned or done anything wrong in his life. He only produced miracles.

I had never known so much about the man who by then had passed from reality into myth. My reading convinced me that we would never know the truth about his enigmatic life.

The course made me reflect on the war, and made me develop some of my own explanations for what happened. It takes two to tango: the Vietnamese and the Americans were both responsible for the war's buildup, and for South Vietnam's collapse in 1975. We should also remember that what many thought was a *civil* war between the North Vietnamese Communists and the Southern Nationalists took place in the context of a conflict between the Communist world and the West that started just after World War II.

On the South Vietnamese side, there were obvious weak points. Early resistance movements led mostly by mandarins and scholars failed to rouse the population. They did not formulate a definite program of social reforms, and lacked sound organization, funds, and foreign support. On the other side, the Viet Minh combined skillful management with a progressive ideology that attracted intellectuals and mobilized the underprivileged. They also had lots of foreign aid from China and the Soviet Union.

In addition, heads of government in the South were not elected in the most democratic way, nor did they emerge through merit; the South did not call forth the leadership to govern a war-torn country. After 1954, the two leaders who lasted the longest, President Diem and President Thieu, remained in power with the help of their powerful sponsor, the United States. Our authoritarian leaders also relied on the police, the army, and the administrative apparatus. What with corruption and the suppression of healthy opposition political parties, successive governments enjoyed little popular support. Resentment was everywhere, and morale was low.

Meanwhile, checks and balances were lacking. Funds that were desperately needed to fight a life-and-death war were mismanaged or misused. Both the National Assembly and the judiciary were under the thumb of the executive branch. Fraud flourished.

Overconfidence and overdependence on handouts of arms and money from our big American brothers brought disharmony to our society. We behaved with excess, exhausting first our checking account, then our savings, and finally our reserve funds. Our karma was unavoidable: a bad ending. This was my humble interpretation and that of most Vietnamese.

On the American side, the administration, without real national support, engaged in a so-called limited war. The president, the military, and the Congress often failed to cooperate during the ten years of their involvement with Vietnam, but instead were pitted against one another. This increased the strength of the antiwar movement. There were errors of judgment on the nature of the war and on the methods to fight it— not enough psychological warfare for a guerilla war, and excessive force that often hit the wrong people. Misunderstanding the culture and the people and underestimating the enemy's mental strength, the Americans implemented inconsistent policies through different administrations.

In the end, the failure of détente with the Russians pushed the latter to send more arms to Vietnam for the final attack, while the Nixon administration was paralyzed by the Watergate scandal.

The McNamara "apology" affirmed these points. Years after my Georgetown experience, Lacy and I were having dinner in Brasilia when I saw on CNN former U.S. Secretary of Defense, Robert McNamara, being greeted by Vietnamese dignitaries in Hanoi. It was early November 1995.

McNamara was smiling at his former enemy, General Vo Nguyen Giap, an old man of eighty-four now, in an olive green uniform.

I watched as the secretary, seventy-nine, his face worn with sorrow disguised as a smile, confessed to the world that, as the main escalator of the Vietnam conflict, he had fought the wrong war. He was trying now to repair his errors of judgment by asking his former adversaries to hold a forum on the Vietnam war. The North Vietnamese director of the Vietnamese Institute for International Affairs was announcing that his government had agreed to such a conference for the following year.

It was a brave gesture. The man who was once the premier strategist of the most powerful country on earth was facing the man whose strategy had defeated both the French colonizers of his small country, in 1954 at Dien Bien Phu, and, in 1975, the American "imperialists." During the conversation, Giap nodded with pleasure as McNamara pleaded guilty and apologized for the "terrible mistake" the United States had committed.

McNamara looked to me like a ferocious hawk turned suddenly into an injured dove. Giap became like a gorilla, breaking off the top of the Eiffel Tower with his left hand and crushing the Statue of Liberty with his right. I saw him brandish the two toys in the air, smiling broadly, his small, slanted eyes half-closed. He appeared to be relishing the moment.

I asked myself what sense it made for McNamara to acknowledge one's culpability to a former enemy, but not to a fellow American. I had been flabbergasted some weeks before to see the same Robert McNamara on TV refusing to apologize to an American woman who was the mother of a Vietnam veteran.

After McNamara had contended that the U.S. commitment was wrong, and said that he knew early on that the war was unwinnable, the woman wanted to know why he had let it drag on for so long, why he had let his countrymen die in vain. She wanted to hear someone say, "sorry," so she, her son, and the thousands of Americans who had perished in the war might attain peace.

Stern in his dark suit and matching mood, McNamara would not yield. The more she persisted, the more he insisted, stubbornly and heat-edly, that it was not his fault. He had followed the policy of his government. So McNamara was trying to have it both ways. But was he right in either case?

I remember McNamara's visit to Vietnam in the 1960s. He was on all of the front pages, his two fingers in a "V" position. He was depicted then as Vietnam's savior, bringing more troops, more dollars, and more arms. That meant more Viet Cong bodies and faster progress toward final victory.

General Tran Van Don, one of the many military officers who helped lead South Vietnam during the war years, remembered McNamara being welcomed at a rally in Saigon. Years later, Don told me a funny story. We were with a small group of Vietnamese "refugees" who had gathered for dinner in Virginia, ten miles outside of Washington, and were reminiscing about our lost country.

Don told me that the year was 1964, a few months before President Lyndon Johnson and the Joint Chiefs of Staff sent the first troops to "Americanize" the Vietnam war. The decision followed the U.S. Congress's Gulf of Tonkin Resolution, passed in the aftermath of a first, then an allegedly second, attack by North Vietnamese torpedo boats against the destroyer, the *USS Maddox*, in August of that year.

Outside, in suburban Virginia, it was snowing hard; a white, soft, velvet blanket covered the ground, the trees, and the windows. Inside, General Don, a well-mannered man in his late fifties, told me that McNamara had wanted to say a few words in Vietnamese to his well-wishers. He tried to say, *"Vietnam muon nam,"* or "Long life, Vietnam." But what came out was, *"Vit Nam,"* or "lying duck." He had used the wrong tone and the wrong pronunciation. What his listeners heard was, "The lying duck wants to lie down." Why couldn't someone have taught him how to say it right before he made a public statement to his Vietnamese allies in their own country?

In fact, the South Vietnamese eventually did exactly that—they lay down—when they were forced by Henry Kissinger and the Nixon administration to sign the 1973 peace agreement. The North Vietnamese Communists, backed by the Soviet Union, were left free to attack the South, while the United States was withdrawing its support.

The funny story of McNamara's faux pas in Vietnam brought tears to my eyes as we sat before the warm fireplace in that Virginia living room, and relived that tormented time.

Was McNamara himself affected as much as the American and the Vietnamese people by his involvement in Vietnam? In the United States, he had been denounced as a warmonger, had endured physical harassment on college campuses, and was caricatured by the media. A public opinion survey showed these figures with the following questions: "Do you think that the United States made a mistake in sending troops to fight in Vietnam?" The responses were 24 percent "yes" in March 1966, 53 percent in April 1968 after the Tet offensive, and 59 percent in January 1971. To the question, "What would you like to see the United States do next about Vietnam? 18 percent responded, "withdraw" in June 1966, 15 percent in June 1968, and 72 percent in January 1971.

In 1995 controversy again surrounded McNamara. The debate over his book, *In Retrospect*, raged everywhere. When Lacy and I were back in the United States that summer for Portuguese language training at the Foreign Service Institute, preparing to go to Brazil, it seemed that the McNamara book came up in every conversation. Almost no one liked it. Antiwar people asked why McNamara had continued for so long to support a war he later said he didn't believe in. Those on the other side thought he was a turncoat and defeatist.

I am with the second group, those who think we fought the right war but fought it very badly. I like the way Bill Colby, the former head of the CIA, put it. Lacy and I had dinner that summer at the Cosmos Club with him and his wife, Ambassador Sally Shelton. We talked about an op-ed piece Bill had done several months earlier for the *Washington Post*, "Vietnam after McNamara." Colby had made the very interesting point that most of the influential books on Vietnam stopped in 1968, the year of the fateful Tet offensive.

That, said Colby, was like ending a history of World War II "before

Stalingrad, Operation Torch in North Africa and Guadalcanal in the Pacific." He acknowledged that the United States and South Vietnam had taken "confused and inappropriate steps" during the McNamara years, but said that, later, they "did indeed learn how to fight the North Vietnamese."

Colby said that McNamara should have given equal treatment in his book to the period after 1968. Colby recalled that a half-million American combat troops had been pulled out between 1969 and 1972, and that the South Vietnamese army then became the principal ground force. The army, backed to be sure by massive U.S. logistical support and punishing air power, did well.

Colby noted, too, that, during this same period, the pacification program freed the rural countryside of Communist guerillas. The refugees were resettled in their original communities and "offered a better life of land reform and local development than the Communists could provide." By 1972, Hanoi recognized that it had lost the "People's War," and started the "Soldiers' War," after the U.S. troops left.

"The fundamental U.S. objective in Vietnam," said Colby, "was achieved—an independent and non-Communist South Vietnam able to defend itself with American support but without U.S. ground combat involvement." It was at that crucial moment, when the North Vietnamese were giving up on the guerilla war and turning to conventional military strategies, violating the 1973 peace agreement, that Congress drastically cut back funding for U.S. logistics support. That led inevitably to the fall of Saigon.

I agree with Bill Colby. If Vietnamization had started earlier, if my own country's leaders had been more united and less corrupt, and if we had not had to endure such a terrible drop in U.S. support, I believe the outcome would have been different.

Ambassador Jacques de Folin agreed with us, too. Jacques headed the French embassy in Vietnam in the 1960s, and devoted his retirement to the history of postwar Vietnam. Among a number of books and articles about Indochina, his last, in 1993, was *Indochine 1940–1955, La Fin d'un Rêve* (*The End of a Dream*).

De Folin had given me Colby's book in French, *Histoire Secrète d'une Victoire Perdue,* or *Lost Victory,* published in 1989, when I spent a week with him and his family at their summer home in Majorca, Spain. It was in the summer of 1994. De Folin and his wife, Marie Laure, were preparing to take a cruise on the *Ocean Pearl* to Vietnam. The arrangement was that he would lead three lecture-discussions on French and American involvement in the Vietnam war for a select group of passengers. So he was thinking a great deal about Vietnam, and we talked about it all through my stay.

We both liked one of Bill Colby's main themes—that the Vietnamization and pacification programs he helped to implement after 1968 should have brought about a self-sufficient Vietnam.

Jacques and I concurred that this was what should have been done in Vietnam at the very beginning, not the end. If rural development had been correctly implemented by South Vietnam's officials, with no excesses or abuses, it would have worked. Support us, we should have said, with the technology and assistance to sustain ourselves. Do not give us an already overcooked fish on a silver platter.

Although I do not think that our root failure was military, it was our inability to counter the last Communist attacks in early 1975 that sealed our doom. The man who laid bare the causes of that final defeat most brilliantly was a soldier—Major General John Murray, the second-to-last American commander in Vietnam. After the war, Murray served as vice president for the Association of American Railroads, from 1974 to 1984. He spent much time helping former South Vietnamese officers who had become refugees in the United States, and we became friends during this period.

Murray also started writing. In 1984, he put his thoughts into an article, "Vietnam Logistics: Who's to Blame?" General Murray had strong words for the U.S. failure to come through at the end. "America pulled the plug," he said. "An army without ammunition is impotent, and the South Vietnamese army's stocks in 1972 fell to dangerously low levels as it thwarted General Giap's 1972 Easter offensive." Because of the way the 1973 Paris Accords limited each country's resupply, the South never caught up again—at least not in the kind of material it needed most.

Murray said that the South Vietnamese—who had turned back both the Tet offensive of 1968 and the spring offensive of 1972—had fought valiantly and well. But toward the end, they started to run out of ammunition. An added problem was American military bungling, which, said Murray, "caused extraordinary flaws in [the South Vietnamese army's] logistics."

So what was McNamara up to with his memoirs? General Ted Serong, who commanded the Australian forces in Vietnam from 1962 to 1965, and later advised the U.S. and South Vietnamese governments on paramilitary operations, agreed with Murray on the redeployment of Vietnamese troops around the Saigon area in the case of a drastic cut in American aid. He said in a 1995 article that McNamara was "preparing for himself a soft landing at the gates of heaven—or history."

Serong saw McNamara as a man with a sketchy and limited military background who suddenly found himself omnipotent—but confused that with being omniscient. Serong himself thought the South Vietnamese could have won with the right strategy.

Hanoi's troops, he thought, could have been contained in the North by blocking the demilitarized zone along the seventeenth parallel west to Savanakhet in Laos on the Mekong River. "This strategy was proposed several times, and supported by General Westmoreland. Each time, it was blocked."

Serong deduced that the late Averell Harriman, as assistant secretary of state for East-Asian affairs, "saw the Laos option as a threat to the position he had built with Russia. He saw it as the linchpin of NATO, and NATO was far more important than Vietnam and SEATO, the Southeast Asian Treaty Organization."

If the first option was not to go into Laos for fear of Russia, the second was to undertake no strategic initiative at all. In major military decisions, said Serong, the primary question was, "How will it affect the president's prospects of reelection?" For Serong, there was "no strategy and no philosophic direction," and "the war drifted on in a wind-down mode for another seven years."

Serong had good reason to bemoan the aimlessness of the Vietnam war: he had spent many years there, and was intimate with the leaders on the South Vietnamese side. I remember an act of kindness by him toward me that I did not recognize at the time for what it was.

Just a few weeks before the fall, I found myself invited to lunch at Serong's house in Saigon. The only other person present was Serong's assistant and confidante, Margarete Weber, who was an officer with the American Defense Attaché Office. It was the end of March 1975, and President Thieu had just ordered a strategic retreat, withdrawing our troops from the northern part of the country to protect what was left, including Saigon. Thousands of Vietnamese from Central Vietnam were streaming toward the capital. I was raising funds for them. I did not think, however, that this was the final agony; in fact, I assured people that the United States would never abandon Vietnam.

Ted and Margarete asked me what I thought of the situation. I said that I agreed with the idea of concentrating our forces to defend the populated area, but doubted that the timing was right. Done during a time of crisis, under pressure from the North Vietnamese Communists, the withdrawal was badly planned and poorly executed. But, I told them, I was still hopeful. I realize now that their question was a way of telling me, gently, that it was the end.

Dr. Henry Kissinger, like McNamara, was stung by Vietnam. I think that he felt, and still feels, that his country betrayed mine.

I had the chance to meet Kissinger the first time he came to Vietnam, in July of 1971, as assistant to the President for National Security Affairs. He stopped in Saigon on his way to China, in the midst of preparations for the Vietnamese presidential election in the fall. President Thieu was campaigning for reelection, and Kissinger was preparing for the first official presidential visit to China, and the possible resumption of diplomatic relations between the two countries. In return, the United States would withdraw its troops from Taiwan and assist the Chinese in gaining admission to the United Nations.

We were at a reception in Kissinger's honor at the residence of the American ambassador, Ellsworth Bunker. It was the first time Kissinger would meet my husband, Nguyen Van Bong, then leader of South Vietnam's major opposition party, the Progressive Nationalist Movement. Kissinger had just called on President Thieu and Prime Minister Tran Thien Khiem.

The following day, Kissinger met privately with Bong. Afterward, the Saigon papers speculated that Bong would be the next prime minister—backed by Kissinger and the U.S. administration. The Vietnamese at that time believed firmly that no South Vietnamese leader could survive without American support. The memory of what had happened to President Ngo Dinh Diem and his brother, Nhu, was still fresh. The two were killed in a coup in 1963 by Vietnamese generals who believed they had American support.

A few weeks after Kissinger's visit, at about nine in the evening, with Bong out for dinner, a strange man phoned to warn me that Bong's life could be in danger. He said Bong should come home right away and then hung up leaving me shivering and speechless.

I knew where Bong was, and I immediately called his host, Khuong Huu Dieu, director of South Vietnam's Industrial Development Bank. He had invited Bong to meet with a group of important people from the private sector, all of whom held key positions and were regarded as young Turks. I asked that they escort Bong home immediately, and they did.

I was not happy with these sensationalist news reports. The papers had speculated more than once that Bong would be the next prime minister. I was now more concerned about his safety than ever. He had already received death threats, and a bomb blast the year before had nearly killed him.

But back to Kissinger. Twenty-four years later, I met him again. It was in September 1995, my first week in Brasilia. Kissinger, now head of Kissinger and Associates, his own consulting firm, was visiting Brazil with executives of a large American telecommunications company.

This time around, I was preparing a luncheon in his honor. My hus-

band Lacy, chargé d'affaires at the U.S. embassy in Brasilia in the temporary absence of the ambassador, was hosting him, his delegation, and
some members of the Brazilian government at the ambassador's residence.

I greeted him and told him that I was from Vietnam. He said, "I feel
sorry when I see a Vietnamese. The United States let Vietnam down."
Andrea Bramson, our in-house photographer, overheard Kissinger and
told me later that that sentence gave her goose bumps every time she
recalled it. I went on to tell Kissinger about Bong, and Kissinger said
that he remembered my late husband.

Kissinger had been touched forever by Vietnam. In his 1979 book,
The White House Years, he begins the chapter, "The Agony of Vietnam"
with the sentence: "I cannot yet write about Vietnam except with pain
and sadness."

Kissinger had come into government with the Nixon administration,
which wanted to end U.S. involvement in Vietnam. In what was then
regarded as a tour de force, Kissinger succeeded in doing so. But his
Paris peace agreement was stillborn. South Vietnam could not remain
independent, because the North would not leave it in peace. Kissinger
had been too eager to negotiate a summit conference with the Soviet
Union and open relations with China. He wanted to manipulate the world
balance of power and end hostility with the two foremost enemies of the
United States. To achieve this détente, Vietnam was sacrificed.

Cynics said that the United States could be said to have withdrawn
with honor if there were a "decent interval"—the title former CIA agent
Frank Snepp gave to his book on the fall of Saigon—between the U.S.
departure and the Communist takeover they thought inevitable.

General John Murray wrote that "Presidents Nixon and Ford fervently
promised that the peace would be enforced by the most powerful of
guarantors: the bombs of U.S. air power and the guns of the U.S. fleet. But
the 'Cooper-Church' amendment, which halted the American bombing,
nullified Kissinger's 'Peace with Honor.' "

In fact, it had been very hard for the South to agree to the provision
allowing the Northern troops that had infiltrated the South to remain

where they were. The agreement allowed them to camp out in the South, arms in hand, and seize as much land as possible, while the South Vietnamese army was to lay down its arms and comply with the cease-fire. It was learned later that Kissinger had made a secret proposal in May 1971 during one of his "back-channel" missions to Moscow. In return for Strategic Arms Limitation Treaty (SALT) ratification, the Soviets would have access to financial credits for purchases of American grain and could conclude a comprehensive bilateral trade agreement. He also agreed with Leonid Brezhnev that the United States would not insist on the withdrawal of Communist troops from South Vietnam. However, Kissinger also emphasized that any North Vietnamese offensive would result in punishing American air attacks.

As a widow, I remember having dinner with our foreign minister, Tran Van Lam, and Hoang Duc Nha, a close advisor to President Thieu, sometime after the signing of the Peace Accords. It was at the foreign minister's official residence on Hong Thap Tu street. Nha asked whether I knew that I was sitting in the same place where Kissinger had sat when he met with Thieu's National Security Council to sell them on the details of the peace agreement.

Nha, a nephew of Thieu, his most trusted confidant, and later minister of information and the youngest person in Thieu's cabinet, had been instructed by Thieu to analyze the agreement. He found that it made no specific reference to the removal of the North's troops from the South. They asked Kissinger about this omission. Kissinger, said Nha, replied that the South should have nothing to fear. The North had already made the biggest concessions in the agreement; therefore, Kissinger did not want to put the entire agreement at risk by introducing withdrawal of the Northern troops.

Nha told me that Thieu had objected strongly, and that he, Nha, had advised Thieu that, if the agreement were not changed, "the Northerners will devour us alive." The North also demanded a coalition government in the South that included the Communist-affiliated National Liberation Front.

Thieu refused to sign. Nixon wrote to him threatening to cut off aid, and Kissinger flared with anger. After successes in his negotiations in Beijing for the presidential visit, Moscow for the arms control treaty, and Paris with the North Vietnamese, Kissinger could not fail now in Saigon.

In November 1972, Nixon wrote in a memorandum of understanding that the United States would "take swift and severe retaliatory action" and "respond in full force" if the North violated the agreement. Finally, in January of 1973, Thieu signed.

The peace agreement won the Nobel Peace Prize for Kissinger and Le Duc Tho, his North Vietnamese counterpart. But it was really the Communists who had won. With Nixon fatally wounded by Watergate and unable to keep his commitment to Thieu, the North did indeed devour the South alive, as the young and perceptive Hoang Duc Nha had predicted.

A quarter of a century after his involvement in Vietnam, Kissinger told me in Brasilia that he was sorry. I had always wondered whether the doctor had diagnosed the disease wrong, like many of his colleagues before him, or whether he knowingly sold us out. Most Vietnamese thought he had. In Paris in the mid-1980s, at a conference organized by Tran Van Tong, the husband of my niece, Bibiche, and other Vietnamese living in France, an angry audience questioned Kissinger about that fateful clause in the peace agreement, and accused him of abandoning their country.

Kissinger replied that their complaint should not be addressed to him but to the antiwar movement and the U.S. Congress. But was he not one of the policy makers, one of the prime authors of the peace agreement? Again, General Murray wrote, "Henry Kissinger and his unnamed palace guard may well be the top contenders for the logistical ineptitude award. His 'peace' pact with the North Vietnamese was a Judas kiss."

I do not think Kissinger deliberately sold us out. He wanted to withdraw American troops while ensuring our survival, but he miscalculated. Aware of the obstinacy of the Vietnamese of both North and South, he thought that peace could be reached if the superpowers stopped providing arms to the two governments in Hanoi and Saigon. The United States would withdraw its troops from the South with honor. China would accept the status quo—partition of Vietnam—if the NLF, its friends, could participate in the Saigon government, and the Soviets would be granted most favored nation status when the SALT I treaty was presented for ratification in the Senate.

Unfortunately, Senator Henry Jackson added a condition to the Soviets' most favored nation provision—they should let the Soviet Jews emigrate freely. The Soviets, furious with that addition, sent more support to the North Vietnamese. The collapse came about when the Americans lost their heart to fight, and the Vietnamese, in 1975, lost their hope in the Americans.

I remember vividly that, in 1980, I had run into Kissinger head-on at the entrance to the State Department. I was there to pick Lacy up after work, as I did every evening. I pushed open the middle glass door and saw Kissinger departing. As soon as I realized who it was, I turned around and followed him. I wanted to ask him just one question: "Are you happy sharing the Nobel Peace Prize with Le Duc Tho?" My heart beat so loudly that I was shaking. I stopped right behind him, tears running down my face, without the strength to say a word. He stepped inside his limousine and was chauffeured away.

At the end of the day, after all the analyzing and agonizing, it is no use assigning blame or pointing fingers or saying, "What if?" At the same time, I sincerely admire people with the courage to admit their mistakes.

How to avoid more Vietnams? The most important lesson is to devise a firm plan, take quick action, minimize the loss of American lives, and then win as swiftly as possible. That was accomplished with the American interventions in Grenada and Haiti, and in the Gulf War. The United States learned from the Vietnam War.

The war holds lessons about America for the rest of the world, as well. One is that Congress is tremendously powerful in U.S. politics— not only the president, as many tend to think. Pressure groups—voters, campaign contributors, special interest groups, and lobbyists—are also influential. This is not to mention the media, which in their powerful scrutiny of the U.S. government became for many the *bête noire* of the Vietnam War.

It is also true, of course, that, unlike the censored press in authoritarian countries, the American media dares to print exposés of the crude truth. Right or wrong, the U.S. press exerts a very strong influence. One effect is that American policies are subject to change and inconsistency, according to the mood of the people as measured by polls. The antiwar protests in the United States, which later spread to other countries, are a concrete example of the press's influence.

The images of those students—protesting, destroying draft cards, burning the American flag—are still clear in my mind. They were beaten, handcuffed, and jailed. But the more they were repressed, the more their anger grew against an administration that failed to explain to them the U.S. national interest in Vietnam. Visions of savage battles, bombing, and the cruelty of the war on both sides invaded American living rooms. People did not comprehend why their husbands and children had to die for an abstract concept—anti-Communism—thousands of miles away. Why should that affect them or threaten their security? As the casualties increased, dissent grew and unrest festered.

That stormy, mid-1960s controversy laid bare the strain on a beleaguered administration; a frustrated military, which was even considering nuclear attacks; and an embittered Congress. The Vietnam War tore the whole American population apart. The Americans lost faith in their government and in themselves.

And yet, President Thieu in April 1975 was still hoping that President Ford and the U.S. Congress would honor Nixon's promise and retaliate strongly against the Northern Communists who were breaking the peace agreement. Did he still believe in *tin*, the loyalty that one head of state should show another in honoring a promise that was solemnly signed? It was not to be so. Thieu had misdiagnosed the American congress and public, and underestimated the power of the media.

At my final exam at Georgetown, I was the third student to appear, for nearly two hours, before a grand jury of four judges. They came from the Pentagon, the Commerce Department, the State Department, and the university itself. Two students had passed through that courtroom that morning. I could hardly eat anything at lunch, and I was trembling with hunger and fear.

The panel of judges made me feel at home by introducing themselves and greeting me with amenities before we got down to business and I felt more confident. They could ask anything they wanted, and we, as potential foreign service officers available for postings abroad, were supposed to satisfy them with our replies. They touched on every issue imaginable. We had to deal with public policy, the trade deficit with Japan, global security, nuclear disarmament, decisions in Congress, U.S.-Soviet relations. Finally, there were questions about the Vietnam War, a subject dear to my heart.

In early 1995, twenty years after Saigon was unified with Hanoi, President Bill Clinton resumed diplomatic relations with Vietnam. In November, the McNamara apology pushed me to write my memoirs. Sometimes I stayed glued to my computer deep into the night, fighting to make my stories bloom in my mind. Sometimes I awoke at three A.M. to put an idea on paper, or to capture a word that had risen to my consciousness while I was sleeping. Sometimes I went for hours or days with no inspiration, no idea of what I was going to write next.

One question stayed with me always: What was the significance of the struggle between Vietnam and the United States during the ten years of the Vietnam War? And what was the legacy of the five American presidents who, among them, spent twenty-five years stuck in what has been called the Vietnam quagmire?

President Henry Truman took the first step in 1950, giving the French $15 million for their war in Vietnam in exchange for French agreement to allow the rearming of West Germany. This was while Mao Tse-tung was conquering China, and the Korean War was erupting. President Dwight Eisenhower, fearing that Asia would succumb to Communism if Vietnam fell, increased U.S. aid to the French to $3 billion, which flowed to Paris until 1954, when the French were defeated at Dien Bien Phu. In the United States, there was a strong, implicit belief in the domino theory.

Following Eisenhower in his support for South Vietnam, President

John Kennedy sent helicopters and other equipment to Vietnam in 1963, doubled the number of advisors to sixteen thousand, and raised aid to a half-billion dollars. Having inherited this larger buildup, Lyndon Johnson got authorization from Congress to send one hundred twenty-five thousand American troops in 1965. That number swelled to half a million by the end of 1967, reinforced by B-52 bombings. By the 1968 election, sixteen thousand Americans had died in Vietnam. The election winner, President Nixon, initiated a dual policy of withdrawing the United States from the war and implementing a "Vietnamization" program. This led to the Paris Peace Accords of January 1973 and the unification of the two Vietnams in mid-1975 under the Communist regime.

After the Communists took over, Vietnam tried to impose a policy of agricultural collectivization. It was a failure, mainly due to poor planning and mismanagement, on the one hand, and the lack of workers' incentives, on the other. Political repression caused a huge outflow of skilled people, who fled to other countries in the mid-1970s as refugees, a political failure with dire economic repercussions.

What then, in the 1980s, were Communist Vietnam's national interests and its prospects for the future? To help pay its $3 billion debt to the Soviet bloc, Vietnam sent half a million "guest workers" to Siberia and other remote parts of the empire. New attitudes surfaced about how Vietnam might feed its population and increase its industrial production. Vietnam cut its army in half, demobilizing a half-million men, and pulled out of Cambodia.

In 1986 the country embraced a program of *doi moi*, or renovation, and introduced economic reforms. It encouraged private enterprise, private production, and private ownership. Now more subdued, Hanoi needed to build more friendships and soften enmities. Australia, France, Hong Kong, South Korea, and Taiwan moved quickly to improve trade with Vietnam. Vietnam restored relations with China, broken in the early 1980s over the Vietnamese tilt toward the Soviet Union, and urged foreign investment.

By 1989, in Europe, the Berlin Wall came down. The Soviet alliance with Vietnam crumbled, too, and three thousand Soviet advisors decreased to fifty by 1992. Trade between the two countries fell drastically. Vietnam was eager for diplomatic relations with the United States. The Communists saw normalization as the key to lifting the American embargo, imposed in 1979 after Vietnam invaded Cambodia. Other benefits would be access to loans from the International Monetary Fund and the World Bank, and an influx of American aid. With normalization, more American corporations could invest in the country and employ thousands of industrious, low-paid Vietnamese workers.

With these hopes in mind, Vietnamese now greeted Americans no longer as imperialist enemies, but with broad smiles, "V" signs, and upturned thumbs. Vietnam saw itself as a potential Asian tiger, following in the footsteps of Hong Kong, South Korea, Taiwan, Singapore, Thailand, and Malaysia.

This vision led Vietnam to drop its demand for war reparations from the United States as the price of normalizing relations. Instead, Vietnam would ask America to help repair the war's environmental and societal effects. Seeking to exploit what it hoped was a lingering U.S. guilt complex, Hanoi cited poisonous Agent Orange, the infrastructure destroyed by B-52 bombings, and the need to rehabilitate war victims as problems with which it needed help.

And what about the United States? What national interests did America have in resuming diplomatic relations with Vietnam? One concerned Vietnam's status as an emerging market. Hundreds of U.S. firms in such fields as oil, construction, telecommunications, and consumer products had been pressuring successive administrations to allow them access to Vietnam's seventy-eight million people (which had reached eighty-six million by the year 2000). They did not want to lose this vast market to other countries.

There was, then, mutual interest in normalization. The only condition the United States imposed was the fullest possible accounting of the more than two thousand two hundred missing servicemen, many of whose remains were being kept by Vietnam as a bargaining tool.

It was up to General John Vessey, a special presidential envoy since 1987, to negotiate a framework for U.S.-Vietnamese cooperation on prisoner-of-war/missing-in-action (POW/MIA) issues. The U.S. government devised a four-step "road map" for normalization, and a step forward was taken in June 1992 when the U.S. allowed commercial sales to meet basic human needs and lifted restrictions on projects by American non-government and nonprofit groups. More U.S. humanitarian aid to Vietnam was also forthcoming.

In February 1994, the U.S. trade embargo was lifted. A year later, in January 1995, the United States opened a small liaison office in Hanoi to seek more information on POW/MIA matters. Finally, in July 1995, the Clinton administration established full diplomatic relations with Vietnam.

But there were still complex issues to be resolved between the two countries. One concerned those soldiers missing in action. The National League of Families of American Prisoners and Missing in Southeast Asia wanted Vietnam to increase its efforts to locate and return their remains. The United States had been pumping $50 to $100 million every year into joint search efforts in Vietnam. U.S. congressional resolutions in early 1996 disapproved of funding for diplomatic relations and the granting of most-favored-nation trading status to Vietnam until Hanoi provided more information on MIAs.

This sensitive issue opened others, as well. The North Vietnamese were concerned about their own three hundred thousand MIAs. And what about the MIAs of the South Vietnamese army?

An issue that remains current is the status of Vietnamese who are American citizens and who return to Vietnam. Under Vietnam's more open economy, over a quarter of a million Vietnamese living abroad have gone back to Vietnam each year to visit. Some have returned to help, to work, or to invest. Our daughter, Annie, was one of them. She had left Vietnam when she was ten years old, and longed to go back to her roots and do something to help rebuild the country.

But once Annie set foot on Vietnamese soil in 1995, despite her American passport, she was a Vietnamese citizen in the eyes of the government there. Vietnamese who had acquired other citizenships were considered subject to Vietnamese law and restrictions. The Vietnamese government claimed that their nationals could become citizens of other countries only after getting its permission to do so. The million and a half refugees who fled the country since 1975, of course, did no such thing. Annie was sent to Vietnam by Ethacon, a subsidiary of the Johnson & Johnson corporation, to help establish the company's first office there. She found herself in a kind of limbo. She was not accepted by local people as a Vietnamese, but rather considered a *Viet Kieu*, "Overseas Vietnamese." She had to use the foreign rate of exchange when she changed her dollars into dong, instead of the more favorable local rate—meaning that everything, from food to housing to taxis, was more expensive for her than for local people.

So Hanoi had it both ways. When it suited the regime, returnees like Annie were regarded as any other Vietnamese. The "Overseas Vietnamese" had to conform to Hanoi's limits on freedom of speech and association. But Hanoi also wanted to milk the much more affluent returnees by using them like it did other foreigners. Vietnam should recognize the right of Vietnamese naturalized in other countries to be treated as citizens of those countries, including when they are in Vietnam.

Another issue has to do with fundamental freedoms in Vietnam for its own citizens. The Vietnamese constitution assigns control to the Communist party in areas such as religion, giving the party authority, for example, over who can teach religion and publish religious materials. That is not freedom of religion, and the regime in Hanoi must address the matter. It must also address the questions of freedom of association and speech; free elections, with non-Communist candidates; and the formation of labor unions. It is up to Hanoi to show whether its behavior is really up to international human rights' standards. Those are the kinds of questions that will continue to come up between Vietnam and the United States, and which the two countries will have to work out. Relations between the Vietnamese Communists and those of us who were on the losing side are another matter, and will be even harder to heal.

Here is another question. Will the pro-Russian and pro-Chinese factions in Vietnam come to terms with each other? Ho Chi Minh professed a policy of equal distance from the two big providers of aid and arms during the war. After his death, we saw the politburo shift toward the

Soviet camp, and it was with this alliance that the North won the war in the 1970s. Afterward, Vietnam tried to copy the Soviets' *perestroika* and *glasnost* reforms.

The collective leadership that had worked so well in the fight against a common enemy—French colonialists and then American "imperialists"— became the victim of a fierce power struggle in the 1990s. There were three factions in unified Vietnam—the government, the military, and the Communist party. Will the pendulum sway toward the conservative, pro-Chinese group, or will the party's strategic goal of industrialization and modernization prevail? The aggressive Vietnamese Communists, instead of embarking on the path of concord and reconciliation they had preached following their "liberation" of South Vietnam in 1975, were continuing their violent and confrontational struggle. They were not only faced with their own domestic problems, but they also had a serious dispute with the Khmer Rouge, the Communists in Cambodia.

And now, one thing seems certain. The thirst for freedom, democracy, individual rights, and progress that the Vietnamese soul has always nurtured is still there, and is growing, especially among young people. Vietnamese from both the North and South, those injured physically and those whose war wounds are inside, are searching for a new and harmonious balance. The healing process continues, in Vietnam and in the United States . . . and within Autumn Cloud and her family.

EPILOGUE

In May 1996, at my mother's funeral in Houston, Texas, her children, grandchildren, relatives, and friends gathered from around the globe to pay tribute and bid her farewell. Standing near her body, I watched over two hundred mourners, her friends and our friends, pass by for one last look. We had all been drawn to the point where life and death, like a total eclipse, crossed paths. Although my mother's body, cremated at her wish, floated and disappeared into the sea at Galveston, her soul would live on in another world. Her Christian friends believed that she would join God in paradise. The Buddhists believed that she would be reincarnated and come back as another being. Who can say whether one is right and the other is wrong? Let us only agree that both are strong, deeprooted beliefs.

I remember a dinner party in honor of my mother in Houston the year before. One of her students from Go Cong—the mother of Therese Phung, my classmate from Marie Curie—was there, and she said to me, "Miss Hanh, your mother, was my third grade teacher and my French teacher when I was nine. I still remember how strict and how good she was as a teacher. She always encouraged us to study hard and do our best." Then she turned to my mother, bent her head respectfully to her teacher, and held her hand. "You know mistress, although I am eightyone now and absent-minded, I still remember some of the French you taught me. Let me practice it with you." It was marvelous to see these two gray-haired ladies, hardly able to see one another any longer, their teeth mostly gone, conversing in broken French mixed with Vietnamese. They reminded each other of happy times now forgotten, in the place where they grew up.

By a miraculous coincidence, Therese Phung and I were reunited at that same dinner. It was at Pauline Loan's house in Houston. We had all been classmates in middle school forty years ago. Following our elders' example, we reminisced about our innocent youth and talked, half in

French and half in Vietnamese, about our other classmates, scattered all around the world, like us.

Pauline told us the story of the bomb blast that almost wrecked her life, leaving her nearly deaf and with her right leg cut short. It was 1960, and a Viet Cong terrorist threw a hand grenade into a movie theater in Saigon. Pauline had just celebrated her high school graduation, and she was engaged to a young man named Hung. Her fiance, undeterred, went ahead and married her and cared for her like a precious baby from then onward. She recovered and, with the help of a wooden leg and a hearing aid, went to work as a translator for Vietnam Press, the South Vietnamese government media agency.

Pauline and Hung had three children, two boys and a girl. The five of them bribed their way out of Vietnam as boat people in the 1980s. During their clandestine flight, her fourteen-year-old son had to carry her on his back, while her husband held the two younger children. They passed through different refugee camps in Southeast Asia before arriving finally in the United States, where both of them had to start out by working as cooks in a restaurant. Now, in 1994, they were the proud owners of a laundromat, and their children were all grown and working in professional jobs.

Another time I stayed with Pauline in Houston, she asked me to call Jolyn, an American woman living in Virginia whom she had known in Saigon in the 1960s. She said she was indebted to Jolyn for helping her after the grenade blast. Unable to hear well, Pauline asked me to talk to Jolyn on the phone and tell her what she wanted to say. So I acted as a go-between, and repeated to Jolyn everything Pauline said, parrot-like.

Pauline told Jolyn that she would be grateful to her for the rest of her life, and that she missed her very much; then she started to cry. So I started to cry, too. And as I sobbed on the phone, I told Jolyn that Pauline was crying. Then Jolyn cried, and I transmitted that to Pauline, as well. Caught in the middle, I wept for the two of them for a good two minutes, to the point that I had to excuse myself and run for a tissue to blow my nose.

Pauline always insisted that I stay at her house when I visited Houston, to keep her company. And I did. We both wanted to bask in our innocent past, and maintain our rare friendship. I had such a strong admiration for Pauline, who, even as I visited her, was working every day from six in the morning until eight at night, moving around with difficulty, whether to serve her customers or cook meals for the needy, with one leg and two ears fewer than normal people. She was a role model for me.

As for Therese, after my mother's funeral, Pauline and I went to visit her husband's grave. He had died of cancer two years before, leaving her working in an electronics firm as a technician, and caring for her mother and her two children. We all prayed that he would be able to protect his family from "somewhere else."

Life swirls around us—love, hate, joy, suffering, unity, division, failure, success. Each person has to go through them all. Each person seems to have a different mission at a given time. We come and go and are replaced. Whether we are like a faint, yellow star, pulsating and shining by itself, or like a giant, luminous blue star joined with thousands of others to form a galaxy, one day we fall into a bottomless pit and disappear. Other stars and other constellations arise, and the cycle continues. The endless wheel keeps turning.

At my mother's funeral, Anh Ba, my only living brother, and my sisters asked me to present her with a rose as our last homage, before the coffin was sealed. I tried to say how grateful to her we were—her ninety descendants—but time was short, and I could not do justice to her life or her accomplishments.

So today, in the spring of 2001 as I finish writing my memoirs, I speak to both my parents, and tell them everything I wanted to say: "I see you both as artists, as painters. You gave us birth, and you passed on to us your strength and your determination to struggle in life. Because we came from your cells, we took on your image. We became strands in your plumage. Now, I would like to report to you what has become of each one of us.

Your eldest daughter, Hai Duc, died peacefully in her sleep only a year after you did, Mother, at seventy-six. She had resettled in Calgary, Alberta, Canada, with four of her children. Mother, she told me with tears in her voice how sorry she was that she could not come to your funeral. She was in a wheelchair, her legs nearly paralyzed. Her youngest daughter, Chi, lives now near Washington with her husband, Tam Pham, the first Vietnamese ever selected to attend West Point.

Hai Duc's five remaining children are still living and working in Vietnam. From her ten children, she had fifteen grandchildren and four great-grandchildren. She was like a mother to me, and told me so many stories about your own parents and about how you were as a young husband and wife. She, of course, knew more about you than any of the rest of us did.

Your eldest boy, Anh Ba, is now seventy-six. It was he, Mother, who visited you every day in your last years and brought you the food which you especially liked, and which he cooked for you himself. He was a model son. Father, you should be proud of him: he lived up to the Confucian ideal of piety and gratitude toward one's parents—the ideal you taught him. He set the example for all of us. Most of us, Mother, lived too far away to be able to give you that kind of care, so we are very grateful to him.

Anh Ba did even more. Even though he was sick with cancer, he defied nature and went in 1994, on our behalf, to the city of Vinh in North Vietnam to unearth and incinerate the remains of your number six son, Trung. Nam Ly, your Communist daughter, helped Anh Ba to find Trung's grave, and went with him everywhere. We can be satisfied now that Trung's remains reside in a padoga in Saigon, and that his soul will rest in peace. All of Anh Ba's nine children are working or studying in the United States. He has six grandchildren. Father, you left me with such a kind image of yourself, and Anh Ba has always lived up to that image. I respect him, too, as a father.

As for Madame Tao—which is how Hue has always been known— she lives in Paris with her four children and her nine grandchildren. She still keeps herself busy with her civic activities. Her daughter, Bibiche, told me that Madame Tao prayed for you every week for seven weeks after your death. She invited her children, grandchildren, relatives, and dear friends to these ceremonies, so they in turn would remember you.

Your fifth daughter, Nam Ly, has written me from Saigon, or, as they now call it, Ho Chi Minh City. She told me stories about your life at Les Terres Rouges plantation so long ago in Cambodia and about her forced wedding to the Japanese officer, Kobayashi. She told me with pride about her time in the *maquis* and in the North with Ho Chi Minh. Both she and her husband, Binh, have retired now. Three of her children are in Vietnam, and one lives with her husband in the United States, although I have not met any of them yet. Mother, Nam Ly sent me a picture of herself standing in front of a street named after Nguyen Duy Duong, your father, and photos of her and her husband in the *maquis* in the 1950s.

Father, I asked Nam Ly her impression of the wars in Vietnam. Here is what she said: "The French and the Japanese were both colonizers. But the Japanese were more cruel and brutal than the French, so they were called Fascists. But the Viet Minh were different. They were revolutionaries who fought for forty years to liberate the nation. I never saw them lay their hands on anyone or treat anyone with cruelty like the French, the Americans, or the Japanese did. They used only righteousness and justice to reform people, and to explain to them the reason why we took up arms to fight against infiltration." That is not what I thought, of course, but that is her view, even today.

Since Nam Ly was not able to come to your funeral, Mother, she, too, paid her respects to you by praying for you. She gathered a group of relatives at a *chung that* celebration on the forty-ninth day after your passing to pray for your soul to be blessed, and for you to be reincarnated in a better being. And she had a *tot khoc* celebration after the one hundredth day, the ceremony that allows the family to "stop weeping" for the dead.

Nam Ly's eldest son, Long Nguyen, whom I babysat, became a doctor but died two years ago. Hoai Chau is an engineer. Hai Yen is a navy pilot, and Hoai Nam is an accountant. She has three grandchildren.

Thu Ha, your daughter number seven, lives in California. Her daughter, Nathalie, works in London and has two daughters. They have visited us in the U.S. Thu Ha has become very thin. She has arthritis, sclerosis, and goiter, but she is taking care of herself, with good medication. We still talk with one another often on the phone.

Mother, I do not need to tell you about your number eight daughter, Thu Cuc, because you lived the last years of your life with her in her house in Houston. We are grateful to her because she took such good care of you and bathed you with her own hands every day. Even though she has not been out of Vietnam long, she has done well as a healing therapist. Three of her children work in California, and three live with her in Texas. Thu Cuc has eight grandchildren. At first she did not want to tell me about her experiences in the *maquis* or her tormented past, but I pleaded with her and now she has. So many adventures.

Thu Thuy, the sister next to me, just retired as a nurse in Paris, and has gone with Christian, her French husband, and her son to live in Nice, on the French Riviera. Her daughter lives in Houston, and she has two grandchildren. Of all my sisters, she has been the closest to me, perhaps because we are not far apart in age. At your funeral, we told each other that if, one day, we were to survive our husbands, we wanted to live somewhere together in a nice apartment and keep one another company in our old age. We have always gotten along so well, from the time we were children.

As for myself, your youngest living child, Miss Littlest, I started writing my memoirs in 1995 in Brasilia, a city I loved. The weather was tropical, warm, and sunny all year round. I found there all the flowers, fruit, and stars I knew "once upon a time" in Vietnam. It was an ideal setting, where I could look out at the rich landscape of my garden, the serene lake beyond, and, out further, the skyline of Brasilia, the country's thirty-year-old capital. There I found the peace to put into print my innermost thoughts and feelings. Now I am back in the United States, in a house on a small lake, and have no desire to move again.

Our children are doing well, and I know you are as proud of them as Lacy and I are. Victor, our eldest, still lives with his wife, Nawa, in New York. He changed jobs again recently, and went to work as marketing manager for a big pharmaceutical company. He and Nawa live right in Manhattan. They work hard, but they like where they are.

And Annie . . . Mother, I am happy to tell you that seven weeks after you passed away, Annie gave birth to a baby, a girl, whom she named after Lacy. We were in the delivery room with her at Fairfax Hospital in Virginia. Little Lacy had dark eyes, and curly hair, like both you and Father did. Right after her birth, as she still lay naked and unwashed, little Lacy put out her hand and caught my finger. I felt she was communicating her innocent life to me, and I felt born again. For us, she is the most beautiful baby you could imagine. She is our first grandchild, and another great-granddaughter for you.

Annie takes good care of her daughter. She has read a lot about how to bring up a child and uses the best available techniques—much better than I did when I gave birth to her. You remember how well Annie did working for a big American company in Saigon and Singapore. She will go back to work when she decides it is time.

And little Alex, who is not so little anymore, is a tall, handsome, and sturdy young man. He, too, is in the business world. After he got his graduate degree from Wharton in Philadelphia, he stayed there and went to work for another large pharmaceutical company. Now he is in New York, and lives just a few blocks from Victor and Nawa. He has taken up body-building! You would hardly recognize the skinny boy you used to know.

I told you I was just finishing the story of our family. It is a bouquet I want to present to both of you. I have taken all the memories I could gather and looked at them through my own eyes and tried to make sense of them. I have tried to show how our lives were changed by the Chinese, the French, the Japanese, and, finally, the Americans, and their wars. I have tried to depict us, not as we Vietnamese appear in movies and books—bystanders in a great drama where the Americans are always front and center—but as real human beings who played our own roles, for better and for worse. I have tried to tell how we lived, what the foreigners did to our lives, and how we fought back and struggled to save our self-esteem.

My bouquet contains all kinds of flowers, from the brightest to the most faded. It contains the happiest and saddest experiences of your lives and my life. It is my last child, delivered with all the joy and pain that accompany a natural birth. It is my last will and testament for my children and grandchildren.

My spring years were spared from World War II, and shielded from the calamities that struck both of you. My summer was tormented by the heat of the American war in Vietnam, the confusion of political upheavals, the assassination of Bong, and the tempestuous passage to my new life in the United States. My autumn was my long voyage around the world with Lacy and the children, in a ship rocked by high waves. Finally, I am approaching a winter of calm, having weathered the cycles of karma that no one can escape.

You witnessed my spring and summer years, but not my autumn with Lacy, our foreign service life. I would like to tell you what happened to me during that time, after our posting in Milan.

One of the most memorable adventures began in mid-1984 with a visit to Washington by Bibiche's husband, Tran Van Tong. He asked me to help find a business partner and a market for Lemaire, the French company of which he was executive director. I found a partner in Baltimore and served as interpreter.

You remember that his father, a well-respected South Vietnamese senator, was assassinated by the Communists in Saigon in the 1960s. His only brother, Tran Van Ba, a student activist in Paris who returned clandestinely to Saigon in the early 1980s to agitate for changes in the regime, was imprisoned, condemned, and executed by the Communist government. His death caused a strong anti-Communist reaction among Vietnamese around the world.

Tong came back to the United States a second time, in the summer after my graduation, bringing with him four of his company's top executives to negotiate a partnership with the company in Baltimore. One of them, Mr. Lefebure, after a week of observing my work as an interpreter and public relations person, offered me the job of finding Asian markets for the Armagnac his company made in France. I agreed.

"Me?" I asked myself that night after I had accepted the job. I did not drink anything stronger than mineral water. What if I were asked to drink my own Armagnac, a liquor akin to cognac? What if I got drunk in front of the macho male executives I would meet? This was a world of men; women, especially Asian women, were not involved in the liquor business. The next morning, I told Mr. Lefebure of my reservations, and said I wanted to withdraw. But he would not agree to it, and urged me to be ready to go to Paris in a week. He had been looking for someone for the job and had found that person in me. His trust revived my confidence, and I started preparing a plan of action that had to be ready before he went back to France in two days.

I spent nearly the whole night thinking and writing a proposal. The next morning, I presented it to him. I proposed going to Bangkok, where I had friends who could introduce me to liquor companies. The next stops would be Singapore, Hong Kong, Taiwan, and Tokyo. The whole trip, including a stop in France, would last a month. I would need Lefebure to contact the commercial sections of the French embassies in each of the countries to make appointments for me with liquor companies. I asked him to prepare brochures and Armagnac samples for me to give out. My job was to promote and market the product; he would take charge of following up if good leads were developed. We agreed.

Although I had scored low in my business courses at Georgetown, I had a good grasp of how to do business in general. I had been helped by a course on how to market that taught me the right techniques. Did the product appeal to the wants of the client? The customer was king, we were taught. We also learned how to do market research, how to present the product, and how to package and promote. I had to consider what the projections were for the product's near- and long-term success, what marketing strategies should be employed, and whether the price was right. I did not have enough facts in hand, or the chance to put any ideas down in writing, before going to France.

I discussed the details with Mr. Lefebure in Paris after he had shown me the hundreds of bottles of Armagnac he kept stored at his vineyard in the city of Armagnac, near Cognac, in the south of France. We had traveled there so he could explain to me the process of making the liquor that the French found so delicious after dinner. He drove me around and introduced me to his colleagues. The city seemed to be a huge liquor store. People produced mostly Armagnac in Armagnac. What else?

I went to Asia and met with the executives with whom my friends and the French embassies made appointments for me. The Asians loved to drink cognac, but they had never even heard the word, Armagnac. In Bangkok, they tasted it and liked it. But they said that it would take a lot of advertising to make it better known. Would Mr. Lefebure invest money to do it with them? I called my boss. No, he did not want to go into that kind of venture.

In Hong Kong, Jim Eckes, the former head of Continental Airlines in Saigon who helped me get out of Vietnam in 1975 and was now again representing airline companies, introduced me to a friend who marketed duty-free products at airports in Asia. The man agreed to go to Paris to meet with Mr. Lefebure to discuss a joint arrangement. He would also market Lefebure's Armagnac in China. Bingo! I hoped it would work this time. The two did meet in Paris, but again Mr. Lefebure was interested only in selling, not in advertising or investing.

In Tokyo, my taxi driver left me on a corner holding two heavy bags of Armagnac bottles. I walked for two blocks, trying to find my destination with my almost nonexistent Japanese. I knew *arigato* (thank you) and *sayonara* (good-bye). I finally made it to the ninth floor of a tall building where three top executives, men in their sixties, received me and listened to my presentation. I talked of the origins of Armagnac, the special soil and particular temperature needed to nurture the grapes, the fine way the Frenchmen fermented and blended the liquor. Finally, I passed out the brochures advertising my Armagnac to these senior citizens.

After the three had listened to me with impassive faces, the man in the middle, the vice-president, told me that they were already selling Armagnac in Tokyo. Red-faced, I asked him where and how. He said it was test-displayed in selected liquor stores to gauge the public reaction, and that sales were still slow. But they were ready to buy in big quantities, in barrels not bottles. They intended to mix the Armagnac with *sake*, the national rice wine, to create a new liquor. They had already tried it in certain bars, and people seemed to like it. Would Mr. Lefebure want to sell in large quantities, in barrels?

The man on the right, the marketing officer, said that he would be willing to sell the Armagnac bottled as it was, provided Mr. Lefebure offered a cheaper price, and that he change the label and the packaging. The vivid colors—red and green with gold lines—looked, he said, like the Italian flag. He proposed a new design, with silver and lilac colors. The new appearance would appeal more to Asians, he said. He was willing to have various labels designed for Mr. Lefebure to chose from.

I was very happy, and called my boss to report the good news. Mr. Lefebure turned the two proposals down flat. His fine Armagnac should be sold in bottles, not in barrels, like beer. He had no intention, either, of changing the labels that he himself had designed, and of which he had recently printed thousands.

That was my last chance to be a success at selling Armagnac. I had gotten a C in my business courses at Georgetown, and now, I thought, I deserved an F for my work in the field. Gone were my dreams of a career in Armagnac.

After more than a month of traveling around the world, exhausted with jet lag, I was happy to be back in my own home with my family. I had not even had time to unpack when, after dinner, Lacy and I went out on our back porch to relax. He was drinking his coffee and smoking a cigar while I recounted my adventures. I was telling him that I had met some Vietnamese women in Tokyo, and that we had made Vietnamese food together. I do not know what happened next, but shortly afterward I remember seeing a man hovering over me and asking me if I knew where I was. I said Tokyo. He asked my name, and I said Jackie. Then I heard the sinister cry of an ambulance siren. The next thing I knew, I was in a hospital, with people scurrying around me.

Lacy told me the next day that I had blacked out and fainted on the porch. He called 911, and within minutes an ambulance had taken me to the Northern Virginia Doctors' Hospital in Arlington. The results of my blood tests and x-rays came back negative, which seemed to indicate that the cause of my fainting had been exhaustion after my long travel. Before the doctor sent me home, however, he asked whether I had ever had a seizure. I said yes, in Milan, eight years before, after falling and sustaining a head injury that required five stitches. The doctor touched my head and right away ordered a CAT scan. It turned up alarming news: I had a meningioma, a benign tumor on the left side of my skull. A neurologist would have to operate on me the next morning.

Lacy wanted a second opinion, and sent my medical records to another neurologist. The reply came back the same: I needed immediate surgery. Dr. Stanislaw Toczek, my neurosurgeon, warned me that I might suffer some side effects from the operation. I might lose the movement in my right arm and leg. I might lose the sight in my right eye, which could also close to half its size. If a certain nerve in the brain was touched, my mouth might be twisted to one side. I might lose my speech. I might be this, or I might be that. I called Lacy and the children, and told them to take good care of themselves and to love each other if the worst happened to me.

That night, all alone, I prayed for everyone I knew in this world, and I asked all our dead relatives and friends to protect and look after my loved ones. Then I suddenly remembered Colonel Y, one of the best Vietnamese astrologers, whose daughter, An, had predicted my marriage to Lacy. I called him and asked whether he saw any danger to my life with the surgery. He consulted my horoscope and called me back fifteen minutes later. He told me not to be afraid of anything. He said there was a brake pedal that would bring the peril to a halt. My ancestors had blessed me with *phuc duc,* good fortune. Not only that, he said, but my future would be much brighter from then on.

Reassured, I slept well that night. The next morning, I smiled and told the surgeon to go ahead. He was a little surprised at my calm, given my worry of the day before. I signed all the papers the nurse presented to me, and was ready for my reincarnation into another life.

As predicted, I survived my trip into the black tunnel. The next day, I woke up and saw the loving eyes of Lacy and the children again. The astrologer was right. I had passed the test. I told myself I was not blindly addicted to astrology. If things had not turned out as foretold, God, my ultimate judge, would not have been offended. I did not lose anything by asking Colonel Y's opinion.

In Vietnam, on the contrary, Bong had warned me not to trust fortune-tellers and the things they said to enchant people. They were used by political brokers to plant ideas in the minds of superstitious men and women. They spread rumors and innuendo to try to change the course of our political life. With their belief in ancestor worship, the Vietnamese relied more on hearsay and prediction and less on their leaders. I should be aware of that, I had been told repeatedly.

But today was a new day. I saw myself reincarnated into a new person.

My two years in Bangkok, Thailand, from 1985 to 1987 were filled with volunteer work for Vietnamese refugees. Visits to the refugee camps and the Suan Plu prison were exhausting but very rewarding. I had promised Bong that I would fulfill my karma by paying my debt to the Vietnamese people for their help to us following his death. I tried, during the twelve years from the fall of Saigon to 1987, to do as much as I could for my refugee compatriots.

My temporary transition to Mexico in 1988 lasted only eight months and was a total failure. I did not even have a honeymoon period with that fascinating country. The pollution and the altitude made me short of breath, and I developed bronchitis and chronic intestinal trouble. On top of that, the window of my car was smashed, jewelry and household effects were stolen from our house, and I was rear-ended at a traffic light by a careless driver behind me. My car was even mistakenly towed from a paid parking lot. But fate intervened. Without my uttering a complaint or asking the State Department for a change, Lacy's miraculous transfer to Trinidad cut short my miserable sojourn in Mexico City.

The following three years in the carnival-loving, twin-island country of Trinidad and Tobago opened a new life for me. Not only did warm people welcome me with open arms; an attempted coup d'état in that tiny place even cleansed me of my war nightmares. During a five-day siege of the capital, Port of Spain, by radical Muslims, I relived the Vietnam War: gunfire, curfews, barbed-wire barricades. It was an exorcism.

I learned in Trinidad how to meditate, to center myself in periods of silence, and to balance the *yin* and *yang* inside me. I began a healing process that I expect to continue until the end of my days.

Jamaica was an intense experience, as well. I spent much of my time on charitable causes, and made many wonderful friendships. When Lacy and I left after four years in 1995, we were treated to the most prolonged and lavish farewell bestowed on any diplomatic couple in living memory. The governor general hosted a classical music show in our honor by Jamaica's best artists at Kings House, his official residence. The mayor of Kingston presented us the key to the city. A multitude of friends flooded us with farewell parties. It was the apogee of our foreign service career. We could not have been more pleased or satisfied.

Brazil was the last of our diplomatic posts. It is a vast country full of people with big hopes who drive too fast. We lived at the end of a quiet street in Brasilia, and our lives unfolded pleasantly, without incident.

So you see, I have become a world citizen; I have traveled far and wide, like you thought I would. But I am still trying to find the right way before I join both of you in the afterlife.

Oh, Ba and Ma, do you know that Lacy and I are celebrating our twenty-fifth wedding anniversary this year. We have renewed the vows of our marriage with a post-nuptial commitment, signed solemnly in our den in front of a statute of Buddha.

So, like butterflies, we sucked the nectar from the most beautiful flowers in our nomadic life around the world. We tried to extract the essence of each country's history and traditions. We learned to adapt to different situations, from the traumatic to the majestic. We visited poor people in slum areas and shook hands with royalty. We were blessed with friends of many nationalities. We got to see a great deal of this large world.

A new beginning awaits us. We are approaching our later years with a sense of assurance. We must now rely on one another for support more than ever. We are looking forward to this last passage.

This morning, in the first year of the new millenium, I wake before Lacy and gaze at him with affection. How amazing to have two people born thousands of miles apart, molded in different customs, bonded together for life in this tiny corner of planet Earth. The wonders of Destiny. I put out my arm and place the palm of my hand on Lacy's heart. I want to communicate to him all my feelings of love and gratitude for steering my damaged boat to safety. With my other hand, I slowly caress his forehead and iron out the deep lines in his face. I stroke his soft gray hair, and think of the wealth of qualities underneath.

Finally, without waking him, I squeeze myself along his side, and kiss his arm. I want to inhale his aroma as if I were smelling a lotus, drinking in the perfume of virtue above the muddy pond. I lie there very quietly next to him and hold him tightly, so tightly that the two of us blend into one.

Suddenly, under the direction of an invisible conductor, hundreds of birds perched on the trees next to my window start their loud serenade in unison, announcing the birth of a new day. I look out and see a cloud dangling in the blue sky, an autumn cloud in spring.

"I do the very best I know how, the very best I can; and I mean to keep on doing it to the end.

If the end brings me out all right, what is said against me will not amount to anything.

If the end brings me out all wrong, ten angels swearing I was right would make no difference."

Abraham Lincoln